The Global Horizon

The Global Horizon

Expectations of Migration in
Africa and the Middle East

Edited by
Knut Graw & Samuli Schielke

LEUVEN UNIVERSITY PRESS

ISBN 978 90 5867 906 2
D/2012/1869/46
NUR: 740

Design: Het Vlakke Land
Cover Photo: Posters on sale in Alexandria, Egypt. © Samuli Schielke

GPRC
Guaranteed
Peer Reviewed
Content
www.gprc.be

Table of Contents

Afterword

Contributors

Introduction:
Reflections on migratory expectations in Africa and beyond

Knut Graw and Samuli Schielke

The visible and the invisible of contemporary migration

In recent years, the topic of migration has come closer and closer to the forefront of public awareness and concern. Issues of labour movement, asylum procedures, border controls, and the 'integration' of new ethnic and religious minorities make headlines in the wealthier (post-)industrial nations, while the issue of 'illegal migration' and the complex dependencies involved in remittances and transnational families are constantly on the agenda in poorer countries. In academia the study of migration has become a social scientific discipline of its own, with exponential amounts of literature being published and specialized conferences being held around the world. In short, it has become nearly impossible to think about the contemporary world without thinking about migration as well. And yet, while migration is all over public and academic debates today, some of its aspects seem over-visible, while others are perhaps under-visible. Two images are helpful to outline this problematic.

The first image is one that has become iconic of contemporary migration to Europe: the haphazardly built boat, half-sinking and filled with refugees/migrants from northern and western Africa undertaking the dangerous journey across the sea to Europe. It is a standard feature in the news and in cultural production about migration. It is a source of humanitarian concern and tightened border controls alike. It evokes strong emotions and associations. And yet it says very little about the protagonists themselves. The image of the boat tells us that lots of people are coming to Europe, that they are taking great risks in doing so, and that there is something *we* need to do about it (for the whole complex concerning the image of boat migration see also Graw in this volume). But why do people take such a tremendous risk? The reasons cited are often highly generic: war, poverty, oppression, hunger. But there has been war, poverty, oppression and hunger before, as well. Why now? Why not before? The image of the boats does not really tell us why. All we get is a vague sense that people have a bad life where they come from, and are trying to get to Europe for a better life. This implicit narrative perhaps appeals to a European self-image as the best place in the world to live, but it is ill-suited to helping us to understand why so many people in our time are so determined to leave behind their homes, their social networks, and their trusted ways of life for such an uncertain and risky project.

The second image, in contrast, is one that is almost completely absent from the European perception of migration but over-visible across the global South: the house built by the migrant, often higher than its surroundings and with walls of reinforced concrete or red brick, built to a good standard of comfort by local measures, often in the outskirts of towns and villages, and often empty for most of the year. Building houses is an almost universal practice among labour migrants who invest a significant part of their incomes in creating a physical presence in a place from which they are absent for most of the time – some for years, others for a lifetime (Dalakoglou 2010, Melly 2010). For the people who live in their vicinity, these houses are often the most immediate and convincing aspect of migration they see. In this regard, houses, not boats, have become *the* symbol of migration in the so-called sending countries, and in fact more than a symbol: they incorporate the very social effects of migration. The houses built by migrants involve flows of money and construction materials, rising prices of land and housing, new standards for a good life, an advantage for migrants and their children on the marriage market, a whole set of possibilities and expectations that mark the path of social arrival. They tell stories of success that are compelling not only for the power of the path they open up, but also because of the increasing difficulty of pursuing any other paths. How else could one build such a house? And how else could one build a respectable life in relative material comfort if not through migration? Yet, like the boats, the houses, too, leave a lot unseen and unsaid. They do not tell of the hardship and alienation of migrant labour, nor of the many cases where people were not successful and did not succeed in realizing the dreams for which they left.

This is the situation we want to investigate in this book: the constant presence of migration as a possibility, sometimes perceived of as an option among many, but more often felt as an almost inevitable necessity. In much of the world, it has become very difficult to think about a better future without thinking about migration to a place where one can make the money needed to realize that better future. Why this is so, and what that inevitable presence of migration, and its becoming synonymous for projects of social mobility, does to social and personal experience is a crucial question if we are to understand the significance of migration in the contemporary world. After all, migration is not just about people migrating. It is a process of change that affects a society at large, and by doing so changes the experiences and perspectives also of those who have not migrated and perhaps never will. The question that we pursue in this book therefore concerns not only the experience of migrants but the experience of migration within the relevant societies, regardless of whether people actually themselves embark upon a migratory project or stay put. What we are concerned with is the question of the changing horizon of expectations that makes migration such a compelling path to so many people despite its well-known risks and adversities.

To our understanding, this question (what makes migration such a compelling path) has been strikingly little discussed or studied despite the tremendous amount of research and public debate on migration in recent years. Until the 1980s approaches to migration had often largely focussed on the socioeconomic and political causes and repercussions of migration. More often than not this perspective also remains characteristic of public debates. While we agree that these are important topics of research, we argue that they need to be complemented by culturally and historically sensitive accounts shedding more light on the subjective and existential side of the causes and repercussions of these migratory processes. Of course, this is not to say that the study of migration would have been blind to the more personal, existential, emotional aspects of migration in general. For one thing, these aspects may always have been central to the personal concerns of people dedicating themselves to the study of migratory processes. Furthermore, there is a growing body of works within anthropology that is explicitly turning towards the personal and existential dimensions, the expectations and experiences of migration (see, e.g., Ghannam 1998; Mains 2007; Pandolfo 2007; Jackson 2008; Piot 2010; McGovern 2010; Alpes 2011; Lucht 2012; Streiff-Fénart and Segatti 2012). In our view, this turn towards more existentially sensitive ways of researching and analysing migratory processes may be crucial for perceiving and understanding what is most central about migration to the individuals and societies involved. In our view, such a more existentially sensitive perspective is helpful in understanding that houses (and the family ties they represent) may be more central to migration than boats, people more central than money, expectations more, or at least equally, important than regulations and border regimes.

In line with this, we see at least three further issues where scholarly and public debates on migration have tended to draw attention to certain issues and away from others.

Although transnational and translocal perspectives have been well grounded in the academic study of migration for at least two decades (see, e.g., Glick Schiller, Basch and Blanc 1995; Mahler 1998; Al-Ali and Koser 2002; Glick Schiller 2005; Glick Schiller and Çağlar 2010; Freitag and von Oppen 2010.), much of the more policy driven research and public debates are often still characterized by a strong emphasis on the so-called 'receiving countries', the countries that have the money and the jobs and that attract labour migrants. As groups of individual migrants turn into diasporic, ethnic communities, they often become involved in new social conflicts, and thus the focus of a tremendous amount of research and social policy. However, initially, migrants are mostly concerned with changing their lives 'at home', and even if they permanently settle in their place of work they continue to be closely connected to their place of origin. In this regard, the life a person lives as a migrant is often but half of his or her reality, and yet the other half remains often invisible to an outside observer, and often seems also less of a concern for national politics which, in turn, influences the distribution of research funding.

Second, research on migration has produced a solid understanding of the economic conditions and financial transactions involved, especially the remittances migrants send to their families (see, e.g. Ambrosius, Fritz and Stiegler 2010). This is in a certain way grounded in the common sense of migrants themselves, whose lives become heavily subjected to the primacy of economy and money. Furthermore, economic interests and financial flows are more accessible to quantitative analysis and political decision-making. However, notwithstanding the tendency to abstraction implicit in the form of money, even in today's extremely financialized world money is more often than not bound up with 'moral, embedded, and special-purpose functions' (Maurer 2006, 17; cf. Simmel 1989 [1900]). The money migrants earn, save, invest, and transfer is not just an abstract movement of finances. It is there to buy specific things, to fulfil specific social expectations – but these things and expectations remain invisible to the observer who will find it much easier to document and analyse flows of money than to grasp the affective sense of obligation and pressure that makes people invest so much of their lives in acquiring certain things.

Third, the study of migration is commonly focussed on people who actually migrate (or their children and descendants). This seems obvious, and yet it hides the fact that people who migrate at first were not migrants. They became so. In order to understand why and how people become migrants, we argue that it is important not only to look at people who in various ways have moved between places, but also those who have not yet become migrants, are in the process of becoming migrants, or will never become migrants at all.

Reacting to these lacunae and based on detailed ethnographic accounts, the contributors to this volume all focus on the imaginations, expectations, and motivations that fuel the pursuit of migration. We foreground, thus, the various subjective dimensions of migration and explore the impact which the different imaginations and practices of migration have on the sociocultural conditions of the various local settings concerned. Scrutinizing the cultural processes underlying and triggering migration in different rural and urban localities across the African continent, this volume also complicates the focus on migration as a question of mobility. We address migration not just as movement but also as processes of imagination and expectation that shape people's lives and lifeworlds from the outset, reflecting not just locally constituted imaginaries but increasingly global horizons.

The new quality of migration in Africa

It is an often repeated insight that migrations are an inherent part of human existence, witnessed most obviously by the spread of the human species across the globe. Stating this fact may not be very helpful, however, in understanding the current dynamics of migration. Although the human species in general is characterized by migrations, the individual lives of humans, their families and communities are often remarkably place-specific over many generations (see Graw in this volume). Why is a young man from an agricultural village in Egypt or Senegal under so much more pressure to consider leaving that village today than a hundred years ago? Or, to put it in more general terms: why are there times when it becomes more compelling to move? What kind of movement is involved here? And what does this movement aim at? The history and genealogy of migration in any given context are neither static nor simple natural or ethnographic givens, but continuously reshaped and reworked. Migratory processes cannot be understood in their full complexity without a study of the cultural genealogy and history of the sociocultural notions and patterns migrants draw upon.

Although contemporary migration in and from the African continent is often related to 'cultures of migration', that is, established forms of interregional and international mobility (see, e.g., Whitehouse 2003; Cohen and Jónsson forthcoming), current processes of migration seem to have taken on a new quality. This is not just a matter of the increased geographic range of migration due to improved means of transportation, communication, and transfer of finances, which make it more likely and feasible to live transnational lives between, for example, France and

West Africa. The more substantial change lies in the way the outlook of the world as a whole has changed.

The world in the experiential sense of everything there is has become a very different place for most people in the past century. This is not to talk about a shift from isolated 'cultures' to global 'flows' (Appadurai 1996). People everywhere on earth have probably always been aware that there are other peoples and other places, including distant and exotic ones. But very often the world beyond one's everyday experience was a very distant and exotic one indeed. In the age of global migrations, in contrast, the larger world is continuously present in the form of returning migrants, globally traded commodities, media, fashion, and most importantly in the form of likely paths of transnational life. In consequence, the rest of the world is not just a distant place, somewhere beyond the boundaries of one's homely lifeworld. It has become a more and more constitutive element of people's lifeworlds and expectations (see Piot 1999). In short, local worlds are increasingly measured against a set of possibilities the referents of which are global, not local. As a result of this, migration gains an almost inevitable attraction as local means are seldom sufficient for one to achieve the demands of a life now measured by global standards. At the same time, however, actual migration becomes increasingly restricted due to labour, border and visa regimes. At the very moment when long-distance migration becomes extremely compelling – inevitable from a subjective standpoint – it also becomes more difficult. And, paradoxically, this difficulty appears to make the pressure to migrate only more urgent.

It would be easy to ascribe this sense of urgency to people being ill-informed about the real risks and chances of migration, or even to put the blame on people and their cultures for erroneously putting their faith in desperate projects of migration that hold them back from pursuing more constructive projects – a critique often voiced in development discourses aiming at discouraging migration. But such critique would overlook how serious the emotional pressure and the lure of migration can be in spite of contrary evidence. In the popular culture of Egypt, for example, there are countless proverbs, songs, films and news features that all repeat the common wisdom that migration is economically and emotionally perilous and that one should stay at home. And yet, amidst all this common knowledge, one chat with a cousin or neighbour who made it to becoming a shop-owner (or so he says) in Italy can be enough to turn the scale and to confirm one in the assessment that going abroad in order to work hard and save some money is the best and only way out of one's current predicament.

This underlying sensibility that propels the urge to migrate requires a theoretical approach that is sensitive to issues of people's outlook of the world, their senses of expectation and their lived experience – an approach that can be called an existential or a phenomenological one (see Jackson 1996; Graw 2012). In what follows, we try to develop some general directions that could serve the development of such a theoretical approach, focussing on the themes of horizon, expectation and experience.

Migration as horizon

As the contributors to this volume met at a workshop at Zentrum Moderner Orient in spring 2009, there was a shared understanding that there is a need for theoretical directions that help to make sense of the processes of imagination and expectation that seem so central to the attraction migration exerts in so many different settings across the globe. Reflecting upon the different contributions to the workshop and the way in which they describe and analyse these specific yet very similar ways of thinking about and dealing with the possibility of migration in the respective local contexts, we started to realize that an important aspect seems to unite all the different contributions and the contexts they are describing: by paying close attention to migratory expectations and the impact of migration on the perception of local realities, they did not just conceive of migration as the result of physical movement but as a horizon of expectation and action. Furthermore, we started to think that the notion of a globalizing horizon, and the various theoretical implications which it entails, could perhaps help us to understand the processes at hand in a way that would account for both the similarities and the differences in the various ethnographic accounts. Having emerged from the workshop meeting and the writing of the individual contributions to this volume, the notion of horizon is not taken up explicitly in all chapters of this volume. Rather, our attempt at thinking about migration as a horizon of action and imagination in this introductory chapter is an attempt explicitly to theorize something that, in our view, emerges in different ways in the different contributions and which, at the same time, looks beyond the specific ethnographic settings. In this section we are therefore trying to make this notion and its uses more explicit, before in the next section returning to the specific questions addressed by the contributors in their individual chapters.

In its most immediate and literal sense, derived from the Greek verb *horízein*, to limit or delimit, horizon refers to the limit or outer rim of our field of visual perception, that is, the distant line where, when one's view is unobstructed by natural or built structures such as mountains, trees, walls, or buildings, the earth or the sea seems to meet the sky. Evoking images of travel, exploration, and open spaces, the term horizon triggers similar associations as the notion of migration itself. In a more metaphorical sense, moving from the realm of physical space and the vision of the eye to the inner world of the person and vision through thought and imagination, the notion of horizon refers not only to what is actually visible but to what is familiar, known, and imaginable for a person in a much more encompassing sense. Here, the word horizon not only describes a limit of perception but becomes almost synonymous with the world itself as that which can be grasped, understood, or thought of by individuals, societies, or cultures in a given moment of life or history.

Drawing on this double meaning of horizon as encompassing the realm of both outer and inner perception, the physical world and the world of the mind, the notion of horizon has been and continues to be employed in everyday usage as well as in more formal, philosophical modes of reflection.

In everyday usage, for instance, a person's horizon is often conceived of as the reach and orientation of her or his knowledge, expectations, or personal ambitions. In this sense, a horizon is not just a static given but also entails something very dynamic, something that can be formed and widened for example through education, working experiences, meeting people, travel, or reading, or a combination of these.

Following the more literal meaning of the term, in philosophy the term horizon was for a long time simply understood as the limit of human understanding or perception. In the 20th century, and especially in phenomenological and hermeneutic thought, the notion of horizon acquired a wider and more positive sense. In one of the few works he published during his lifetime, the founder of phenomenology Edmund Husserl described objects and acts of perception as defined not just by the properties of the act or object itself but by their horizon (*Horizont*) or *Hof* (halo, a term describing a circle or circular space around something, derived from the Greek *halos*, originally a threshing floor), that is defined by the objects and perceptions that precede, come after or surround it (Husserl 1976 [1913]). In a similar vein, but drawing more on the metaphorical meaning of the term and moving from objects and acts of perception to the cultural 'objects' of texts and reading, Hans-Georg Gadamer made use of the term horizon to describe that which characterizes the meaning of a text beyond its literal sense; that which can often not be grasped immediately but which has to be approached through a careful process of reading that is sensitive not just to what a text seems to say explicitly but also to the understandings which informed and made a particular text possible in the first place (Gadamer 1960).

It is in the form of such more nuanced conceptualizations that the notion of horizon becomes productive for the understanding of migration and migratory expectations in particular. Understood as being part of the larger sociocultural horizon of a given society or person as well as constituting a specific horizon in themselves, migration and migratory expectations cannot be understood in an isolated or abstract way but rather within their social, cultural, economic, and historical context. In this regard, the very diversity which characterizes not just migration studies but artistic and literary works on migration alike, can be seen as the outcome of the conscious or intuitive understanding of the fact that migration implies much more than can be conveyed by describing migration as a function of economic difference alone.

It is in this context that the attribute 'global' becomes crucial. This is, of course, not to say that everything becomes globalized, or that the notion of globalization in itself would provide an answer to all our questions – on the contrary. Semantically and empirically, a concept or category such as a 'global horizon' is in fact not free of contradictions. If one remembers the original meaning of the term horizon as the (limit of the) spatial extension of the visual field, the notion of horizon implies a person who views his or her surroundings from a specific vantage point. In so far as any horizon shifts as soon the person moves, horizons are necessarily specific. In this sense, there could be no such thing as a global horizon unless the differences between the different vantage points were to get smaller and smaller and finally disappear. But is this the case? This question seems to bring us very close to the question whether globalization leads to homogenization, flattening out cultural differences, or, on the contrary, to heterogenization, producing as many varieties of responding to globalization as there are people, cultures, locales, etc. Looked at from a 'horizontic' perspective, however, this is no longer an either-or question. The experience in question is essentially ambiguous, whereby the notion of a global horizon may offer a way of better comprehending that ambiguity (or dialectic, perhaps).

On the one hand, the hermeneutic properties implied in the notion of horizon transgress any attempt to essentialize cultural perception: the world as horizon is not just a locality or place but reveals itself as the way reality shows itself to the person in any given situation. Given its changing and perspective-dependent character, the notion of horizon also points to the fact that migratory expectations may not be identical even within the same sociocultural location, but dependent on the situation, perspective, understandings, experiences, and biography of each individual.

On the other hand, a horizon implies not only a person's gaze but also a landscape or space being looked at. Horizons of expectation – be they related to migration or not – are therefore both structured by the reality as it is perceived and structuring that very reality. As lifeworld, that reality cannot be comprehended without reflecting the person's personal and cultural perception of his or her situation. In this regard, it is not so much the vantage points that become homogenized – or at least this is not what seems to shape this process in the first place – but rather the landscape or space being looked at. With regard to this dynamic, dialectical relationship between world and person, the notion of horizon thus makes clear that, insofar as a world is necessarily constituted by a horizon and cannot exist without it, the way the world and one's own life are perceived and experienced is always already the result of a complex process of mediation, integration and expansion.

The notion of horizon, thus, corresponds with the observation that contemporary sociocultural worlds are never fully autochthonous, endogenous or local, and probably never have been. What the attribute 'global' emphasizes in this context is the fact that what constitutes the horizon of many locales today is no longer just another adjacent locality with its own seemingly autochthonous sets of meanings, but instead notions and concepts that are either attributed to abstract, not easily localized concepts such as modernity, development, or progress, or projected onto geographical settings that are seen as setting the standards for these concepts. This is significant in at least two regards.

First, the formation of personal and cultural horizons implies both individually and locally distinct experiences, structured by particular conditions as much as by local symbolic, religious, or sociopolitical networks of meaning, *as well as* the reconsideration of local situations in relation to much less localizable notions and processes. Speaking about a global horizon, we thus want to point out that the effect of globalization is not so much the replacement of one horizon by another but a gradual actualization along conceptual vectors. Such vectors have specific histories, but due to the colonialist and capitalist expansion of the past centuries, they have now gained such a currency and scale that they have become commonplace among various peoples across the planet.

Arjun Appadurai (1996) famously proposed an understanding of these processes that exceed the boundaries of particular places and national states in both scope and quality as 'flows' and 'scapes' of finance, technology, politics, and more. James Ferguson (2006), in contrast, argued that Appadurai's model of global flows does not do justice to the extremely stratified and unequal ways in which globalization is experienced, not least in many African contexts. Trying to get a visa to the Schengen area from Senegal, Egypt, or Cameroon puts global flows into perspective in a way that is hard to ignore. But while the returns of globalization are very unequally shared, or not shared at all, the promise of these returns has spread all over the world. By showing how the expansion of the scope of what can be expected is shaped but not diminished by the dramatic 'gap between the actual and the possible' (Weiss 2009), the notion of a global horizon may actually allow one to describe both the significance of the expansion of global flows and the expansion of conditions excluding people from the flows of globalization they are exposed to.

Second, the notion of global horizon allows us to see that these processes, relational and implying different vectors and sets of meaning as they are, are not likely to be uniform. Without being uniform, however, horizons do become increasingly comparable and similar through their relationship with the elements that shape them: concepts, conditions, mediations, economical and power relations that transgress local, regional, and national settings. A marriage between a Senegalese migrant man in Spain and a woman from his home village or region in Senegal, for instance, is no longer a local event in the conventional sense, even if the marriage takes place in the village or home region of the partners in question. In addition to its immediate setting, such a marriage is related to European wages and remittances, Chinese household goods bought by the groom for the bride, as well as expectations of love and romance echoing Mexican or Brazilian telenovelas as much as local custom. In the specific case, this relationship is at once unique to the individuals involved in that particular union in that particular place, and similar to many others in many other settings worldwide. And, most importantly perhaps, this is usually well known by the people involved. It is this similarity, not homogeneity, between the interplay of conditions, expectations, and material elements of social practice which explains why migration movements in very different locations worldwide have started to look so similar.

Expectation and experience

What does it, then, mean in practical terms to live, to hope and to struggle under the conditions of a global horizon of migration? This is the question which the contributors to this volume pursue in different ways, with case studies reaching from West and Central Africa to the Middle East. The volume as a whole is divided into three parts. Opening with the chapters by Knut Graw on Senegalese migration to Spain and the question of cause, and by Maybritt Jill Alpes on the disconnections of information about 'the bush' (that is, places to migrate to) in Cameroon, the first part of the volume focuses on the perceptions and sensibilities through which ideas of migration, the outside world, progress and self-realization become powerful – so powerful indeed that migration is often held to be the only viable alternative to nothingness. The second part describes and analyses specific modalities and trajectories – both spatial and temporal – resulting from these processes of sociocultural imagination and practice. The issue of departures and possible destinations is thereby entangled with the problem of non-departures – getting stuck and waiting, as shown in the chapters by Filip De Boeck on the history of ideas of migration in the Democratic Republic of Congo, Denise Dias Barros on rural-urban migration in Mali, Gunvor Jónsson on immobility and the problems of social becoming in Mali, and Paolo Gaibazzi on time and waiting in Gambia. With chapters by Ann Cassiman on the meaning of the image of the Eiffel Tower between Paris and Ghana, Aïssatou Mbodj-Pouye on literacy and mobility in Mali, and Samuli Schielke on gazing at the other side of the sea in Egypt, the third part turns to the question of how ideas of migration and the wider world contribute to transforming people's horizons of action regarding the social worlds they live in. Finally, an afterword by Michael Jackson concludes the volume.

Partly but not fully overlapping with the structure of the volume, five aspects emerge as central to the enquiry developed in the chapters of this volume. First, there is the seemingly ubiquitous power of migration as a source of expectation and longing in times when non-migratory trajectories appear to be increasingly unfeasible. This is the more problematic as actual migration has at the same time often become more difficult. In her study of involuntarily immobile Soninke youth in a Malian village, for instance, Jónsson reveals the discontents and troubles of men who do not make it abroad, and who therefore remain in a state of limbo, unable to accomplish full male adulthood. Regional rural-urban migrations seem to have been less troubled by visa regimes. In her study of the rural-urban migration of Dogon in Mali, Dias Barros shows how being a migrant in the city has become a fundamental element of being a Dogon man. And yet while migrating to the city is much easier than migrating to Europe as in Jónsson's account, the perpetual state of migrancy creates problems of its own when the social ideal of circularity (of migration and return) becomes unfeasible.

Second, there is the often tragic nature of migratory expectations, as that which constitutes an important source of hope easily turns into the source of misunderstanding, hardship, and feelings of failure. For those who fail to fulfil the expectations and to return wealthy with plenty of gifts, this is a very traumatic experience, since failures are very likely to be seen as personal ones, and not as inherent to the project itself. As Alpes shows with the case of the (mis)communications about migration in Cameroon, such experiences are often actively downplayed in a situation where international migration has become practically identical with success, and not to desire to migrate would be like having no ambitions in life. Migration thus comes along with a compelling but also problematic force of optimism – whatever the cost. Writing about Senegalese and Gambians who undertook the path of travel and eventually found themselves working in southern Spain, Graw looks at the situation where, having arrived in Europe, one is compelled to think about what one expected and what one got – a process of reflection which is often difficult to convey to people back at home, and which comes at a moment when crucial decisions have already been made.

Third, there is the temporal nature of the expectation of migration and the cultural practices relating to it, involving powerful ideas of personal future and one's movement (or non-movement) in time (Graw 2005 and forthcoming). The problem of incomplete circularity in the contribution by Dias Barros, for instance, is very much a problem of time. Another powerful and problematic temporal sensibility is taken up by Gaibazzi in his study of Soninke men in the Gambia waiting for an opportunity to migrate. Perpetual waiting and its corresponding frustrations, it becomes clear from his account, are the intimate counterpart of the expectation of rapid and significant progress through actual migration.

Fourth, there is the imaginative, world-making character of migratory expectations which runs through the whole volume. Looking at literacy in Mali, Mbodj-Pouye shows specifically how the practice of keeping notebooks creates and accompanies different forms of mobility. Linking literary to migratory imagination, Schielke, in turn, shows that the imagination of a different life on "the other side" is an ambiguous one, partly oppressive when migration narrows down one's imagination to the need to make money, but partly also a creative site for developing alternative paths of action. Writing about the Eiffel Tower, brought as a souvenir from France to Ghana, Ann Cassiman argues that the tower and the experience of 'having one's eyes opened' which it embodies open up a space in which to think about migration and modernity as the reconnection and actualization of local lifeworlds to global landscapes of possibility.

And fifth, all contributions are reflective of the fact that migration, and the expectations and dreams connected to it, is both a reaction to as well as an attempt to overcome socio-economic situations felt as being restricted or repressive. This fact emerges particularly vividly in De Boeck's contribution on migratory trajectories in and from the Democratic Republic of Congo. There he describes the aspirations of those who follow the 'siren's call of migration' as a continuous struggle to maintain and develop the capacity to act despite often adverse conditions. A struggle also, as Jackson elaborates in his afterword, that forces anthropologies of migration to go beyond the apparitions of public discourses and pay close attention to the complexity of how the contemporary world is experienced and imagined in a multiplicity of locales today.

Acknowledgements

This volume is based on a workshop entitled *Migration at Home: Migratory Imaginations and Imaginary Cosmopolitanisms in Africa and Beyond* which was held at Zentrum Moderner Orient (ZMO) in Berlin from 11 to 13 March 2009. Almost all the contributions to this volume are based on papers presented at the workshop. We thank all the contributors for their dedication to the project of this book. We also thank Stefania Pandolfo who presented a text continuing her reflection on migratory expectations in Morocco and Hans Lucht who presented a chapter of his then forthcoming monograph on Ghanese migration to Italy (Lucht 2012). We thank Heike Liebau and other members of the working group 'Actors in Translocal Spaces' for providing both an initial framework for debate and practical assistance for the workshop. The workshop and the book proposal received the continuous support of the ZMO which also allowed for the translation of Denise Dias Barros' text from the original French. We thank Doreen Teumer, Katharina Zöller, and Saboura Beutel who in their function as student assistants have taken care of a lot of crucial logistical matters around the workshop and this book. We also thank Marike Schipper and Veerle de Laet from Leuven University Press for their interest in this book project and their careful editorial work.

References

Al-Ali, Nadje and Koser, Khalid. 2002. *New Approaches to Migration? Transnational Communities and the Transformation of Home.* London and New York: Routledge.

Alpes, Maybritt Jill. 2011. Bushfalling: How young Cameroonians dare to migrate. PhD thesis, University of Amsterdam.

Ambrosius, Christian, Barbara Fritz and Ursula Stiegler, 2010. O potencial das remessas dos migrantes para a governação e o desenvolvimento financeiro no contexto EUA-México. In *Migrações, Coesão Social e Governação – Perspectivas Euro-Latino-Americanas,* eds. Andrés Malamud and Fernando Carrillo Flórez. Lisboa: Imprensa Ciências Sociais.

Appadurai, Arjun. 1996. *Modernity at Large: Cultural Dimensions of Globalization.* Minneapolis: University of Minnesota Press.

Cohen, Robin, and Gunvor Jónsson. 2011. Connecting Culture and Migration. In *Migration and Culture,* ed. Robin Cohen and Gunvor Jónsson. Cheltenham: Edward Elgar.

Dalakoglou, Dimitris. 2010. Migrating-remitting-'building'-dwelling: House-making as 'proxy' presence in postsocialist Albania. *Journal of the Royal Anthropological Institute* 16 (4): 761-777.

Ferguson, James. 2006. *Global Shadows: Africa in the Neoliberal World Order*. Durham and London: Duke University Press.

Freitag, Ulrike and Achim von Oppen, eds. 2010. Translocality: *The Study of Globalising Processes from a Southern Perspective*. Leiden: Brill.

Gadamer, Hans-Georg. 1960. *Wahrheit und Methode. Grundzüge einer philosophischen Hermeneutik*. Tübingen: J.C.B. Mohr (Paul Siebeck).

Ghannam, Farha. 1998. Keeping Him Connected: Labor Migration and the Production of Locality in Cairo. *City and Society* 10, 1: 65-82.

Glick Schiller, Nina, Linda Basch and Christina Szanton Blanc. 1995. From Immigrant to Transmigrant: Theorizing Transnational Migration. *Anthropological Quarterly* 68 (1): 48-63.

Glick Schiller, Nina. 2005. Transnational Social Fields and Imperialism: Bringing a Theory of Power to Transnational Studies. *Anthropological Theory* 5 (4): 439-461.

Glick Schiller, Nina and Ayşe Çağlar, eds. 2010. *Locating Migration. Rescaling Cities and Migrants*. Ithaca: Cornell University Press.

Graw, Knut. 2005. Culture of Hope in West Africa. *ISIM Review* 16 (Autumn): 28-29.

Graw, Knut. 2012. Divination and Islam: Existential Perspectives in the Study of Ritual and Religious Praxis in Senegal and Gambia. In *Ordinary Lives and Grand Schemes: An Anthropology of Everyday Religion*, eds. Samuli Schielke and Liza Debevec, 17-32. New York: Berghahn.

Graw, Knut. Forthcoming. Divination in Times of Migration: Globalization, Subjectivity, and the Path of Travel in Senegambian Divinatory Praxis.

Husserl, Edmund. 1976 [1913]. *Ideen zu einer reinen Phänomenologie und phänomenologischen Philosophie*. The Hague: Martinus Nijhoff.

Jackson, Michael, ed. 1996. *Things as They Are: New Directions in Phenomenological Anthropology*. Bloomington: Indiana University Press.

Jackson, Michael. 2008. The Shock of the New: On Migrant Imaginaries and Critical Transitions. *Ethnos* 73 (1): 57-72.

Lucht, Hans. 2012. *Darkness Before Daybreak: African Migrants Living on the Margins in Southern Italy Today*. Berkeley and Los Angeles: University of California Press.

Mahler, Sarah J. 1998. Theoretical and Empirical Contributions toward a Research Agenda for Transnationalism. In *Transnationalism from Below*, eds. Michael Peter Smith and Luis Eduardo Guarnizo, 64-100. New Brunswick, N.J.: Transaction Publishers.

Mains, Daniel. 2007. Neoliberal times: Progress, boredom, and shame among young men in urban Ethiopia. *American Ethnologist* 34 (4): 659–673.

McGovern, Mike. 2010. This is Play: Popular Culture and Politics in Côte d'Ivoire. In *Hard Work, Hard Times: Global Volatility and African Subjectivities*, eds. Anne-Maria Makhulu, Beth A. Buggenhagen and Stephen Jackson, 69-90. Berkeley: University of California Press.

Maurer, Bill. 2006. The anthropology of money. *Annual Review of Anthropology* 35: 15-36.

Melly, Caroline. 2010. Inside-out houses: Urban belonging and imagined futures in Dakar, Senegal. *Comparative Studies in Society and History* 52 (1): 37-65.

Pandolfo, Stefania. 2007. 'The burning': Finitude and the politico-theological imagination of illegal migration. *Anthropological Theory* 7 (3): 329-363.

Piot, Charles. 1999. *Remotely Global: Village Modernity in West Africa*. Chicago and London: University of Chicago Press.

Piot, Charles. 2010. *Nostalgia for the Future: West Africa after the Cold War*. Chicago: The University of Chicago Press.

Simmel, Georg. 1989 [1900]. *Philosophie des Geldes*. Frankfurt: Suhrkamp.

Streiff-Fénart, Jocelyne and Aurelia Segatti, eds. 2012. *The Challenge of the Threshhold: Border Closures and Migration Movements in Africa*. Plymouth: Lexington Books.

Weiss, Brad. 2009. *Street Dreams & Hip Hop Barbershops: Global Fantasy in Urban Tanzania*. Bloomington: Indiana University Press.

Whitehouse, Bruce. 2003. *Staying Soninke*. Providence, Rhode Island: Brown University.

On the cause of migration: Being and nothingness in the African-European border zone

Knut Graw

But we cannot know the truth apart from the cause.
Aristotle

Homo migrans and the question of cause

Few topics dealt with in the social, political and economic sciences have received as much academic and public attention in recent years as the topic of migration. Research centres and networks, conferences, journals, books, research and policy reports, news features, documentaries, as well as artistic projects dealing with the topic of migration, have multiplied with great speed and, given corresponding processes on the ground, this is unlikely to change soon. Already due to its sheer size, to characterize in a few lines a field as vast, complex and multidisciplinary as this is thus problematic, and bound to provoke the criticism that it is selective or biased in some way. In this regard, this text is not written against specific empirical or theoretical works contributing in different ways to the analysis of contemporary migrations, but responding to certain tendencies within that field which, without completely homogenizing it, seem nevertheless to dominate the discourse on migration today in important ways.[1]

One of these tendencies is the priority granted to economic and policy related aspects of migration. The problem with this is, in my view, less a simple lack of attention to or empathy for individual situations and testimonies but, rather, that the concrete ways in which migration is experienced seem to have no, or at least very few, consequences for the analysis and theory of migration processes as such. In other words, what can be observed is less a lack of individual accounts as such than their reduction to either something calling for humanitarian action or what in journalistic parlour is referred to as of 'human interest', that is, a category with considerable journalistic appeal but with little or no consequence for the general understanding and theoretization of migration as such.

Another problematic tendency in the writing about migration seems to be what one could call the normalization or naturalization of migration, that is, the tendency to describe and characterize migration, by reference to either historical precedent or the wide range of migration processes in a multitude of sociogeographic contexts today, as that which is the norm in human behaviour, not its exception.[2] In its most explicit form, this tendency to describe migration as a typical rather than exceptional trait of human nature seems to result in an argument which can perhaps best be described as viewing the human being not as sedentary but as a kind of 'homo migrans'. In terms of its epistemological direction, the homo migrans argument can take on different guises, defining migration either almost biologically as an expression of mobility characterizing human beings from prehistoric times or, more historically, as a human practice that has occurred on so many occasions and in so many contexts that it should be considered a normal state of affairs. With archaeological and historical evidence apparently on its side, at first sight the argument appears convincing. What is more, by pointing out the 'normality' of migration, the homo migrans argument provides an important argument against xenophobia, racism, and other forms of exclusion migrants and refugees are regularly exposed to, and the argument is often employed in this way. However, even if politically useful, the argument is also highly problematic, both epistemologically and politically.

The epistemological problem of such a homo migrans argument lies primarily in the fact that it tends to gloss over important differences between, on the one hand, the seasonal and predominantly circular character of migration among hunter-gatherers and pastoralists, among whom migration functions as a way of responding to and dealing with the ecological and climatic conditions in a particular geographic setting, and, on the other hand, modern day labour migration as a response to conditions which are, in essence, not geographical or ecological but political and economic. What is politically problematic about this is that the equation or likening of historical forms of subsistence-oriented seasonal migrations or transhumance with labour migration or the displacement of refugees leads to the representation of processes as normal and part of human nature which are really political in nature. This important differentiation is of course not a new insight but has informed Marxist and world-system theory-oriented analyses of migration for many decades. Drawing on his work on migration in West Africa in the 1970s, Samir Amin, for instance, has argued that even if migrations have occurred throughout history, modern migration should not be conflated with earlier displacements or movements of people because of its intrinsic link to a globalizing capitalist economy. Amin insists, thus, on the need "to distinguish between the movements of people and labour migration" (Amin 1995: 29). In other words, the consideration of migration as a normal or natural trait of human behaviour depoliticizes the phenomenon of migration and, as a result, the question why an increasing number of people engage in (not just) transnational migration needs no longer to be asked.

However, Amin's position also implies a very critical question about the significance of the study of migratory expectations and subjectivities. According to him, questions concerning the personal motivations of migrants, their cultural patterning or individual psychology are structured, if not determined, by the political economic processes in question from the outset and therefore of little theoretical relevance for the understanding of what migration is (Amin 1995: 30). Amin is very categorical on this point. "Individual motivations", he writes "are well known. Their 'revelation' by a sociological investigation is mere empty talk" (Amin 1995: 32). Amin argues that the motives and motivations given by migrants and their communities have to be seen as rationalizations of the conditions they are faced with but not as what causes migration in the first place. Surprisingly, the point Amin makes here is rarely addressed in studies arguing for the importance of studying migration from within and taking cultural and individual motivations and experiences into account, and perhaps already represented a dissident point of view when he first expressed it in the 1970s (Potts 2010: 41). While agreeing with Amin that migration processes must be considered in relation to the structuring effects of economic production and the underlying political economy at play, this chapter argues that it may nevertheless be crucial to pay attention to the ways in which migration is conceived of and experienced by the individual in order to understand the actual working of the conditions in question beyond their importance as abstract economic parameters. Focusing on the motivations and ideas underlying the migratory projects of young Mandinka-speaking migrants from Senegal and Gambia, this chapter thus explores the ways in which globalizing socioeconomic conditions translate into individual aspirations. In this regard, the chapter considers individual perceptions and aspirations as an important form of social commentary on the conditions shaping the realities of contemporary postcolonial lifeworlds. The chapter first presents a brief historical sketch of migration from Africa toward Spain, before turning to a consideration of its underlying motives and the question of cause.

Beginnings

The history of undocumented African-European migration via the Strait of Gibraltar and, subsequently, by boat crossings to the Canary Islands, can be traced back to the capsizing of a small boat just off the coast of Los Lances, a beach close to Spain's southernmost town of Tarifa, in November 1988. Of the 23 people who had been on board the vessel only five survived. Eleven bodies resurfaced and were washed onto the shore during the next few days. The bodies of the remaining seven passengers were never recovered. While the small blue vessel that capsized at Los Lances was probably not the first boat used to cross from Morocco to Spain, it was the first attempt of, in this case Moroccan, migrants to reach Spain which, due to the shocking death toll, interviews with some of the survivors, and pictures taken and published of at least one of the corpses, received major public attention, and has become the publicly remembered beginning of a process which still continues, albeit with changing routes, today. In this context, it is also important to remember that the first African migrants coming to Spain did not arrive via the Strait of Gibraltar but had come overland from France. Entry by boat became predominant only once it became clear that there were plenty of labour opportunities in Spain while, at the same time, French visa and immigration policies became more and more restrictive.[3]

During the early nineties most of the arrivals were from Morocco itself. From the mid 1990s onwards Moroccan migrants were increasingly joined by sub-Saharan migrants, mostly from West Africa. In order to embark upon the short but dangerous crossing of the Strait of Gibraltar, most migrants had first to travel overland through Mali, Niger, and Algeria in order to reach Morocco. The reason for this particularly long and often arduous journey overland was and continues to be twofold. On the one hand, due to the military conflict between the Polisario movement and the Moroccan state in the region of Western Sahara, including a system of fortified walls more than 2,500 kilometres long built by Morocco, the coastal route to Morocco through Mauritania has in practice been blocked. On the other hand, flying into Morocco, although possible with Moroccan tourist visas which are reportedly obtained more easily than visas to European countries, is perceived by many as being too great a financial risk because many migrants are denied entry even with a valid tourist visa and thus forced to return directly to their home countries, negating almost at once their own as well as their relatives' financial efforts in obtaining visas and airfares.

The financial risks of the inland route are no lower, however. The costs involved in crossing the Nigerien-Algerian and the Algerian-Moroccan borders are high, often involving arrest and expulsion to Niger and Mali by Algerian and Moroccan border controls – whereby migrants are often stripped of their valuables before being expelled. Many sub-Saharan migrants arrive in Morocco with few or no financial means. In consequence, they are unable to pay to cross to Spain by boat and are virtually stranded in Morocco. While many found themselves in one of Morocco's major cities and urban agglomerations such as Tangier and Casablanca, others tended to stay on the Moroccan Mediterranean coast in improvised, make-shift camps, avoiding the inevitable costs of lodging in the cities, in some cases saving whatever is left from their travel budgets and waiting for a perhaps cheaper chance to cross, in some cases simply trying to hold on.

Given the precariousness of this state of suspension in a kind of permanent transit, in 2005 an increasing number of migrants started to avoid the sea passage and to enter European territory directly by crossing the fenced, barbed-wired and guarded borders of the Spanish enclaves of Ceuta and Melilla. The eventual series of attempts by especially sub-Saharan migrants to climb over the fences of the Spanish enclaves in the autumn of 2005 involved several deaths and many injuries, and received major media attention. These events propelled the issue of African-European migration into the public arena in a hitherto unprecedented way. On the level of public debate reactions to these events were mixed, invoking concerns about the precariousness of the situation of African migrants as well as about Europe being threatened by an uncontrolled influx of migrants, potentially destabilizing social and public security. The practical reactions and measures taken on the political level were more of one mind, emphasizing the necessity of effective border control. As the most immediate result of this tightening of security efforts, the fences around the Spanish enclaves were fortified, making further crossings impossible. At the same time, negotiations with the Moroccan authorities had to secure tighter controls at the Moroccan-Algerian border.

While the crossing of the fences of the Spanish enclaves seems to have been effectively stopped, the same does not hold for (West-) African-European migration in general. As a matter of fact, the most immediate result of these policies was that the points of embarkation and arrival moved further south. With the routes through and from Morocco increasingly blocked, an increasing number of open but much larger fishing boats started to depart from Mauritania, Senegal, Gambia and even Guinea-Bissau, directed now not towards continental Spain but towards the Canary Islands. The Canary Islands were not an entirely new destination for migrants attempting to get to Europe. Smaller boats, similar to those used for crossing the Mediterranean and referred to as *pateras* in the Spanish media, had been used earlier in order to cross from Morocco and Spanish Sahara to the Canary Islands.

These smaller boats, however, were not suitable to make the longer crossings from Mauritania and Senegal. Larger fishing vessels, however, were suitable. This passage was first tried in 2004 by an experienced Senegalese fisherman originally from Saint Louis upon the request and purchase of his vessel and services by a Malian organizing clandestine travel to Europe (Sall and Morand 2008: 38). Since 2006, larger pirogues or *cayucos* (as this type of boat is referred to in the Spanish press) have been used for passages of 1,000 kilometres and more. As a result of this change in means of transport, the number of African migrants arriving in the Canaries leaped from 4,700 in 2005 to more than 31,000 in 2006.[4]

All these developments have been followed up extensively in the media and have formed the topic of numerous reports by government and non-governmental agencies. And yet, culturally and historically sensitive descriptions and analyses of its economic, political, and sociocultural causes are less readily available, not to speak of detailed accounts of the cultural and personal motives and trajectories behind the official statistics. This is not meant as a general critique of the way these developments have been covered by the media. As a matter of fact, journalists and film-makers have been among the first actually to look at the individual stories behind the news, including detailed documentation of the conditions many migrants endure on their travels and the ambivalent ways European states have reacted to their arrival in Europe.[5] It is rather that the perhaps inevitable reduction of these events to numbers of arrivals and deaths in the daily news seems at least partly to obliterate the descriptions of the conditions and dynamics aimed at in longer formats of journalistic writing and film making. In a similar way, the use of quantitative rather than qualitative approaches to the understanding of human realities on the one hand, and approaches that answer perhaps too promptly to government and administration-induced interests concerning issues such as integration and public security, on the other, has had a problematic impact on the way current African-European migration has been dealt with in certain branches of the social, political and economic sciences. The quantitative and policy-oriented approaches seem to stand in the way of more complex and nuanced accounts and analyses of the ways in which these processes are experienced by the protagonists themselves. As the editors of this volume remark in their introduction, it is only recently that the social sciences and especially social and cultural anthropology have developed an increased attention to the more personal and cultural dimensions of these processes, including the ways migration and migratory experiences are perceived of and voiced in local settings and the embeddedness in and relation of these experiences and local conceptualizations and practices to the wider field of a globalizing political economy.[6]

Drawing on ethnographic research in Senegal and Gambia between 2002 and 2005 and ongoing research with Senegalese migrants in Spain (since 2006), this chapter aims at contributing to this growing body of literature through a culturally and historically sensitive analysis of the reasons and motives underlying the migration of Mandinka-speaking young men (originally) from the region of Yacine and the neighbouring area of Pakao in the Casamance region of Southern Senegal. The analysis of the imagination, practice, cultural dynamics and impact of migration outlined in this chapter was first developed in the context of the research I conducted in Senegal and Gambia, which mainly focused on the cultural logic and existential significance of divinatory practices such as geomancy and cowrie divination⊠practices frequently employed for coming to terms with and facilitating migration projects as well as confronting problems caused by the absence of sons and husbands due to migration.[7] These attempts to understand the motives underlying the current dynamics of migration in Senegal and Gambia are reconsidered through conversations with Senegalese migrants in Spain during which these earlier ideas were explicitly addressed and discussed. This has resulted in an increasingly dialogical and retrospective mode of analysis, moving back and forth between different settings, voices and theoretical perspectives.

Questions

During the research on the personal significance and cultural logic of divination which I conducted in Senegal and Gambia from 2002 to 2005, I was struck by the fact that many of the consultations I had the chance to witness centred round the question of 'the path of travel' or simply 'the path', as migration was referred to by diviners and their clients.[8] By 2002 and 2003, the more dramatic scenes at Ceuta, Melilla, and the Canary Islands had not yet emerged and the issue of African-European migration had not been mediatized to the extent that would push it to the forefront of public debate and awareness by 2005 and 2006. Initially, I had therefore not been aware of the extent to which the idea and practice of migration had started to capture especially young people's minds, increasingly shaping their personal perception of their lives and economic possibilities. Of course I had heard people inquiring about the possibility of obtaining invitations and visas for travelling to Europe, and in fact already on my first trip to Senegal in 2001 at least two young men had mentioned to me their wish to travel to and look for work in Europe. However, it was only during my apprenticeship with several diviners, and in the consultations I witnessed and the subsequent conversations I had with them and their clients that I became fully conscious of the acuteness of the role that the issue of migration had started to play in Senegalese and Gambian society, extending far beyond the ethnic and religious groups international migration had until then been associated with in the Senegalese context, such as the Soninke from the upper Senegal valley and the Mouride brotherhood.[9] What was especially striking to me – and this point has been confirmed to me during many later conversations with Senegalese migrants in Spain – was that the degree to which migration is considered a feasible option was not easily linked to categories such as 'youth' or activity in the informal sector. From what people told me it became clear that the appeal of the idea of migration was not limited to people without employment, or to a clearly definable condition of poverty, or to a particular age group. While statistically men under 30 years old with little or irregular income probably do constitute the majority of those who will actually leave and try to get to Europe, many middle-aged men (older than thirty) and even people with salaried work told me they were considering migrating to Europe if possible, and some of them did. As a matter of fact, the distinction between unemployment and employment loses much of its immediate heuristic value as a means of sociological distinction when the percentage of those having regular salaried work is, as in the case of Senegal, comparable to the average rates of (youth) unemployment in most Western European countries, causing an almost complete reversal in income stability if one compares sub-Saharan and western European household economies.[10] A similar problem exists in relation to the category of 'youth' if associated with a specific age group, such as, for instance, in the definition used by UNESCO defining a youth as a person of 18 to 24 years of age, or definitions associating youth with unmarried marital status. In fact, many of the 'young' migrants are actually older than 24. At the same time, even if they are younger than 24 at the time of departure, they may nevertheless already be married and have children, enjoying a much more adult status in their communities than unmarried individuals.

In this regard it was not so much the fact that migration had become an important option for individual economic praxis in Senegalese society that I felt needed to be addressed, but the question of what precisely constituted and constitutes the rather generalized appeal of the idea of migration as perhaps *the* only remaining option, obliterating any other. This question is all the more relevant as Senegal is considered to be one of the more stable political and economic countries of the region, ruling factors such as military conflicts, civil unrest, or major food shortages out of the list of factors causing people to move. Although there had been a military conflict in the Western parts of the Casamance region for some time and teenagers told me that especially in the bigger towns and cities such as Serekunda, Kaoloack, Thiès and Dakar you eat, but you never eat until you are full, people would generally not consider themselves refugees or starving. Still, the main motive for migration in Senegal and Gambia is clearly economic, most people's economic situation being chronically tenuous and money being the one element dominating any conversation on the topic of migration. At the same time, there seemed and seem to be other factors and rationalities at play as well. Rationalities that transcend simple economic reasoning but refer directly to the way one sees oneself, oneself and others, oneself and the world.

Globalization as absence

One of the possibilities in thinking about current migration processes is to consider migration as one of the major outcomes and functions of globalization, pragmatically defined as an increasing movement of goods, ideas, capital, and people world wide. The one element uniting the different aspects of this pragmatic definition is a generalized increase in mobility. This concerns the mobility of material objects, especially through trade, of immaterial elements such as ideas and images, and of people. Several related but distinct aspects are worth mentioning with regard to the globalization-as-increased-mobility-formula that disturb clear-cut distinctions such as between push and pull factors, cause and effect, agency and structure.

It is clear in the above and other definitions of globalization that mobility and movement are not just seen as the outcome or effect of globalization processes but are, simultaneously, constitutive of the processes they are described as being part of. Blurring the distinction between effect and cause, it becomes clear that, in the same way as globalization and mobility, the process of migration, as one of the most visible ways in which mobility seems to manifest itself, is also not just caused by globalization but very much part of it. The significance of this becomes even clearer if we include another relationship, both facilitating and hampering current analyses of migration processes, in the analysis: that between agency and structure. Depending upon which dimension one chooses to focus on, one's analysis will arrive at different conclusions. Echoing with the critique of studying subjective motives for migration by Amin, approaches emphasizing the agency of migrants and other sociocultural actors in current social, cultural, and economic practices are, in this regard, increasingly criticized for confusing issues of cultural difference with what are actually issues of economic and political inequality.[11] At the same time, however, it should not be overlooked that approaches emphasizing agency, cultural creativity and people's capacity to resist have been developed precisely as a reaction to approaches that, by closing in on questions of economic dispossession and constraint, seemed to victimize people to an extent that often appears in contradiction to the ways people see themselves and conceive of their own actions.

Things become even more complex when one considers the fact that – quite in contrast to the emphasis on mobility and movement characterizing most conceptualizations concerning the nature of globalization, and despite factually increasing volumes of national, international and intercontinental transport – what the majority of people in Senegal, Gambia, and elsewhere are confronted with and experience is not mobility but *immobility*. They face the difficulty of affording even rudimentary means of transport, often increased by a lack of or deteriorating transportation infrastructure, and the virtual impossibility of obtaining visas for travel to Europe or the US. As a result, globalization is by many people primarily experienced in its absence, in the form of the non-arrival of change, unfulfilled promises and aspirations rather than in an actual increase of mobility or flux of goods. As I have argued elsewhere (Graw, forthcoming), the various forms in which globalization manifests itself as absence – for example in the trade with fake commodities or second hand clothes – reveal the effects of abjection and annihilation which directly impact upon the ways in which personal and local realities are perceived. Not only do these experiences add considerably to the idea that migration is perhaps the only way of realizing the future one hopes for. They also affect the imagination and practice of migration more generally.

The precise impact of these processes of annihilation and abjection and their significance for understanding current processes of migration is not easy to define. It may even be disguised by self-designations used by migrants themselves, such as the description of migration as '*aventure*' (adventure) in Francophone contexts, or 'hustling' in Anglophone settings – terms that emphasize the ability and decisiveness to act, the will to take risks and to realize oneself, rather than expressing the underlying conditions, vulnerabilities or afflictions.[12] In contrast to these self-designations as adventurers and hustlers, the diviners I worked with insisted that in order to identify and understand the nature and cause of their clients' wishes, difficulties and aspirations – concerns and longings which are usually not revealed to them by their clients beforehand but which it is the diviner's task to identify through the divinatory procedure – they had to look for what they referred to as '*niitooroo*', literally, the 'injury of the soul', that is, the underlying affliction forming the basis of a person's longings and intentions (Graw 2006). The question that arises here is that of the cultural reality, emotional substance and personal significance of what appears to be possible to be addressed only in the interstitial cultural space opened up by the divinatory encounter. Drawing on a conversation with one of my Senegalese interlocutors in Spain, I will in what follows address the questions where, outside the divinatory encounter, experiences of annihilation express themselves and become manifest and how the experience of absence is mediated and transformed into migratory projects.

Absence and nothingness

Roquetas de Mar, 5 May 2008. Having socialized for a few hours and having had lunch with the other inhabitants with whom A. shared a flat in the neighbourhood of Doscientas Viviendas, one of the neighbourhoods with the highest percentage of North African and sub-Saharan migrants in Roquetas de Mar, a small town 20 kilometres south-west of Almería, A. and I decided to go out for a walk and perhaps have a coffee somewhere outside. At around half past three in the afternoon, it is still hot in the streets but not uncomfortable. Still a little tired from lunch, however, we decide not to continue down to the corniche but first to have a coffee and to continue to the seaside later in the afternoon. At this time of the day, the café is not very busy and we find a table right in one of the large windows facing the street. When the waitress brings our coffees, we start reminiscing about how, after dinner, back in his uncle's village in the Casamance, we often used to have *attaya*, the strong and sweet Mauritanian style tea popular in all of Senegal and Gambia, finishing the day by sitting together, waiting for the tea to be ready, listening to the last sounds coming out of the neighbouring compounds, engulfed in the tremendous dark of a night untainted by electric light. As things go, reminiscing about one thing brings up other memories, of other friends, family members, et cetera. Pausing for a moment, lost in the comfort of memories of what one has known best, he says that sometimes he wonders why on earth he had wanted to come to Spain in the first place. If he had known how difficult things were and how different from what he had expected, he would never have come.

'What did you expect to find?', I asked.

Without giving me a direct answer, he asked if I remembered what I had asked him when, still in Senegal, we once talked about his wish to go to Spain and join his relatives there. Answering his question himself, he said, 'You asked me why I did not use the money I would need for the trip to Spain to start something at home.' Pausing again he continued, 'You know, what surprised me most is that I couldn't find work. When I got to Zaragoza, you know, where I stayed with my mother's niece and her husband, I stayed there for months and there was no work at all. I had to ask my relatives for money if I wanted to catch a bus or go and drink coffee when I had thought I would start working immediately, taking whatever chance opened up, earning money and start sending money home for my wife and my mother. Like that...', the last phrase being accompanied by an energetic and slightly resigned finger snapping. 'You know,' he continued, 'once I have made enough money here, I will go home and invest my money in Senegal. Perhaps I will throw myself into agriculture, buy a tractor perhaps. Something like that.'

The question why the possibilities of doing something at home are often not even explored and why the idea of migration often seems to shut out any other thoughts still hanging in the air, I told him that I had often been asked by friends working for development agencies about what to them appeared to be a rather passive and uninterested attitude towards the agricultural and health projects they were offering and pursuing – for instance, growing vegetables to provide a more varied diet for the people and their children.

'What did you tell them?'

I answered that my standard answer had been that people were not disinterested in these things in general, but that growing more tomatoes or other vegetables in their backdoor garden would not allow them to buy a new zinc roof for their house, not to speak of a car or a house in town. It was just not what people were looking for. Now, pausing for a moment myself, I added that I thought the fact that especially young people would often no longer consider local economic options but instead focus directly on migration might have to do with other things as well. 'For instance?', he asked. 'A certain degree of frustration because of having to buy Chinese or Korean copies of certain electronic products, for instance', I suggested, referring at the same time to similar facts like being forced to buy imported second hand rather than new clothing, the growing frustrations when seeing returning migrants coming home with money, TV-sets, and gifts, and the increasing feeling of pressure to achieve the same.

'Do you know what they call dealing with second hand clothing in Wolof?', he asked.

'*Fuuk diaye*. Right? Selling stuff from which you first have to shake the dust off.'

'Yeah. Do you know what we call something like a second hand shirt or other cheap stuff in Mandinka.'

'No.'

'*Feng kati baloo*. A thing without body. And do you know what some parents say to their sons when they don't work or when their work doesn't pay off? *I manke fenti*. You are nothing.'

The question of cause

I had sometimes wondered about the extent to which the economic logics of remittances and new levels of gift-giving introduced by migrants actually shaped people's perception of their own situation. I was now shocked at the degree to which, according to what I was told, these effects had actually penetrated not just individual minds but the social tissue of kinship groups, families and, one may add, society at large. Perhaps pointing in a similar direction, it has been argued that part of the reason for migration in the Senegalese context has to be looked for in the relations of competition existing between co-wives in polygamous households and the corresponding obligations of their sons towards them (Bouilly 2008: 20-21). In terms of analysis, part of the problem here results perhaps from the fact that the same social relations that explicitly or implicitly exert pressure upon the individual are the same relations upon which the individual socially, emotionally, and in most cases also economically depends upon, a situation triggering different reactions in different individuals.

My interlocutors have unanimously described their obligations towards their relatives and their wish to help their families as an important reason for having come to Spain, emphasizing social relations and the resulting obligations as positive motivational elements. In a different vein, the Senegalese psychologist Mamadou Mbodji cites a young migrant repatriated from the Canary Islands to Senegal who, in contrast to my interlocutors, mentions escape from social obligations and control as part of what motivated him to migrate (Mbodji 2008: 310). Even if this statement may be exceptional, it shows that personal reasons and motivations may not be identical with structural settings, and thus need to be taken into account in order to understand the current dynamics of migration in Africa as well as elsewhere. This holds true even if, as Amin has argued, these motives can be read as rationalizations of decisions which are not self-determined but become necessary due to political economic conditions. In fact, part of the tension that seems to exist between structural and more agency-oriented approaches towards migration may have to do with a somehow restricted understanding of the notion of cause.

The term 'cause' cannot just be used to describe that which causes a situation or the movement of an object mechanically, but also that which an individual or a group of people envisages and intends to defend as their 'cause', allowing for describing, for instance, the idea of social justice as the cause of voluntary social work or the idea of equality as the cause of socialism. In order fully to appreciate the significance of the semantics of the term cause for the theoretization of migration it is important to remember that these different usages of the term 'cause' are not coincidental but reflective of attempts to come to terms with the nature of being and causality in philosophy that go back to Aristotle's famous reflections in the *Physics* and the *Metaphysics,* where he distinguishes between four types of cause necessary in order to understand the nature of an object or action: (1) the efficient cause as the force or instrument by which a thing as produced; (2) the formal cause constituting the specific form or shape of an object or action; (3) the material cause encompassing the elements or matter from which an object is produced; and (4) the final cause as the end or purpose for which something is produced or done.

It is clear that our most common understanding of a cause is identical to the first category, that is, the efficient cause. In regard to the tension between structural and agency-oriented approaches toward migration that interests us here, it could be argued that the contradiction between these approaches seems to arise precisely from the disagreement on the question of what forms the efficient cause of migration as that what makes a person move and leave his or her familiar geographic and social surroundings. In such a view, structural approaches would thus be seen as approaches which identify the economic conditions as efficient cause, while agency-oriented approaches would appear to be viewing the subject itself as the efficient cause of his or her decisions and actions. However, agency-oriented authors are unlikely to ignore the importance of structural conditions as efficient cause of migration. Instead, they would argue that while conditions are of course crucial for understanding migration, migration cannot be reduced to a simple reaction to economic conditions but involves many more aspects, including prior or existing historical and cultural experiences of migration, culturally specific understandings of selfhood and agency, notions and patterns of intrafamiliar and intergenerational solidarity, social competition within and among social groups and many other aspects, all of which are important in order to understand migration as a social praxis, and in order adequately to describe the way social actors themselves perceive their own decisions and actions. In a similar vein, authors more concerned with the structural causes of migration are likely to respond, as Amin does so eloquently, that they are not ignorant of personal and social motives for migration but that these motives do not cause the processes in question but are, in fact, caused by the politico-economic conditions, not vice versa.

While these clarifications may bring structural and agency-oriented approaches closer together, the basic tension seems to remain and the respective accounts and analyses are likely to be perceived as insufficient by either side. How can this dilemma be resolved? Drawing on the ways migration is experienced and conceived of by my interlocutors, I would argue that what causes the tension between structural and agency-oriented approaches is perhaps not just a disagreement on the question of what constitutes the efficient cause of migration but also a tendency not to distinguish between the efficient and the final cause of migration, that is, between that which produces migration and that for which migration is pursued.

Migration and finality

Within the order of causes given by Aristotle, the fourth or final cause is traditionally held to be 'first in dignity' (Enriques and de Santinella 1932: 235). The main reason for this is that Aristotle bases his reflections on causality on examples concerning the meaning of the production of human artefacts and human action more generally, actions which regularly acquire their meaning through what Aristotle refers to as the *to on eneka*, that for which a thing is done, or *telos*, that is, their end, purpose, or function. One of the famous examples of the significance of the final cause concerns the meaning of walking, or rather going for a walk or stroll:

> Cause means ... the same as "end"; i.e. the final cause; e.g. as the "end" of walking is health. For why does man walk? "To be healthy," we say, and by saying this we consider that we have supplied the cause. (Aristotle, Metaphysics V, 2, 3)[13]

In other words, the reason for considering the final cause to be the first in dignity is that without understanding the end or *telos* of a person's action, this action may appear strange and without meaning. Once we understand the end for which something is done, we understand its sense, and by doing so recognize that the person as acting for a reason, for or towards an end that can be grasped and understood.

What, then, is the *telos* of migration in the Senegalese case? Asked for what reason someone would leave Senegal and try to go to Europe, the most common answer by my interlocutors in Senegal and in Spain was and continues to be 'in order to earn money'. Money (Mandinka *koddoo*) is given as the main reason or cause (*sabuu*), referring, in essence, to the wish to earn money and gain access to the economic and social possibilities it is associated with, from supporting one's family to being able to afford to marry, to start a small business, to build a house, etc. In this regard, the reason for migration is clearly economic, or at least finds its starting point in an economic situation and the way in which this situation is experienced. If one looks more closely at what is being said here, however, one sees that the end or purpose of going to Europe is not simply money as a material gain but overcoming the experience of lack of money and the social impasse which insufficient economic means implies for the person or family concerned. While this may seem rather obvious, it is important to keep this nuance in mind in order to understand the difference between the efficient cause of migration, be it perceived in the socioeconomic conditions or in the person's own decision and decidedness to leave, and its final cause, that is, its finality and underlying reason or motivation. In other words, what the distinction between efficient and final cause allows us to see is that even if migration may primarily need to be viewed as caused by economic conditions and the political economy producing these conditions, the conditions constituting migration's efficient cause do not form the sole element that needs to be taken into account. Instead, analyses of migration need to be complemented by a consideration of the final causes of migration, that is, the reasons which turn migration into a logical and dignified response to the conditions encountered. It is only in such a more nuanced perspective that it becomes clear that the final cause of migration is not simply socioeconomic conditions as such but the wish and decidedness to overcome them. And it is from such a more nuanced understanding of migratory causalities that one is able to start to develop modes of understanding migration that are not solely external but which resonate with the aspirations and motives expressed by its protagonists.

In this context it may be worth noting that the differentiations offered by an Aristotelian understanding of cause are useful not only in relation to the question of the *causa finalis* of migration. While different modalities and focuses of migration research are often described as competing, many of them could be considered under the rubric of one of the two other forms of causality described by Aristotle. The increasing interest in the sociocultural patterning and specificity of migration as a social practice in different locales and among different social, ethnic, and national groups, for instance, could be perceived as representing an interest which in its epistemological direction comes very close to the question of the *causa formalis* or formal cause in the terminology derived from Aristotle. In a similar way, studies describing the way migration is actually carried out, that is, by the use of what means and under what kind of conditions, could be described as investigating the *causa materialis* or material cause of migration. The challenge which this complex understanding of causality poses for the understanding of migration, and in fact any other practice, is the fact that for Aristotle all forms of cause may be relevant to understanding a given object or phenomenon. However, without the inclusion of the *causa finalis*, it is difficult to arrive at an understanding of migration that is existentially sensitive, and it is from here also that the terms and notions migrants employ in describing their undertakings start to make sense and start to lose their seemingly arbitrary character.

The use of notions such as 'travel' in Mandinka (*tamoo*) or 'adventuring' in West African French for referring to migration, in terms both of the actual journey and the later moves between different towns, cities and places of work, is precisely an expression of the insistence on the dignity of migration as an attempt to counter marginalizing economic conditions, not a sign of naïveté concerning the impact of these conditions or their political economic causes. In other words, the insistence on agency on the part of the migratory subject is not simply an expression of what within a political economical analysis may be understood as false consciousness. Instead, insistence on agency and self-determination is the expression of existential claims in the face of conditions that may indeed sometimes leave little choice. If all other ways appear blocked or dead-ended, migration becomes a promise, offering a way out, and simultaneously an expression of the claim to economic participation and well-being. And it is in this regard also, that is, as a claim to participation, access, and recognition, that the nature of the processes of migration we witness worldwide is not just factual, economic, or cultural, but also deeply political. Also in this regard, the question of cause cannot be avoided.

References

Adams, Adrian. 1977. *Le long voyage des gens du Fleuve*. Paris: François Maspero.

Amin, Samir. 1995. Migrations in Cotemporary Africa. A Retrospective View. In: Baker, Jonathan and Tade Akin Aida (eds.), *The Migration Experience in Africa*. Uppsala: Nordic Africa Institute, 29-40.

Bakewell, Oliver and Hein de Haas. 2007. African Migrations: Continuities, Discontinuities, and Recent Transformations. In: Chabal, Patrick, Ulf Engel and Leo de Haan, *African Alternatives*. Leiden: Brill, 95-117.

Bilger, Veronika and Albert Kraler, eds. 2005. African Migrations. Historical Perspectives and Contemporary Dynamics. Special issue of *Stichproben. Wiener Zeitschrift für kritische Afrikastudien* 8.

Bouilly, Emanuelle. 2008. Les enjeux féminins de la migration masculine. Le collectif des femmes pour la lutte contre l'immigration clandestine de Thiaroye-sur-Mer. *Politique africaine* 109: 16-31.

Dia, Omar and Rennée Colin –Noguès. 1982. *Yâkârê. L'autobiographie d'Oumar*. Paris: François Maspero.

Diop, A. Moustapha (1990) L'émigration murid en Europe. *Hommes & migrations* 1132 : 21-24.

Ebin, Victoria. 1990. Commerçants et missionnaires: une confrérie musulmane Sénégalaise à New York. *Hommes & migrations* 1132 : 25-31.

Enriques, F. and De Santinella, G. 1932. *Storia del pensiero scientifico. Il mondo antico (Vol. 1)*. Bologna: Nicola Zanichelli Editore.

Ferguson, James. 2007. *Global Shadows. Africa in the Neoliberal World Order*. Durham and London: Duke University Press.

Graw, Knut. 2005a. Culture of Hope in West Africa, *ISIM Review* 16, 28-29.

Graw, Knut. 2005b. The Logic of Shells: Knowledge and Lifeworld-Poiesis in Senegambian Cowrie Divination, *Mande Studies* 7: 21-48.

Graw, Knut. 2006. Locating *Nganiyo*: Divination as Intentional Space, *Journal of Religion in Africa* 36 (1): 78-119.

Graw, Knut. 2009a. Beyond Expertise: Specialist Agency and the Autonomy of the Divinatory Ritual Process, *Africa* 79 (1): 92-109.

Graw, Knut. 2009b. Divination as Hermeneutic Encounter. Reflections on Understanding, Dialogue, and the Intersubjective Foundation of Divinatory Consultation. In: William Christian and Gabor Klaniczay eds. *'The Vision Thing' - Studying Divine Intervention*. Budapest: Collegium Budapest, 459 - 477.

Graw, Knut. Forthcoming. Divination in Times of Migration: Globalization, Subjectivity and the Path of Travel in Senegal and Gambia.

Hahn, Hans Peter and Georg Klute. 2008. *Cultures of Migration: African Perspectives*. Münster: Lit Verlag.

Jackson, Michael. 2007. Migrant Imaginaries. With Sewa Koroma in southeast London, Chapter six of *Excursions*. Durham and London: Duke University Press, 102-134. (A shorter version of this chapter has appeared as Jackson, Michael. 2008. The Shock of the New: On Migrant Imaginaries and Critical Transitions, *Ethnos* 73 (1): 57-72.)

Martínez Veiga, Ubaldo (2001) *El Ejido. Discriminación, exclusión social y racismo*. Madrid: Catarata.

Mbodji, Mamadou. 2008. Imaginaires et migrations. Le cas du Sénégal, in Momar-Coumba Diop, ed. *Le Sénégal des migrations: mobilités, identités et sociétés*. Paris, Dakar, and Nairobi: Karthala, CREPOS, and ONUhabitat, 305-320.

Moura, Paulo. 2005. *Passaporte para o Céu*. Lisbon: Dom Quixote.

Pandolfo, Stefania. 2007. 'The burning'. Finitude and the politico-theological imagination of illegal migration. *Anthropological Theory* 7(3): 329-363.

Potts, Deborah. 2010. *Circular Migration in Zimbabwe and Contemporary Sub-Saharan Africa*. Woodbridge, Suffolk and Rochester, NY: James Currey at Boydell and Brewer.

Sabry, Tarik. 2004. Young *Amazighs*, the land of *Eromen* and Pamela Anderson as the Embodiment of Modernity, *Westminster Papers in Communication and Culture* 1 (1): 38-51.

Sabry, Tarik. 2005. Emigration as Popular Culture. The Case of Morocco, *European Journal of Cultural Studies* 8 (1): 5-22.

Salazar, Noel B. 2010. Tanzanian Migrant Imaginaries. *Working Papers of the International Migration Institute* 20: 1-29.

Sall, Aliou and Pierre Morand. 2008. Pêche artisanale et émigration des jeunes africains par voie piroguière, *Politique africaine* 109: 32-41.

Sarró, Ramon. 2007. La aventura como categoría cultural: apuntes simmelianos sobre la emigración subsahariana. *Working papers of the Instituto de Ciências Sociais Universidade de Lisboa* 2007 (3): 1-16.

Schmidt di Friedberg, Ottavia. 1994. *Islam, solidarietà e lavoro. I muridi senegalesi in Italia.* Torino: Edizioni della Fondazione Agnelli.

Schmitz, Jean, ed. 2008. Migrants ouest-africains vers l'Europe: Historicité et espace moraux. *Politique africaine* 109: 5-15.

Simoncini, Stefano. 2004. *Frontiera Sud. Marocco/Spagna: viaggio nei non-luoghoi dell'immigrazione "illegale"*, with photographic work by Giancarlo Ceraudo. Rome: Fandango.

Suárez-Navaz, Liliana. 2004. *Rebordering the Mediterranean. Boundaries and Citizenship in Southern Europe.* New York and Oxford: Berghahn.

Žižek, Slavoj. 2005. *The Ticklish Subject. The Absent Centre of Political Ontology.* London and New York: Verso.

Žižek, Slavoj. 2008. *In Defense of Lost Causes.* London and New York: Verso.

Notes

1   Earlier versions of this chapter were presented at the international workshop 'Migration at home: Migratory Imaginations and Imaginary Cosmopolitanisms in Africa and beyond', organized by Knut Graw and Samuli Schielke at the Zentrum Moderner Orient in Berlin, 11-13 March 2009, and the lecture series *Africa and Beyond: Translocal Perspectives*, organized by Achim von Oppen at the University of Bayreuth and the Bayreuth International Graduate School of African Studies, 28 January 2010.

2   For a similarly critical argument emphasizing the importance of the study of internal migrations in comparison to views presenting migration primarily in terms of outward, international migration see Bakewell and De Haas 2007.

3   It is unclear in which year precisely boats were used for the first time or started to be used regularly for crossing to Europe. However, it was during the mid-1980s that North African workers started to be employed in the growing economy of glasshouse agriculture in the

region of Almería in southern Spain (Martínez Veiga 2001: 41). At the same time, immigration controls in France and Gibraltar were tightened, making regular entry into Spain more and more difficult and triggering clandestine crossings of the Strait of Gibraltar with the use of small boats or *pateras* in the first half of the 1990s (Suárez-Navaz 2004: 172-174). In this regard, the tragedy at Los Lances in 1988 was probably not coincidental.

4   Between 2002 and 2005, the number of arrivals ranged between 9.900 (2002) and 4.700 (2005). After its peak in 2006 and allegedly due to the tightening of controls, numbers dropped to 12.624 in 2007 and 9.089 in 2008. Simultaneously, also the number of arrivals in the Balears and the Spanish peninsula dropped from 7.502 in 2006 and 5.779 in 2007 to 4.243 in 2008 causing the Spanish Ministerio del Interior to speak of continuous success in what it refers to as its 'fight against illegal immigration' (*lucha contra la inmigración ilegal*).

5   See, for instance, Simoncini 2004, Moura 2005, Naranjo Nobel 2006, Brinkbäumer 2006, et al.

6   See, for instance, Sabry 2004 and 2005, Bilger and Kraler and contributors 2005, Pandolfo 2007, Jackson 2007, Schmitz and contributors 2008, Hahn and Klute and contributors 2008, Graw, forthcoming, and the further references in the introduction to this volume. For an account of migratory imaginations in an East African setting see also Salazar 2010.

7   For analyses of different aspects of these practices see Graw 2005a and b, 2006, 2009a and b. For the relationship between divination and migration see Graw, forthcoming.

8   *Taama siloo* or *taamoo* in Mandinka, *yoonu tukki* or *yoon* in Wolof. For a more encompassing discussion of this notion see Graw (under review).

9   For early accounts of the importance of migration in Soninke communities see, for instance, Adam 1977, and Dia and Colin-Noguès 1982; for early accounts of the developing transnational trade networks of the Mouridiyya see Diop 1990, Ebin 1990 and Schmidt di Friedberg 1994.

10 The last available rate for salaried employment in Senegal having been 17.4 % in 2005 as indicated by the Africa Brief of the 2010/2011 Global Wage Report of the International Labour Organisation (ILO).

11 For one of the most trenchant critiques of agency-oriented approaches in the social sciences see Ferguson 2007. For a similar insistence on the analysis of global inequalities in the field of political philosophy see, for instance, Žižek 2005 and 2008.

12 For an interesting discussion of the notion of adventure see also Sarró 2007.

13 Cited in the translation by Hugh Treddenick, Aristotle, *The Metaphysics, Books I - IX*. Cambridge, Mass. and London, Engl.: Harvard University Press, 1933.

Bushfalling:
The making of migratory expectations in Anglophone Cameroon[1]

Maybritt Jill Alpes

For an entire year, my 25-year-old research assistant Delphine refused to take her salary because she wanted to save it up to be able to travel.[2] She was determined to add to her salary money she received from boyfriends, ex-boyfriends and family members in order to travel out of the country. She wanted to study in either South Africa or Europe. Based on what she had heard from others abroad, she planned to study and hustle. Hustling in Cameroon means to try and be ready to do any kind of work.[3]

The topic of out-migration is imminently present in Cameroon and referred to by the term 'bushfalling'. Bushfalling is the act of going out to the 'wilderness' (bush) to hunt down meat (money) and bring the trophies back home. A bushfaller is expected to 'hustle' – which means that he or she will accept any kind of work so as to be able to 'work money'.[4] Bush is the term used to describe '*white man kontri*' – largely understood as the 'West' (Nyamjoh and Page 2002). Any place where there is money can be called 'bush'. The most popular places to fall bush are Europe and the U.S. However, under certain circumstances, it is also possible to gain status and success in places like South Africa, Dubai or China.

To achieve the goal of studying and hustling in bush, Delphine was willing to give money to a migration broker. In the midst of the transcription of yet another interview on the hardships, struggles and sufferings of an undocumented migrant woman whom I had interviewed in Europe, Delphine jumped up, laughed and proclaimed: 'Je veux go a tout prix!'[5] In her exclamation, she made reference to a Cameroonian film entitled 'Paris à tout prix' that came out in 2008. The film portrays the risks and potential downfalls of migration, such as unwanted sex work, money swindlers, failure and deportation. After watching the film, Delphine just shrugged her shoulders, viewing these issues as the 'bad luck' of the protagonists. Delphine was ambitious and determined: 'Bush a tout prix!' She was going to go at any cost and in any way. If others had been unlucky, she would work hard on getting bush right. She was going to have success and bush was the only means and place to get there.

In our research, Delphine and I repeatedly came across migration brokers who failed to send out their clients and families who had invested money in vain into the bushfalling projects of their children. Yet, Delphine would not change her mind about wanting to go to bush. Half way through fieldwork, one of the informants whose bushfalling trajectory Delphine had been transcribing was deported back to Cameroon. Delphine saw first hand how impossible Manuella's life had become in Cameroon. Although they became friends, Delphine did not trust, believe or take Manuella's advice seriously. Whatever the odds, she wanted to see bush with her own eyes.

Delphine is not an isolated case of extreme fixation on bush. The level of enthusiasm about the possibilities of bushfalling is high in Cameroon in general and in Anglophone Cameroon in particular. Eighty percent of all respondents in a survey that I conducted said that they would like to fall bush[6] and twenty-nine percent had actually tried in concrete ways to go abroad (see graph 1).[7] Above all, young Cameroonians – not yet married and of both genders – are eager to try to make their lives outside the country.[8] Most bushfalling in Cameroon takes place via the airport and not overland.

Graph 1   Wanting to and trying to fall bush

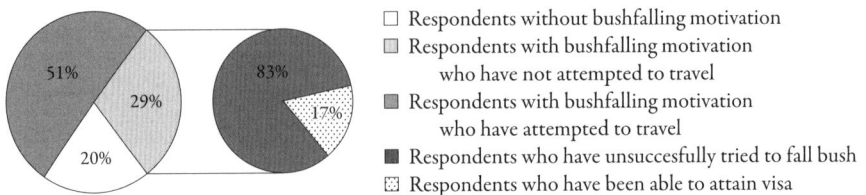

☐ Respondents without bushfalling motivation
▨ Respondents with bushfalling motivation
    who have not attempted to travel
▦ Respondents with bushfalling motivation
    who have attempted to travel
■ Respondents who have unsuccesfully tried to fall bush
⊡ Respondents who have been able to attain visa

Source: Quantitative survey conducted in May 2008 amongst 100 respondents in different neighbourhoods in Buea, South West Cameroon

Although families are willing to mobilize considerable sums of money for both their daughters and sons to go to bush,[9] the gap between desire and capacity to travel abroad is vast. In my survey, only five percent of all respondents had actually been able to travel to bush. In relation to bushfalling, the experience of having tried, but failing to travel out is extremely common. Cameroonians perceive the world as closed off. Possibilities for air travel out are referred to as *lines, openings* and *programmes*. To understand the eagerness of Delphine and others wanting to fall bush at all cost, the gap between aspiration and capability needs to be taken into account.[10] Many young Africans today experience their place in the world as having been abjected (Ferguson 1999: 236; Piot 2010: 77 & 94).[11] Central to this particular sense of exclusion is not the cost of migration, but the absence of visas (Rosny 2002).

This chapter seeks to contribute to the discussion on how people come to evaluate scopes of possibilities for themselves both in Cameroon and abroad. It will do so by tracing the emergence of the phenomenon of bushfalling, as well as by analysing flows of information and their respective evaluation. Why do young Cameroonians persist in pursuing success in emigration? Why was the 'information' of the film and my research not relevant or trustworthy for Delphine? Through focusing in particular on flows of information and their respective evaluation as trustworthy or not, this book chapter seeks to contribute towards the discussion on questions of visibility and migratory expectations. In the introduction of this volume, Schielke and Graw evoke the image of migrants' houses in their home villages. In my chapter, I set out to explain why and how migrants' hardship abroad and cases of failure cannot become visible in a place of departure, such as Anglophone Cameroon.

The data that I draw on were generated during 13 months of fieldwork in 2008 and 2009 in Buea in the South West Province in Anglophone Cameroon. All interviews and conversations were conducted in Pidgin, the lingua franca of Anglophone Cameroon. Buea owes its size and dynamic character to the university that was constructed there in the early 1990s. As a university town, Buea is densely populated with young people – which is one of the main reasons I chose to conduct my study there. Buea is furthermore interesting as a key city in Anglophone Cameroon. Past patterns of labour migration mean that most of my informants are considered as 'foreigners' in Buea. Finally, it is interesting to examine the migration expectations of Anglophone Cameroonians who often entertain an ambivalent relationship with the mainly Francophone state (Konings and Nyamnjoh 2003).

As attitudes towards migratory risks need to be considered from the standpoint of risks in everyday life within the context of departure, this chapter will start by outlining the historical and geographical emergence of bushfalling in Anglophone Cameroon. In his work on involuntary immobility, Jørgen Carling takes into account not simply people's aspirations, but also their respective ability to emigrate (2002). So as to understand the migratory expectations and attitudes of Delphine and others, I suggest we need to consider not just people's ambitions of mobility, but also the hurdles and obstacles that render geographic mobility so difficult. It is also the hurdles and obstacles to (legal) migration that feed into the emergence of bushfalling.

In this chapter, I furthermore propose that, in order to explain both people's aspirations and their ability to travel, we need to consider what I term as the economy of migratory knowledge. With the economy of migratory knowledge, I refer to cultural and societal factors that structure flows of information and influence the construction of meaning within this sphere. Migration choices and strategies are developed under circumstances more complex than being informed or not informed about obstacles and downsides of migration. Instead I propose to examine trust in information. An in-depth understanding of how information on migration flows and is validated also puts into questions the deployment of ever greater financial resources into prevention and sensitisation campaigns that try to convince aspiring migrants to merely stay at home.

The making of bushfalling

So as to understand migratory expectations, I suggest we need to consider not just people's ambitions of mobility, but also the hurdles and obstacles that render geographic mobility so difficult. In an age of supposed 'globalisation', the movement of large parts of the world population remains remarkably restricted. Whilst the free flow of capital and commodities is often celebrated, little attention is given to the (un)free circulation of labour (and thus people) (Malkki 2002, 352; Kearney 1986). It is also the hurdles and obstacles to (legal) migration that feed into the making of migration expectations. In particular, it is the structural difficulty of migration that here has given birth to the emergence of migration in Cameroon under the term of 'bushfalling'.

'Bushfalling' is a very new expression and only started being used in the 1990s.[13] It is in the last two decades that the desire for out-migration on the part of Cameroonian youths has become rampant. In the late 1980s and early 1990s, policies related to the structural adjustment programme drastically changed the economic situation in Cameroon. As a consequence, salaries and profit margins are low in Cameroon. Civil servants are often paid little. Publicly employed teachers working at secondary schools, for example, earn on average between 60.000 and 100.000 CFA (90 to 150 Euros). A person who has been to bush has in many ways a higher social status than somebody who has a high level of education. Given the work prospects in Cameroon, many young Cameroonians firmly believe that the best place to work one's money these days is in bush.

The language in which Cameroonians talk about the world of travelling and migrating is revealing of the sense of exclusion in which ambitions of mobility have to be formulated. A priori the world is perceived as closed off and thus a possibility to travel out is referred to as a 'line' or an 'opening.' Given the a priori impossibility of mobility, it takes a 'programme' to be able to aspire to even try to leave the country. The word 'migration' is very rarely used. Rather people talk about wanting to 'travel' out. In other words, both this choice of word and the symbolism of bushfalling do not imply the idea of wanting to leave the country to 'settle' and permanently live elsewhere.

Originally, the bush refers to the rural hinterlands. In contrast to the term bushfaller, to call somebody a 'bushman' is an insult. It designates the person as 'primitive' and 'backward'. It is hence surprising to note that the big dream of migration of is talked about in terms of 'bushfalling'. In fact, 'to go bush' means to go hunting or to go to the farm, to work there, to sweat and then to bring back food to eat. People who 'fall bush' go to Europe to work there, to find money for survival, to send back that money for their family members to eat. It is the essence of food and money that joins the two seemingly contradictory meanings of 'bush' as in farm and 'bush' as in *white man kontri*' or the 'West' (Nyamnjoh and Page 2002). Both are a source of livelihood. Both are places of productivity.[14]

Ever since the early 1990s when the terminology of 'bushfalling' first emerged, 'bush' itself has come to define more and more the very notion of success. The status of a bushfaller (somebody who has travelled out) is so very high precisely because he or she has been able to overcome this exclusion.

The imminence of departure: secrecy, jealousy and bad luck

Delphine was the first in her family (and one of the very few in her compound) to graduate from university. She is from a modest family. Both her parents are illiterate and augment the father's pension by working the soil.[15] In the fifties, they moved from the North West Province to 'work money' on the plantations at the coast.[16] In the South West Province today, families from the North West Province are looked on as 'strangers'. Due to tensions between North and South Westerners, Delphine's mother was forced to give some of the land she was farming to feed and educate her children to South Westerners who claimed that it was theirs. Delphine's father also lost a plot of land to a group of South Westerners who claimed it had not been rightfully purchased.

Bush is today's version of what was then migration towards plantations at the coast. While migration as a means of integration into the money economy is part of the family history of all North Westerners in Buea, actual exposure rates to what it takes to get and be in are low. I will demonstrate how information on migration pathways does or does not flow, as well as how it is received and interpreted. While enthusiasm for migration is predominantly discussed in terms of lack of information about realities in Europe, at stake is whether and how information is trusted as credible.[17] I will demonstrate how decisions to migrate are based not on knowledge, but on interpretations of knowledge.[18]

Every time my landlady was absent for more than one day, my neighbour would jokingly ask whether she had fallen bush. Despite endless repetition of the joke, her question never failed to entertain the people in our compound. 'Where have you been all this time? I haven't seen you in ages. As if you had left for bush!?'[19] I often overheard such conversations and was once in shock myself when I could no longer contact an informant of mine. None of her telephone numbers worked and her house was deserted. Now that Mamie Comfort had left, I remembered the times she had confidently shared with me that she might try to rejoin her brother in the U.S. A few weeks later, I discovered that her visa for the U.S. had been denied, yet, I had learned a lesson. Preparations for international journeys are largely well-guarded secrets.

As pointed out earlier, few actually make it to bush. Many travel attempts falter. Thus secrecy is paramount to avoid embarrassment and gossip in cases when travel projects come to an unexpected halt. Secrecy in the preparation for leaving for bush is furthermore crucial as it increases the chances of actually being able to make it out. In Cameroon, witchcraft is often said to cause the failure of migration. Because migration is related to success, jealous people can seek to prevent the success of others through witchcraft attacks.[20] Secrecy can prevent the jealousy of others and thus render migration safe.

I was often told stories about mysterious disasters happening to people on their way to the airport. Delphine told me, for example, the story of a girl from her quarter who, after many failed migration attempts, sought out the spiritual protection and prayer of her pastor and finally received her visa. On the day that she was meant to leave, something strange happened in Cameroon so that no aeroplanes could come in or out. The girl's flight got delayed and she was able to leave only a few days later. People afterwards said that if the girl had left on that particular day, she would have died. A witch had been waiting for her at the airport on that day.

Fears of jealousy and witchcraft mean that only secret emigration trajectories are safe emigration trajectories. Given that also the extended family is seen as a possible source of jealousy and occult dangers (Geschiere 1997), even close friends and family members will often only be informed a few days before the departure date. As a consequence, the departure of people for bush always seems imminent. Anybody can be suspected at any time of secretly preparing to travel out. A standard greeting is: 'what are you so busy with? Are you chasing down your papers?'[21]

Yet, even when negative news about bushfalling does circulate, information can be interpreted in ways that do not change dominant views and contemporary understandings of migration. Those who have succeeded in getting to bush and proceed to talk negatively about bush are said to speak to prevent the success of others. Their warnings about bush are considered to be the fruits of jealousy. As another informant called Florence put it '*White man kontri* is paradise on earth. [...] If anybody says *white man kontri* is not good, that person is a witch.'

Lines and openings: in search of scholarships, cyber massas and doki men

Delphine's choices after graduation were either bushfalling or marriage. So she started applying for MA programmes abroad. Even were she granted admission with a university in Europe, she was going to need a *doki* man. Doki men are migration brokers specialized in the production of the papers needed for emigration. 'After all', Delphine explained to me, 'not everyone can get a visa.'[22] She meant that it took special powers to be granted this privilege. I encouraged Delphine to apply for scholarships. For her, scholarships were a highly unlikely route to bush. Instead of researching the scholarship institutions I wrote down for her, Delphine often came back with stories of men from international dating websites.

Delphine knew people who had succeeded in getting to bush with the help of a doki man. She also knew people who had succeeded in getting to bush with the help of a cyber mass, that is, a husband found on the Internet. Yet, scholarships were to her a relatively unknown access route to bush to her. Thus, it did not seem a reliable or trustworthy means of making it to bush. Scholarships were for others and something only I could believe in. Being a foreigner and newcomer to Cameroon, I do not think she trusted me to know what it really takes to fall bush. To browse dating sites, instead, was a more ordinary procedure to her.

A year of arguing over bushfalling at all cost finally came to an end when Delphine actually – against all odds – did win a scholarship for a Master's programme in Europe. A former teacher of hers had forwarded her the information for the application. When Delphine found out about having won the scholarship, she exclaimed that she was now on a different level: 'My level now na different level.' She declared that she now no longer had time for those Internet dating websites – or even men in general. She now no longer needed either to get what she wanted. She was eligible for a visa.

When the visa had not become available on the first promised date, Delphine became nervous. Whether for externally funded studies or otherwise, Delphine's path to bush was marked by fear and anxiety. Secrecy remained of the essence even for the scholarship route of falling bush. Delphine only confided only in her immediate family and others who had been to bush before. Beyond that, Delphine kept her bush preparations a secret, and by extension I had to do so as well. Delphine traveled back and forth to the Embassy. Yet, when close informants of ours asked how Delphine was, I had to say that she was around and that things were as ever.[23]

It was awkward to have to keep a secret from close informants who had shared many intimate stories with us.[24] Not until Delphine arrived in Sweden could I finally speak openly again. I explained to neighbours and informants that Delphine had won a scholarship. Yet, despite my explanations, a doubt always remained in people's minds. What I was saying did not have the same weight as what everybody had been seeing. For the past year, Delphine and I had been side by side every day. Now Delphine had disappeared and people knew that I was about to leave soon.[25] It was clear that I must have been instrumental in aiding Delphine's departure. The rumour in Delphine's neighbourhood was that the 'white lady' had brought her over.

Delphine had disappeared and because her departure had been a secret, few people beyond her immediate family actually knew how and why she had been able to go: 'Delphine has left for the white world.'[26] That is the part of her migration trajectory that has become visible in her quarter. While Delphine's brothers and sisters knew she had received a scholarship, her mother simply knew that a *njangi* group had decided to give money to her daughter. In Cameroon, njangi groups are weekly savings groups. The word scholarship does not exist in Pidgin.

Closure and the limits of credible information

Eleven months after Delphine's arrival in bush, she sent me an e-mail telling me about a phone conversation with an old friend in Cameroon. This friend had just come back from Nigeria to Cameroon. He had wanted to go to Spain overland via Libya with four male friends. In answer to Delphine's question whether they had not heard how people were dying on that route to Europe, he replied 'Some have died, some have succeeded. No risk, no money. We wanted to try our own luck.'

Delphine never considered reaching Europe by the overland route. Even my informants who were the most eager to go and fall bush tended to acknowledge the physical dangers associated with this route. The only people I came across during fieldwork who had attempted this route were men. In principle Delphine's shocked reaction was not connected to her new geographical position in Sweden. She shouted at her friend and told him never to try to fall bush in this way again. Delphine now began to talk to her friend about the dangers of bushfalling in terms of papers (residence and work permits) and issues of legality.

During our period of doing fieldwork, Delphine had persistently waved away the relevance of any negative aspect she was told about bush, as well as anything she would hear about legal frameworks of migration control. Delphine and many other young Cameroonians consider that it takes luck and/or a connection to be able to overcome closure and travel to bush. In this mental worldview, legality cannot explain the respective success or failure of migrants. As a consequence, Delphine's new narrative of how difficult it is to get papers in Europe did not fall on fertile ground with her friend. Delphine told me that her friend responded to her warnings about illegality in bush in these terms:

> How about those who have documents? How did they manage to get theirs? The ways that those who have succeeded – we would have also used the same ways to succeed. Because we were very prepared for anything. We are men and men are smart.

In e-mail to me, Delphine complained that her friend was unlikely to change his opinion about bushfalling at all cost. None of her explanations about the difficulties experienced by Cameroonians in bush, she complained to me, 'mean [t] anything' to him. For the first time in over two years of ongoing discussions between the two of us on bushfalling, I found her expressing fear, as well as a sense of concern that bushfalling could also have negative consequences:

> I am so afraid because I know that they will not give up and they will only try again. My fear is what may happen to them if they even succeed to cross Morocco. How will they manage? Oh my God!

The passionate advocate of migration at all cost had turned – largely due to her stay in bush – into a person warning people not to go. She had ardently defended bushfalling as a precious dream and important ambition. Yet, in this e-mail from Sweden, she talked about bushfalling as an 'illness' that needed a 'cure'. This is a radical shift in Delphine's migratory expectations.

Yet, her new attitude was in line with a discourse I had already encountered with a small group of elite students in Yaoundé organising into an NGO that was largely sponsored by the Swiss Embassy to fight 'illegal migration'.[27] As young students of a much more privileged class background than Delphine, the NGO staff had themselves a better chance of being granted a visa at the embassy. What distinguished the members of this NGO from Delphine was not their level of education, but the degree to which they were already connected with people and institutions in bush. It is connections rather than education that can lower migratory expectations and that can make migration projects through other channels more attainable.

By fully appreciating the shift in 'level' and status that comes with having had and having access to the international level we can grasp why Delphine's new views migratory risks would not speak to and be relevant to her friends in Cameroon. Upon receiving an MA degree, Delphine was in a position to sign up for a second MA degree in order to prolong her residence permit. With only a university admission letter, her friends in Cameroon by contrast would have only had a small chance of being granted a visa. If Delphine was changing her views on bushfalling, it was also because she now had other means of achieving social and geographical mobility.

After a two page e-mail describing her horror and despair at the Cameroonian madness of wanting to fall bush at all cost, Delphine added in a short note that she was preparing to send money home for Christmas, but also to buy phone credit so that she could call and greet friends and family in Cameroon. She sent home 175,000

CFA (almost 300 Euros), equal to a good monthly salary of a well-positioned person in Cameroon. The money was able to take care of the school fees for her younger brothers and sisters, which must have been a considerable relief to her aging parents who receive 10,000 CFA – roughly fifteen Euros – every three months from their pension. They work as farmers to be able to pay for the rest of their expenses.[28]

Both the financial gifts and the phone calls demonstrated to everyone in Cameroon the power of bush. Before falling bush, Delphine would not have had the capability to pay the school fees of her family members. Now that she was in bush she had the power. Through being in bush, Delphine was on a different 'level'. All those connected to her through kinship ties or friendship benefited from the occasional money streams or even just the added prestige of receiving phone calls from a bushfaller.

By performing the ritual of calling from bush during Christmas, Delphine elevated the social status of those whom she called. Any connection to bush has its worth – particularly when migration is possible because of connections and not because of information and knowledge on procedures. As a bushfaller, Delphine can now raise the status of her family both financially and through the additional prestige of making international connection visible and apparent through phone calls.

When Delphine became a bushfaller – that is, when she was in Sweden – her attitudes towards bushfalling at all cost changed. Over the phone, she talked to her friends for the first time about the difficulties of living and working 'illegally'. Delphine knew, however, that she had only a small chance of being taken seriously. Her new position in bush meant that she was no longer a trustworthy source of information on bush. Successful bushfallers might want to prevent the success of others and thus spread information that was not to be trusted. Those Cameroonians still hoping to travel out of Cameroon consider the complaints and stories from bushfallers about the difficult realities in bush as mere signs of wickedness.

Conclusion

Bushfalling constitutes a particular form of contemporary mobility. Tensions between what people want and what is possible have created a situation in which any kind of desire for emigration (whether for studies or for work) has to be sought out against all odds. Migratory risks are internal to the concept of bushfalling and need to be considered in the context of conceptions of risk in contemporary Cameroon. At the same time, bushfalling has started to encapsulate the very notion of success itself. In Cameroon, the desire to fall bush at all cost is largely considered to be a sign of ambition and the determination to be successful in life. Giving up on wanting to go to bush is like giving up on the pursuit of success, wealth and hope itself.

Looking at the case study of Delphine, I have suggested that a close analysis of the economy of migratory knowledge helps to explain the feverish pursuit of emigration against all odds in important ways. Values and norms in Anglophone Cameroon impede information from flowing freely. If negative news or simply contradictory pieces of information reach Cameroon, these are either not recognized as valid information or interpreted in ways that do not question the concept of bushfalling itself.

Jealousy, fear of witchcraft and the consequent imperative for secrecy can help to explain high degrees of optimism among young Cameroonians of certain classes about the transformative potential of bushfalling. Aspiring migrants have to fear the jealousy of people in Cameroon who might want to stop their travel projects. Jealous acquaintances can engage in witchcraft to prevent the success of others. Failure of travel projects is thus often explained through and blamed on witchcraft.

Fears of jealousy, witchcraft and failure also mean that aspiring bushfallers must keep their travel projects secret when trying to leave the country. The circle of people allowed to know about a departure project can be very selective. Within the moral economy of departure in Cameroon, it is not information, but secrecy, that can render migration safe. It is secrecy that protects aspiring migrants from the jealousy of others and thus from witchcraft.

The economy of migratory knowledge is not a mere question of 'mis'-information. The pursuit of these ambitions of mobility is marked not so much by mere ignorance or naïveté, but by a particular kind of interpretation of the reality of migration, including notions of risk and success. One should ask, not what people know or do not know before departure, but how they come to trust and interpret the information that they do have.

References

Alpes, Maybritt Jill. 2011. Bushfalling: How Young Cameroonians dare to migrate. Ph.D. thesis, Universit of Amsterdam.

Apter, Andrew. 1999. IBB= 419: Nigerian democracy and the politics of illusion. In Jean and John L. Comaroff, eds. *Civil society and the political imagination in Africa-critical perspectives.* Chicago: University of Chicago Press.

Carling, Jørgen. 2002. Migration in the age of involuntary immobility: Theoretical reflections and Cape Verdean experiences. *Journal of Ethnic and Migration Studies* 28 (1): 5-42.

Chernoff, John .M. 2003. *Hustling is not stealing: Stories of an African bar girl.* Chicago: University of Chicago.

De Rosny, Eric. 2002. L'Afrique des migrations: les échappées de la jeunesse de Douala. *Etudes* 396 (5): 623-633.

Evina, Roger Charles. 2009. *Migration au Cameroun: Profil national 2009.* Genéve: IOM.

Ferguson, James. 1999. *Expectations of modernity.* Berkeley/ Los Angeles: University of California Press.

Fischer, Peter A., Reiner Martin and Thomas Straubhaar. 1997. Should I stay or should I go? In *International migration, immobility and development: Multidisciplinary perspectives*, eds. Tomas Hammar, et al. New York: Berg Publisher.

Fleischer, Annett. 2012. *Migration, marriage and the law: Making families among Cameroonian 'bush fallers' in Germany.* Berlin: Regiospectra Verlag.

Geschiere, Peter. 1997. *The modernity of witchcraft.* Charlottesville, VA: University of Virginia Press.

Geschiere, Peter and Francis Nyamnjoh. 2000. Capitalism and autochthony: The seesaw of mobility and belonging. *Public Culture* 12 (2): 423-52.

Jua, Nantang. 2003. Differential responses to disappearing transitional pathways. *African Studies Review* 46 (2): 13-36.

Kalir, Barak. 2005. The Development of a Migratory Disposition: Explaining a New Emigration. *International Migration* 43 (4): 167-196.

Kearney, Michael. 1986. From invisible hand to visible feet: Anthropological studies of migration and development. *Annual Review of Anthropology* 15: 331-61.

Konings, Piet and Francis Nyamnjoh. 2003. *Negotiating an Anglophone Identity: A study of the Politics of Recognition and Representation in Cameroon.* Leiden: Brill.

Malkki, Liisa. 2002. News from nowhere: Mass displacement and globalized 'problems of organization'. *Ethnography* 3 (3): 351-360.

Martin, Jeannett. 2005. *'Been-to', 'Buerger', 'Transmigranten?' Zur Bildungsmigration von Ghanaern und ihrer Rückkehr aus der Bundesrepublik Deutschland.* Münster: LIT.

Nganghi, Alphonse. 2006. *Billet retour.* Yaounde: Masseu.

Ngwa, Lydia and Wilfred Ngwa, eds. 2006. *From dust to snow: Bush-faller.* Princeton: Horeb Communications.

Nyamnjoh, Francis. 2005. Images of Nyongo amongst Bamenda grassfielders in whiteman kontri. *Citizenship Studies* 9 (3): 241-269.

Nyamnjoh, Francis and Ben Page. 2002. Whiteman kontri and the enduring allure of modernity among Cameroonian youth. *African Affairs* 101: 607-634.

Piot, Charles. 2010. *Nostalgia for the future: West Africa after the cold war.* Chicago: University of Chicago Press.

Roitman, Janet. 2005. *Fiscal Disobedience: An anthropology of economic regulation.* Princeton and Oxford: Princeton University Press.

Séraphin, Gilles. 2000. *Vivre á Doualá: L'imaginaire et l'action dans une ville africaine en crise.* Paris: L'Harmattan.

Notes

1 This chapter is based on fieldwork done from September 2007 to January 2009. A more elaborate version of this paper can be consulted under "Bushfalling at all cost – the economy of migratory knowledge", *African Diaspora*, (forthcoming 2012). Both pieces form part of my Ph.D. project entitled *Bushfalling: How young Cameroonians dare to migrate* (Ph.D. thesis, University of Amsterdam, 2011).

2 In order to save money Delphine first kept it a secret that she was working for me and later pretended that her salary was about a third of what it actually was. This way she was under less pressure from her siblings and her wider family to make financial contributions.

3 For the use of the word hustling in Nigeria see (Chernoff 2003).

4 Cameroonians in bush might capture the at times excessive pressure for remittances and gifts through references to specific forms of witchcraft, i.e. *nyongo* (Nyamnjoh 2005; Jua 2003). Yet, those still in Cameroon are extremely eager to be the ones that go out for their family to 'hustle' and '*work moni*' in bush.

5 As Delphine was referring herself to this Francophone film, she mixed the title of the film 'Paris a tout prix' with both Pidgin and French. Linguistically, contemporary Cameroon is divided into an Anglophone and a Francophone part. In every day life, people in the Anglophone part of Cameroon speak Pidgin, rather than English.

6 This number also includes people who want to go to bush for holidays or studies. Not all of these respondents wanted to go to bush to work or stay.

7 These emigration attempts stretched from applying for admission with foreign universities abroad to engaging in conversations with family members abroad about whether they could 'bring them over'.

8 Fleischer has pointed to a gendered difference between the pre-migrational marital behaviour of men and women. According to her research, Cameroonian men are able to migrate alone even after they are married, while married women face more difficulties in leaving the country without their husbands (2012). Yet, just like women, men nevertheless prefer to fall bush when they do not have a family in Cameroon.

9 In a survey conducted in the 1990s, Seraphin established that more than half of the people

questioned in Douala would like to migrate or at least travel out of the country. Most who would like to emigrate are young, of a higher level of education and are not yet heading a household (2000: 200- 201).

10 Carling has equally argued for the importance of an understanding of involuntary immobility for the study of migration (2002: 5).

11 Ferguson has defined the state of abjection as the act of 'being thrown aside, expelled, or discarded' (1999: 236). In this sense, abjection is different from mere exclusion.

12 Those who have already reached bush might capture the at times excessive pressure for remittances and gifts through references to specific forms of witchcraft, i.e. *nyongo* (Nyamnjoh 2005; Jua 2003). Yet, those still in Cameroon are extremely eager to be the ones that go out for their family to 'hustle' and *'work moni'* in bush.

13 Migrants in the 1970's and 80's, for example, were referred to as 'been to's'. For usages of the term 'been to' in Ghana, see (Martin 2005).

14 Roitman notes that to 'work the bush' is to work unregulated markets (Roitman 2005, 26).

15 Having Ngie, Ngwo and Pidgin as their main three languages, neither parent speaks English.

16 To *work money* is an expression in Pidgin that I have chosen to keep, as it reflects well the idea that prior to migration, her parents had worked the soil. Delphine's parents were not the only case in which mobility was closely related to a further integration into the money economy.

17 While Fischer, Martin and Straubhaar, for example, mention that people process information differently, they have very little so say about how and why different interpretations occur (1997: 65).

18 For other discussions of migration choices see (Carling 2002 & Barak 2005).

19 Original: 'How you loss so? A don stay for see you like se you go na bush!'

20 The 'notion of effortless gain at the expense or even consumption of others is echoed in various witchcraft beliefs and feeds into cultural imaginings of migration' (Apter 1999). Urban migrants can, for example, be suspected by members of rural communities of origin to have used occult forces to enrich themselves (Geschiere & Nyamnjoh 2000).

21 Original: *'Ha you over busy so? You de follow na doki?'* To go to bush above all means following up on one's papers. These papers can be attained in any manner, both through official procedures, as well as through financial motivations.

22 Embassy requirements for visas are restrictive and in 1995 consulate officers considered they had to reduce the quota of granted visa demands by 50 percent (Rosy 2002).

23 Original: 'I dey.'

24 From among our closest informants, Delphine decided to tell only Manuealla about her scholarship. She would have confided in Pamella, too, but an occasion did not present itself before her departure.

25 Foreigners do not need to keep their departure a secret. Instead, I was advised by my assistant and host mother to keep further arrivals a secret. For them, this secrecy was an extra guarantee of my safety.

26 Original: 'Delphine don go white man kontri.'

27 For public treatments of the theme of bushfalling in Cameroon that also include negative aspects of the phenomenon see (Ngwa & Ngwa 2006; Nganghi 2006). *From Dust to Snow* is an edited volume that gathers mainly the voices of Cameroonian students abroad. As such, the edited volume is not at all a reflection of the views and attitudes of Cameroonians still in Cameroon. *Billet Retour* was written by a Francophone student migrant in Russia who overstayed his visa after his studies and was after a period of imprisonment repatriated back to Cameroon. Another example that includes a more critical stance on migration is the academic volume edited by the Cameroonian scholar Pondi. After a conversation with Professor Pondi, my research assistant disqualified his arguments as representing a typical *ajebotar* perspective. By ajebotar, Delphine referred to Professor Pondi's privileged socio-economic position in Cameroon (see also glossary). Whereas Delphine and other informants were reasoning on an individual or family level, Pondi was concerned in his argument on bushfalling with development on the African continent as whole. His main reference was the nation state or the African continent.

28 At the national level, the average monthly salary that stems from the exercise of the principal working activity is 26, 800 CFA. In the public sector, the average monthly salary in public administration is 124,300 CFA. In the formal private sector, the average monthly salary is 103,600 CFA. These data stem from a report on employment and the informal sector ('Enquete sure l'emploi et le secteur informel (EESI)) by the Institut national de la statistique (INS) (Evina 2009: 37).

City on the move:
How urban dwellers in Central Africa
manage the siren's call of migration[1]

Filip De Boeck

Introduction

Over the last three decades Kinshasa, the capital of the Democratic Republic of Congo, has grown into a megalopolis of more than 8 million people. And yet, this mega-city, which was once heralded as an international pinnacle of colonialist modernity, and which is Sub-Saharan Africa's second largest city today, is often perceived as a place of distance and 'remoteness' (Piot 1999), a local 'shadow city' (Neuwirth 2006), 'off the map' of the global cityscape, under the radar of formal modes of globalization, and seemingly disconnected from the rest of the world. At best, Kinshasa often seems to exist only as an eccentric landmark in a planetary geography of slums, filled with 'excess' or 'surplus humanity' (Davis 2006). Mutatis mutandis, this also applies to the African continent as a whole. What, to take but one example, does it mean when Manuel Castells (1998) writes that Africa constitutes the 'black hole of the information society'? Being defined as global or local, connected or disconnected, powerful or powerless, rich or poor, it seems, has everything to do with the ability to be visible, with the power constellations in which one is inscribed and entangled, with the (im)possibility, also, of constructing and putting into broader circulation an objectified identity of oneself. Unable to give a more global voice to its own identity constructions, Kinshasa, like many other non-western cities, and in spite of its considerable size, therefore seems to occupy a very weak and peripheral, even invisible, position on the formal map of the territories which constitute the global city and make it visible.

And yet, these urbanscapes are often leading cities within an alternative global network of material as well as mental territories that are interconnected, entangled, and transposed by more informal infrastructures and cultural imaginaries which, as Simone puts it, 'destabilize the prevailing terms of social stratification' (Simone 2006, 1). The 'worlding' of African cities (Simone 2001) often follows unexpected trajectories. Inhabitants of the kind of urban contexts under discussion are indeed increasingly embedded in extremely complex and mobile fluid networks of exchange and interdependence, which are situated beyond the level of the city as geographical entity and which often take them into the uncharted territories of more invisible or clandestine, sometimes even illicit or illegal, spaces.

In recent years mobility, and old or new technologies such as cars or cell phones which facilitate that mobility, have become an increasingly central topic in the Africanist social science research (cf. Archambault 2010; de Bruijn, van Dijk and Foeken 2001). A focus on mobility is central to understanding how urban dwellers design their own lives by 'navigating' or cruising through different, often nebulous, circuits made up of composite locales. As shown in my own research on Kinshasa (De Boeck and Plissart 2004) but also in the recent work of fellow researchers such as AbdouMaliq Simone (2004; 2010) and Dominique Malaquais (2006), urban life cannot be understood without paying attention to the ways in which people move in, through and beyond the city. In the current globalized world, though, movement and migration have become complex processes. How exactly do people steer their lives between here and there? How do these various 'heres' and 'theres' interconnect and impact on each other? What does this do to notions of identity or difference, or to definitions of territory and locality? How does this impact on our understanding of 'the local', a trope so central to our anthropological investigations for such a long time? How do roots and routes interconnect? How do these migratory trajectories challenge our understanding of cities in the Global South as increasingly poor (pre- or post-) urban outposts outside the globalized network of the new information age? How does it force us to rethink the notions of order (or, more precisely, the lack thereof) that we all too easily apply to these urban contexts? How does it impact on our received wisdom about what is functional or normal and what is not?

Using the city of Kinshasa as a starting point, the following pages attempt to provide a short history of various alternative patterns of migration that have characterized pos-tcolonial Congo from the moment of its independence until now: from the dream of the West, exemplified by a migration to the former metropole (the 'Mwana Poto' or 'Mwana Mayi' model'), the emergence of alternative migratory itineraries, most recently towards the Arab world and China (the 'Guangzhou model'), the emergence of local alternatives (the 'Mwana Lunda model'), and the migration of the imagination offered by new religious models (the 'Visa for Heaven model') as well as by the links between the rise of the occult in relation to (colonialist) modernity and its economies of desire (the 'Shege-Shengen model'). In the final part of the chapter I will offer some ideas for reading the traces of lives on the move.

Routes: A short history of Congolese models of movement and migration

The 'Mwana Poto' model

Effectively barred from travelling abroad during the colonial period, Congolese were quick to insert themselves into waves of increasingly intensive migration after independence. This mobility intensified and was accentuated by the gradual economic decline that started to manifest itself in the latter half of the 1970s and that reached mind-boggling dimensions towards the end of Mobutu's long and disastrous reign. The breakdown of the Zairean state and the increasingly harsh living conditions in Kinshasa and the country at large prompted a huge exodus. From this period onwards, the city also started to materialize as a huge machine of evacuation, and develop complex (semi-)informal economies, involving the production, selling and buying of those rare but much desired goods called visas, passports, *prises en charge* and all the other documents and stamps needed to enter the 'rally' of migration and move out and beyond the increasingly confining horizon of sheer survival that Kinshasa has become (cf. Mayoyo Bitumba Tipo-Tipo 1995).

Almost invariably, the first stop along the often difficult path of diasporic existence was Belgium, and even today the focal point of Kinshasa's diasporic mirror remains, to some extent, the Congolese neighbourhood of Matonge in the Brussels municipality of Ixelles. In many respects this Belgian Matonge continues to be the social and cultural nexus of Europe's Congolese migration. Both a simulacrum of Kinshasa and a re-invention of Brussels, it is named after what used to be one of Kinshasa's most vibrant neighbourhoods, the fast-beating heart of the city's night life and popular music scene, with its effervescent central square, Rond Point Victoire, and its famous night clubs such as La Crèche, its open air bars and *ngandas*... .

The migratory movements towards the former Metropole, or to Paris and other Western destinations, partly illustrate Kinshasa's complex relationship with the outside and the beyond of a more global, transnational world, with the real and imagined qualities of modernity and of the wider, whiter, world of the West.

In Congo, as elsewhere in Africa, the mirror of the West conjures up the property of the marvellous. The collective social imaginary concerning the West (referred to as *Poto* or *Putu, Miguel, Mikili, Zwenebele*, or *Lola* – literally 'heaven' in Lingala; also the name given to Belgium) is rich in fairy tale images that evoke the wonderland of modernity, and the luxurious, almost paradisiacal lifestyle of the West. One would do almost anything 'to die' (*fwa ku mputu*) in this Poto.[2] 'The West', as a topos of the Congolese imaginary where one enjoys the benefits of endless sources of wealth for free, sums up all the qualities of the good life. This oneiric image of Europe is amplified by the figure of the Sapeur which emerges in the late 1970s and early 1980s and which is famously portrayed in the songs of the leading Congolese musician of those days, Papa Wemba. In signature songs of that period, such as *Matebu*, the Sapeur, this elegant urban Kinois youngster, offers a self-invented Congolese version of the cosmopolitan, and opens up dreams of accessing an idealized Europe in Technicolor. Seemingly unhindered by any economic or political reality, the Sapeur strolls the Parisian Champs Elysées in his expensive designer clothes and addresses his girlfriend at home: *Matebu / Listen to your husband / Who calls you from the Eiffel Tower / What a joy! / Do you hear the children of the country in the background?* And he calls his girlfriend to Paris, so that they can get married there: *My love, I'm waiting for you, mama / The day of the wedding / That day, you know / The day of the wedding, listen / They will be wearing* Torrente */ They will be wearing* Giorgio Armani */ They will be wearing* Daniel Hechter */ They will be wearing the shoes of* J.M. Weston!

The lifestyle of a rich Congolese urban elite and of a large part of the white expatriate community in Congo confirms the reality of this Idea of the West, an idea further reinforced by broadcasts on the numerous Congolese TV channels. Some years ago, for example, one of the many local Kinshasa TV stations broadcasted a widely watched programme by the popular journalist Zacharie Bababaswe entitled *Mputuville*, a programme that further mythologized Congolese life in the European Diaspora, showing parties and receptions amongst the Congolese rich and famous throughout Europe. And when, in 2006, Bababaswe tried to counter the critique that he misrepresented the reality of the Congolese Diaspora by making a reportage called *Vanda na mboka* ('Stay at home') which portrayed Congolese illegal aliens in Belgium, he was fiercely attacked by the Congolese community in Belgium for what they perceived to be an insulting attempt to demythologize their diasporic existence in Europe. Rather than deconstructing this myth for the home front, people who themselves experience in the flesh the often harsh realities of Diaspora life usually go to great lengths to deny this grim picture and to confirm the exactitude of the collective imaginary about *Lola*. Admitting that life in the West not only offers opportunities but often turns out to be a life full of poverty and hardship does not invalidate the topos of the Western Paradise for those who remained behind on the home front. Instead, lack of success in Europe is often interpreted as a sign of personal failure and weakness of the *mikiliste* who followed the trail abroad. Rather than revealing that life in the Diaspora is not that easy, Congolese living abroad often prefer to send home pictures of themselves in front of a Mercedes, neglecting to mention that the Mercedes actually belongs to the neighbour. Europe (or the United States and Canada, as 'the White Man's Poto', the ultimate Land of Cocaigne) thus continues to be framed in these positive terms.

Nevertheless, this myth of the West is increasingly losing its attraction. A phrase of one of the songs made famous in the 1990s by Empire Bakuba, a popular band until the untimely death of its lead singer Pepe Kalle in 2002, goes as follows: *Bakende Putu, bakweyi na désert*, "They go to Europe but land in the desert instead." The phrase conveyed the demythologization of the idea of Europe as Paradise. It signified the unpleasant discovery that diasporic existence in Europe did not correspond to the multi-colour version which the Sapeurs' songs herald. It signalled an awakening to the harsh black-and-white realities of Europe, a Poto revealing itself to be a desert rather than a Paradise, a place where one's life is filled with poverty and problems concerning money, jobs, papers and housing, where one feels unwanted and undesired, where one is often confronted with racism and with the huge human cost of broken marriages, families and friendships, in short, with all the collateral damage of migration... .

The classic song *Voyage na Poto* (*The Journey to Europe*), interpreted by Pacha and Papa Wemba's band Viva La Musica addresses these issues. The singer talks to his wife Julie, who remained behind in Kinshasa.[3]

> *I am leaving on a trip to Europe*
> *'Cause I've heard my friends there have been doing well.*
> *I'm going to run the risk*
> *I'm thinking of my children's future*
> *Wait! I'll be back, dear Julie, wait for me, I say!*

Europe, however, turns out to be very different from his expectations:

> *Julita, in this Europe where I arrived today,*
> *There are no scraps, not a crumb to be found*
> *The economic crisis is everywhere, I'm unemployed*
> *I don't have the means to send you gifts from Europe*

Julita, in these societies where I came to find
Those who arrived before,
Today they are thrown out.
If tomorrow you learn that I am in Kin or Luanda,
You will know that I've been expelled.

Julie, the acquaintances who greeted me
Felt I brought too much heat down on them
To get rid of me, they pretended
To require that I do the laundry
I refused, and they chased me out!

Julita, in White Europe,
The pocket money I had with me,
They made me waste it.
But there are always kind people
Who find me a place to sleep in a 'ghetto'

[in French :] *Oh, chérie Julie, je pleure, j'ai trop de soucis*
J'ai maigri, il y a trop de souffrance,
je n'attends que toi
Oh, chérie Julie, en quittant chez nous j'avais un visa
Maintenant, il est périmé, pour rester en Europe , je dois devenir réfugié

Oh, dear Julie, I thought I could live where I pleased
God created just one world, humans divided it
They call me foreigner, sweetheart
Julie, the little crumb I scraped together
Pays little for hard work
I have to eat and pay the rent
Before saving some for you
Wait for me to save up a bit, my love

Julie, there are those, dear, who have gone to Europe
They sold their family lots
They came in the hopes of recouping their money
But are blocked on this side, honey.

Julie, in Europe, they don't want the Blacks
There are good people, and there are racists
Who treat the Blacks badly.

"If you're not happy, go home"
Many want to go back, they've had it up to here.
Europe is so eminent, manual labour
Won't get you by
They chose to die in Europe

Julie, for some among us
Going to Europe means success
I don't want to go back to Africa to be bewitched
But Europe is no Paradise

Oh, dear Julie
This Europe of which you hear is not in colour
Everything costs, and nothing gets collected
There are no presents, my love

In this world of Europe
Where you will come, don't trust what our own people say.
We don't love each other, jealousy,
No one wants another's success

Only in Europe, one grasps the truth about Europe
Come see the truth for yourself.
Europe is no Paradise
Nothing is collected here
There are no presents

Pacha's song is a poignant rendition of all the hardships of the diasporic existence, but more than any other song, perhaps, it is *Lubuaku – Pénitencier* (The Penitentiary) by Bozi Boziana, which expresses the final disillusionment with Europe. The protagonist of the song finds himself stuck in a European prison, with shattered dreams, totally penniless, and abandoned by his Parisian girlfriend who took another lover: *Look at me now, in this gloomy house, what sorrow! / The Penitentiary...*

Both Pacha's and Bozi Boziana's songs, both from the 1980s, foreshadow the 'desert' phrase made famous by Empire Bakuba in the mid 1990s. But Empire's song line 'They go to Europe but land in the desert instead' also conveys another message:

> We Congolese started our insertion into a global oecumene of modernity as defined by the White World, but we never attained our goal. Somewhere along the way our plane ran out of fuel and we crashed in the desert.

The world of modernity as it was (and is) defined by the colonial ruler, the missionary, the post-colonial state, the white expatriate development worker or today's UN peacekeeper, with its tempting promises of boundless consumerism embedded in a vision of an expansive and global capitalism, has become a vague chimera which is out of reach for most in a country such as Congo. Blame for the impossibility of accessing this western version of the good life is not only laid on the excesses of the Mobutu era, or the incompetence of the current ruling class, but is increasingly also laid on the doorstep of the West itself. A couple of years ago, I noticed a sign painted on the wall of a shop in Kinshasa. It read: *"A qui la faute? Chez le blanc!"* ("Who is to blame? The White Man!"). The shop's motto quite poignantly translated a growing breakaway from the world of modernity as defined by the former colonial powers, a definition which reduces an increasing number of people in Congo to a subaltern status, forcing them to become part of a swelling army of Third World Proletarians, the excess humanity that Mike Davis talks about, living in the shadow of, but excluded from, the global neoliberal world-order and its promises (Ferguson 2006).

The 'Guangzhou model'
In reaction to the tendency of Fortress Europe to heighten its walls and deepen the waters that surround it, Congolese have turned into 'practical cosmopolitans' (Mbembe 2001, 11) and have started to focus their expectations on other 'elsewheres'. Even in the Mobutist years, various migratory itineraries existed that not only took Congolese into the promised land of the former Metropole (although that was usually seen as an ideal terminus of one's migratory dreams) but also propelled them into other places on the African continent itself. Sometimes these destinations came into existence because of the political alliances existing between the Congolese leadership and that of other countries (as in the case of Togo or Cameroon, for example, countries which became popular destinations for – often female – traders from Kinshasa). Sometimes people moved to particular places because the prospect of a good life seemed more promising there, as in the case of

South Africa, which saw a huge (and legal) influx of wealthy and educated Congolese in the 1980s, followed in the 1990s by waves of far less wealthy migrants who sometimes even walked their way through Angola, Zambia and Namibia in order to reach Johannesburg or Cape Town. Huge Congolese communities live in these cities to this very day (the Johannesburg Tower and the surrounding Hillbrow neighbourhood have become symbols of inner city decay for which, according to many in South Africa, Congolese and other African illegal immigrants, or *makwere-kwere* as they are locally referred to, are to blame.) As it became increasingly difficult to access these destinations, other routes opened up. In recent years, Dubai and Abu Dhabi have become important transit points for importing cars and many other goods from China and the whole of (South-east) Asia into Congo.

Figure 1: Inside the Ponti Tower, Johannesburg, 2006. Photo by F. De Boeck.

An increasing flow of literature documents the new economic position that China, and to a lesser extent India, Vietnam, Thailand and Indonesia occupy on the African continent. Very little, however, has been said so far about the routes that this Chinese presence has opened up for Congolese and others on the African continent. Far less of a fortress than Europe, China, and especially the Pearl River Delta, has become an important destination for many in Congo in recent years. In 2005, 26 year old

Bibish, one of the daughters of the household in which I live when in Kinshasa, decided to try her luck and travel to China. Three years before, she had married a young Luba Pentecostal preacher who was making a name for himself among the youngsters of the neighbourhood after setting up his own church. She herself was an ardent believer, nicknamed Ayatollah and *Dame de fer* by her sisters because of her unwavering faith (as attested by the Contract with *La Royale*, God's own insurance company, which hung in her room at that time – cf. Fig. 2). Before long, Bibish and her husband had two children, but then he was offered a job in Mbuji Mayi and left, returning regularly to Kinshasa to visit his wife and children. In time, however, the intervals between his visits became longer and longer. By then the news was spreading through Kinshasa that there were plenty of business opportunities in China and that a visa was not even needed. Bored with sitting at home waiting for her husband, Bibish made up her mind to go to China with the plan of buying baby clothes there in the hope of reselling them at a small profit in Kin. And so Bibish, who had never travelled abroad before, had never even set foot outside Kinshasa, and could not speak a word of English, left for Ghuangzhou, with the help of some of her Pentecostal relationships and her faith in God, the 'King of kings' (see clause 4 of the abovementioned Contract: "The insurance contract with *La Royale* is everlasting and cannot be exchanged. It permits the holder of such contract to travel in any part of the world, guaranteeing him/her eternal life.").

An increasing number of (indeed often female) Congolese have followed Bibish's example and have started to travel to cities such as Shenzhen, Dongguan, Huizhou, Hongkong, and especially Guangzhou, looking for trading opportunities, or buying goods and commodities for retail in Kinshasa. An important Congolese community which is already numbered in the thousands, has sprung up in Guanzhou, and there are almost daily flights connecting Kinshasa to these cities in southern China.

Yet, this Guangzhou model, i.e. the ability to inscribe oneself in different, often less visible and more informal, globalizing streams that open up more possibilities than the increasingly inaccessible destinations in the former colonial centres seem able to offer, is not necessarily perceived as a new *Lola* either. In *Ma personnalité*, a song from his 2002 hit album *A la queue leu-leu*, Werrason, Congo's most popular contemporary musician, sings: *The White Man says that he invented the turkey! / For he eats the turkey's breast / The Ethiopians eat the drumsticks / The Chinese eat the wings / Ah! And we eat misfortune/ the fat of the turkey's behind!* In these lines Werrason toys with the word *libabe*, which means 'misfortune', but in this context also refers to the *tiges*, the small (imported) sticks of roasted turkey fat that have

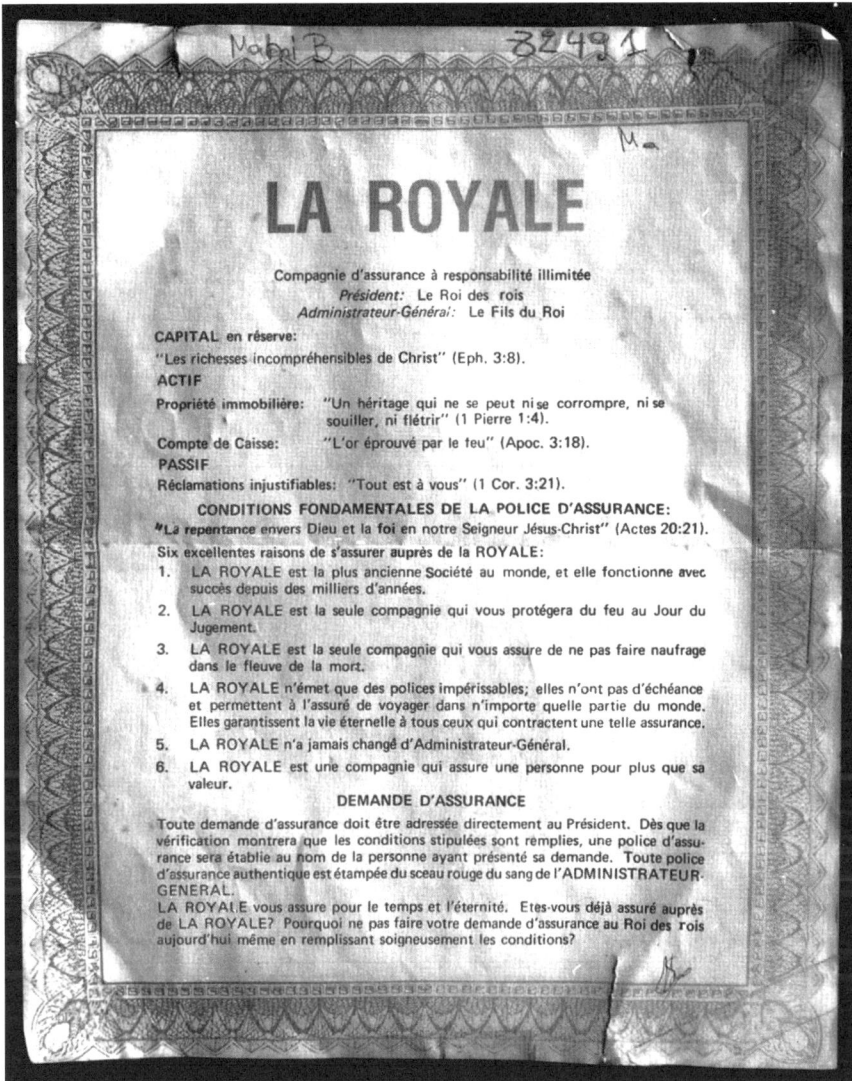

Figure 2: Contract with La Royale, *God's own insurance company. Photo by F. De Boeck.*

become part of the Kinois' diet in recent years, mostly because they are so cheap. These lines, which were immediately picked up by Kinshasa's youth, are indicative of the complex and multi-faceted relationship that Congo continues to maintain with the outside and the beyond of a more global, transnational world (from the White Man and the West to Ethiopia and China).

Local alternatives: the Mwana Lunda model

What the criticism implicit in the Werrason lyrics indicates is that Congolese have become highly critical of certain imported models which impose on them a (colonialist) modernity or an ideological hegemony of a version of the good life defined not by Congolese, but for Congolese, over and above their own heads; models in which they eternally remain subaltern and second class citizens, much like the *évolué* of former colonial times who was condemned to remain a 'mimic man', to cite Naipaul, a second rate, inauthentic version of the white role-model. At times this criticism has led to a rebellious rejection of these imposed modernities, as in the wave of lethal yet also ludic lootings that swept through Congo in 1991 and again in 1993, and that have been commented upon by some observers as a radical break with the West and with a more global world (cf. Devisch 1995). Yet, this tendency to turn away from the 'modernist' position, in a true spirit of resistance to domination from the outside does not at all mean that people in Congo resist or reject the material fruits promised by and inextricably interwoven with modernity's notion of the good life. These fruits are embodied by the TV set, the stereo-chain, the DVD player, the electric fan, the car or the refrigerator to which everybody aspires, even in Congo. But a shared economy of desire does not necessarily go hand in hand with the same patterns of accumulation, expenditure and consumption. Elsewhere (cf. De Boeck 1999), I have described the emergence of autochtonous modernities in the movement of the Bana Lunda, the Children of Lunda, which peaked in the mid 1990s, at a time when the war in Angola between UNITA and MPLA was still in full swing. The Bana Lunda were and are Congolese youngsters trekking to the diamond fields of northern Angola, especially the provinces of Lunda Norte and Lunda Sul, where they engage in artisanal diamond mining and, in doing so, in a reinvention of capitalism (Bayart 1994) and of a Europe in their own terms. Diamond digging and smuggling offer access to a *savoir vivre* to those for whom the privileged world of Poto has become inaccessible. Those who cannot access a visa, or who cannot afford a ticket to Europe walk their way to Tembo, Kahemba and other destinations along the border with Angola; that is, they walk to their own accessible version of the promised land (or Terra Nova, as Lunda Norte is referred to), where the Poto model is redefined along lines that leave room for a continuity with one's own social reality and past. The diamond frontier has become the space par excellence in which to generate a more accessible version of colonialist modernity, with its own form of accumulation and maximization of profit, its own ways of capturing money and consumer goods, and its own modes of expenditure and upward social mobility. The Bana Lunda use the modernist language of progress and development by referring to themselves as *kuntwalistes* (from kiKongo *kuntwala*, to go forward) but their 'progress' unfolds along lines that are no longer imposed from outside and defined by the former Metropole or the post-colonial Congolese state. As such, the Bana Lunda reconstitute static and closed concepts of the unidirectional relationship between modernity and tradition, city and countryside, the West and its offshoot, Africa, in terms of shifting lines of partial (translocal as well as local-global) connections and patterns of de- and reterritorialization. This offers them the possibility of inverting the (neo-)colonial experience. In a 1948 novel, entitled *Terra morta* the Portuguese novelist Castro Soromenho described the exploitation of the local population by the Portuguese colonizers in Lunda Norte. Today, the Bana Lunda have redefined this violent and exploitative colonial space, in which the colonial subject occupied a subaltern position, in terms of a 'New World', a *Terra Nova* that can be accessed and designed through one's own agency. At the same time, *Terra Nova* is also the name of a suburb of Luanda, the Angolan capital. Bana Lunda thus define their occupation of the province of Lunda Norte as an access to an urban space from which they are otherwise excluded. Here the Bana Lunda echo the colonizing dynamics of earlier urban youth movements such as the Bills in Kinshasa. In Léopoldville in the late 1950s, the Billism movement, inspired by Hollywood westerns, grouped together various competing youth gangs who used the image of the cowboy as culture hero to colonize, claim and rename various neighbourhoods of the city, in an often ludicmove to overthrow and invert the Belgian colonizer's segregationist urbanization that denied this youth access to the city (i.e. the white central downtown area, referred to as 'la ville') and relegated them to the peripheral areas of the 'cité indigène'. Similar, though much more violent and radical, movements exist today in Kinshasa. In recent years street gangs have increasingly colonized the different areas and neighbourhoods of the city, imposing their own law and order onto these urban spaces. These urban youth gangs are referred to as *koluna* or *kuluna*. They (also physically) attack elders, state agents, priests and other figures of authority, often on the occasion of youngsters' funerals, to impose their own law, 'the order of disorder' on the city (cf. De Boeck 2008; 2009). The popular etymology of the word *koluna* is twofold: it refers to the verb 'to colonize', as well as to the military term 'colonne' (column). Like a column of soldiers, youngsters violently recolonize and take hold of the urban space, overthrow its (colonialist, white) order, and impose their own moral grids and action schemes onto it. Rather than migrating abroad, it is in the here and now of one's own familiar neighbourhood that the chance of a new beginning and a better life is opened up.

In summary, the model proposed by the Bana Lunda (or in its more extreme form by the *koluna* street gangs of Kinshasa) puts all the stress and effort not on a physical migration to the promised land of Poto, but on the generating and accessing of a Poto at home. That this model is consciously proposed as a real alternative to the earlier Poto model is attested by the circulation of a number of locally produced tele-serials such as *Mwana Lunda contre Mwana Poto* (see Fig. 3). Produced between 2002 and 2003 by Groupe Salongo, one of the most popular theatre groups in Kinshasa, this serial was broadcast weekly on a local TV channel and was also made available on video cassette. It tells the story of a young Kinoise who is courted by two men. She has to make up her mind which one of the two she will marry. The first is a *Mwana Poto*, a young Congolese man who migrated to Paris, and returns to Kinshasa to marry his sweetheart. Because he can offer her the prospect of what he depicts as a wealthy life in Europe he is pretty sure that she will not refuse him. At that moment, the second candidate, *Mwana Lunda*, shows up. He recently returned from Angola, his pockets full of diamond dollars. It signifies the start of fierce competition between the two candidates, and in the end it is *Mwana Lunda* who wins the contest.

Figure 3: Posters of tele-serial Mwana Lunda contre Mwana Poto. *Photo by F. De Boeck.*

The prayer model

Apart from the rejection of the older *Mwana Poto* migratory model and the creation of a new, homebrew variety of that model, there are also other pathways of – physical but often also imaginary – migration available to the inhabitants of Central Africa's urban centres. As Bibish's story above already indicated, religion offers one such powerful possibility. As elsewhere in Africa, Congo's neo-pentecostal churches are embedded in transnational and global networks of religious movements that define themselves not so much in relation to local autochtonous pasts and traditions, but in relation to a global modernist oecumene. Belonging to one of these churches and becoming an authentic Christian along the ideological lines set out by these prayer movements offers the prospect of inserting oneself into this more global world and tapping into its sources of prosperity. Here prayer has become the surest way to inscribe oneself into new migratory channels leading to Europe, Asia and the United States. During prayers and church meetings, preachers will invariably stress that a visa is within reach of all those who pray hard enough, and travelling abroad is seen as a Divine reward to those who are true Christians. At the same time, though, these church movements have also opened up the prospect of more imaginary routes of migration which do not necessarily lead to physical elsewheres abroad, but propel one straight into the celestial paradise instead. As 'Ambassadors of Christ', preachers routinely promise their true followers the ultimate visa, a 'visa for heaven'. Or, as JB Mpiana, another musician who is very popular in Kinshasa, frames it in one of his songs: *L'élévation ne vient ni de l'orient ni de l'occident, l'élévation vient de l'éternel* (Salvation does not come from the West or the East, salvation comes from the Eternal).

Travelling inside one's head: Shege and their Shengen

As the previous example indicates, movement and migration is no longer solely defined, generated or contained by physical geographies and the material covering of distances. Movement has increasingly also become a mental activity, a form of mind travel, turning specific locales in both the North and the South into virtual and imagined sites, or states of mind, that are given a content in historically situated urban imaginings, longings, dreams and desires which are generated by and in turn generate this urban flow.

Today, some in Kinshasa engage in specific creations of more global modernities that find their origin in local imaginings without necessarily materializing in the real world in which one lives. Street children, for example, are referred to as *bashege* (De Boeck 2004; 2005). Although the word *shege* is originally a derogatory Hausa term, children's own popular etymologies connect the word *shege* to Shengen, the town in Luxemburg where European Union member states signed a treaty to abolish the inner frontiers and create a free and open European zone which can be accessed in its totality by means of one single visa. For Kinshasa's *bashege*, for whom travelling to Europe is not an option, the street is viewed as an alternative Shengen territory: It is the space where food, freedom, sex, drugs and money can be freely accessed. To them, the world of the urban *cité*, which is referred to as *Belesi* (derived from *Belgique*, Belgium being the name of one of Kinshasa's neighbourhoods during colonial times), is a world full of constraints, a backward world which belongs to the past. Significantly, Kin's modern housing style was referred to as *Belesi* during colonial times because living in these durable brick houses with their corrugated iron roofs was perceived as accessing the ideals of colonialist modernity as it was thought to exist in the metropole itself. In contrast to this, Kinshasa's street children now consider the street to be 'modern' and exciting. The street and the night form the spatial and temporal zones in which the young generate and dream up their own identities in self-invented processes and narratives of globalization.

These dreams of living in a free and boundless, globalized world often come hand in hand with a presumed knowledge of, and power over, the forces of the occult. In Kinshasa, for example, many street children end up in the street because they were accused of witchcraft by parents and other adult family members. Such beliefs have also spread to Congolese Diaspora worlds, as attested to by recent and highly mediatized court cases in London (cf. La Fontaine 2009). But as early as in 1994, in Brussels, I accidentally came into possession of a videotape which triggered my interest in what has by now become a widespread belief in 'witch-children' (Lingala: *bana bandoki*).[4] The videotape featured three Congolese boys between the ages of eight and twelve. They were being cross-examined by a number of Congolese adults and two Belgian men, members of a Neo-Pentecostal prayer movement in the Congolese Diaspora setting of Brussels. The three children had recently been sent from Kinshasa to Belgium, and had started going to school in Brussels. The tape shows how the three children are accused by the adults of the deaths of eight of their relatives in Kinshasa, one of whom is the mother of one of the accused boys. During the (at moments rather violent) cross-examination, of which the tape offers a one hour long summary, the three kids acknowledge that they indeed 'ate' a number of people in Kinshasa. They explain in detail how they 'exited' their bodies and flew back to Congo in a 'nocturnal helicopter', which they had fabricated out of a match-stick, using their own urine for fuel. In Kinshasa, they had been helped by older witches and nocturnal friends. Finally, the three gave a morbid account of how they killed their victims, chopped them up, and distributed the body parts amongst witch friends to 'eat' during a nocturnal feast, dancing naked around their victims' houses.

In these and other witnessing accounts that children accused of witchcraft almost routinely give, the empowering witchcraft idiom of eating, formerly the prerogative of elders, illustrates the nocturnal possibilities of immediate access to the fruits of modernity. Not only does the power of the occult allow these children to travel freely and overcome all the know boundaries that block them in the real world, but the nocturnal consumption of one's elders also gives straight access to, and is quite literally the incorporation and ingestion of modernity's technology, its bourgeois aspirations, and its spaces of consumption. This is fully illustrated by children's own accounts of the importance of 'eating' their victims' bodies. In these accounts they compare their victim's head to a swimming pool or the glass from which the rich *patron* drinks, the backbone to a radio or satellite telephone, the eyes to a television set, the skin to a carpet for the living room, sperm to grease for the maintenance of motor and car parts etc... .[5]

In the impossibility of ever possessing all of these things, or initiating a migratory trajectory in real life, the realm of the imaginary opens up these occult economies of desire and offers unexpected possibilities of mobility and achievement. At the same time, however, the material horizon, the singularity of these children's spaces, and the social geography of their lives often only extend to the corner of their street or the borderline between their neighbourhood and the next.

That in itself raises another question: what does the local and the global, or movement and migration, mean for people who are physically and materially confined to a spot, a street, a neighbourhood, or a village, but who mentally conquer space and imagine lives for themselves in distant and different elsewheres? What does it mean for a city to be filled with people who are mentally no longer there? Kinshasa's streets are extremely full of bodies, but the minds inhabiting these bodies are absent. They have already evacuated the place, dreaming of living a life in Brussels, Paris, the States or China. Where, then, does a local entity begin or end? What does movement in such a case mean? What does it mean when locality, longing and belonging do not coincide? Geographically, the city of Kinshasa has exploded into multiple fragments; other Kinshasas that now also exist in Brussels, Paris or London, much as the former kingdoms on the frontiers of the Central African savannah exported and reproduced themselves elsewhere (cf. Kopytoff 1987). But what do place, locality and identity mean to those who do manage to escape and now inhabit these other Kinshasas, inscribing themselves in various Diaspora movements and 'shedding their bodies' (Lingala: *kobwaka nzoto*), as the process of migration is referred to in

Lingala. In other words migrating literally means to become a no-body, an illegal alien (*ngunda*, 'stranger', 'migrant'), or a living dead in Europe or elsewhere... .[6] What does place, locality and identity mean for young men moving back and forth between rural Angola, Kinshasa, Tel Aviv, Johannesburg and Antwerp? What does it mean for Kinshasa's witch-children (see De Boeck 2005), who claim to leave their bodies behind at night and fly back and forth between Brussels and Kinshasa in the world of the occult? How many localities can one manage in a world where flux seems to be so much stronger than place or belonging? What could be the forms and limits of the local in a world that is increasingly formless and limitless, a world that is shaping up in between the contradictory processes of constant unfolding and contracting, in the friction zones or folds between inside and outside, private and public, internal and external, centrifugal and centripetal forces, the real and the imagined?

The local and the line: Locating traces of lives on the move

All of the possibilities of movement outlined above are invariably coupled to what often seem to be new and inventive forms of community building. Not only do the networks generated by city dwellers interconnect various geographical spaces, they should also be read as forces with a concrete expression in diverse, often intersecting, associational networks, each with its own life span, its own functionality, and its own impact. These networks are not necessarily anchored in any precise geographical location or territory. In this respect, it is a highly significant fact that a city such as Kinshasa has geographically exploded and that, as I pointed out above, there exists a Kinshasa in Brussels, London and Paris, while Brussels, London and Paris have, in some ways, also become suburbs of Kinshasa, Lagos or Dakar. Certainly, also, it is important to appreciate the geopolitical fact that there are more Congolese merchants travelling between Kinshasa and the Chinese cities of Guanzhou or Shenzhen these days than there are between Kinshasa and Brussels. It means that these networks are often open-ended sites of flux, of contact, transmission, networking, circulation and migration, generated by the opportunities of the moment, and capable of quickly changing directions and adapting to new situations. Through these various 'streaming' realities, information and connectedness are being channelled, reoriented, and transformed and new forms of 'social navigation', to use this currently popular term (cf. Vigh 2006; Christiansen, Utas and Vigh 2006) are being generated.

But what exactly does this 'navigation' entail? Given the fact that more often than not the sea is rough, how does one sail to other shores, and where, in the end, can one moor the ship of one's existence?

Mudimbe, in a beautiful text on lines and the paradoxes about allegories of identity and alterity, states: "Our physical geography, the whole domain of our culture, including mental configurations and our relations to nature, are topographies structured by lines." (Mudimbe 2008, 25). In his essay, he starts off with the idea that the lines generated by the movements and physical interactions of people, ideas, commodities, etc. can no longer be described or interpreted as *straight* lines. Indeed, post-colonial subjects' lives do no longer unfold as 'straight stories', to paraphrase film director David Lynch's movie title; they often take the form of a 'Lost Highway'... In popular cultural practices and narratives, linearity has come to mean something else. Local biographies and physical interactions are not, and probably never were, generated as straight lines. Rather, they develop into cultural topologies that basically are deviations fromof straightness, and are often marked by instability (in economic terms certainly, but also politically, or morally). Living in the local often means that one cannot afford to live with the safety net of steadiness and durability. The local, in this respect, is anything but static.

Consider the complexity of the lines described by many Congolese throughout their life-times. Two such lines are provided by the biographies of Shayibunda and his uncle.[7] The lines of their lives do not start in Kinshasa, but somewhere on the borderlands between Congo and Angola, where I conducted field research between 1987 and 1994:

> Shayibunda was born in Congo in the mid-fifties, the son of an important Luunda paramount title-holder who had 32 wives and over fifty children in the course of his life-time. As a boy he was sent to a Catholic boarding school, run by Belgian missionaries, in Southern Congo. There he completed his primary education and the first three years of his secondary school, making of him one of the first Luunda 'intellectuals' in the area. He then returned to his father's village and started living in a number of other villages in the border area between Congo and Angola. In the early 1980s, his father died. In 1984, his maternal uncle, Kasongo Lunda, was enthroned and became paramount titleholder Kateend II. In this new capacity Kateend set up a royal village, situated in Congo's Upper Kwango area (province of Bandundu). Kateend was born in the Belgian Congo as well. He never received formal school training and

could barely read or write, nor speak French, although he mastered rudimentary Portuguese. As a young man he had moved to Angola to become
a soldier in the Portuguese colonial army. He was even sent to Portugal
for a brief period of military training – or so it was said. After Angolan
independence in 1975, Kateend, an authoritarian but intelligent man,
was appointed by the Angolan authorities as *regidor* or 'traditional chief'
in Lunda Norte, but later he got into trouble because of his UNITA
sympathies. The MPLA killed one of his sons, and when he avenged
himself by capturing and executing an MPLA soldier, he had to flee to
Congo. There he became locally famous as a renowned elephant hunter,
before becoming a paramount titleholder. In this capacity too he made
quite a name for himself, and eventually he was decorated as a Knight in
the National Order of the Leopard by Mobutu. The latter even invited
him to the presidential palace in Gbadolite in the late 1980s.

In the early eighties, in the meantime, surging on the waves of newly
developing diamond traffic, Shayibunda had started to travel between
Lunda Norte, Kinshasa and Brazzaville, trading diamonds. Along the
way he married his first wife, a Mbala girl from the town of Kikwit, where
he had bought a house with the money from his diamond transactions.
After a couple of years, he returned to the village, bringing her back with
him. By then, he had also started a career in local Luunda politics, as an
advisor to the new paramount titleholder, his maternal uncle. Because
of this, the royal court pressured him into marrying a second wife, one
of his own matrilineal cross-cousins, a daughter of Kateend II. Shayibunda agreed to marry her, but insisted that she should first be sent
to Kinshasa for a couple of years to obtain a diploma as a nurse. Upon
her return, conflict broke out between Shayibunda's two co-wives. As
a result, his first wife, together with her children, moved back to the
house in Kikwit, while his second wife moved out of the village and set
up a household in the local border town of Kulindji, where Shayibunda
built a new house for her. This forced him to move between his uncle's
village and the households of his two wives, each hundreds of kilometres
apart (distances not easy to bridge in Congo today). Then, in the early
1990s, he was sent by the royal court to Kinshasa, to act as a representative of the Luunda paramount ruler at the National Sovereign Conference that accompanied the country's opening up to a multiparty system.
Contrary to what he had expected, his stay in Kinshasa lasted not three

weeks but three years, during which he was unable to visit his wives and children, mainly because he lacked the funds to do so. As a result, his senior wife, who lived in total poverty in Kikwit, abandoned her five children and left for Tshikapa, in the Kasai region, where she remarried and got pregnant again soon afterwards. In Kinshasa, in the meantime, Shayibunda himself got involved with another woman. Then, in the late nineties, he finally managed to move back to his uncle's village, and from there started travelling again between Angola and the household of his second wife, who refused to return to the royal village with him. In 2002, after a long political struggle and much lobbying during another long stay in Kinshasa, he was appointed as a local district commissioner by the central government, which enabled him to move to the town of Kulindji and pick up his life with his second wife again. He also started to try and reassemble the children from his first marriage who by now were dispersed between Kikwit, Kinshasa and some villages along the border with Angola. Two years later, his uncle, paramount Kateend II, died after a long illness. His death left the court weakened and divided. Shayibunda, in spite of his reluctance and even refusal to become the new paramount, became entangled in a fierce succession fight with two of his own brothers (who through their mothers also had different political allegiances and were backed up by different clans within the royal lineage). In 2004, then, Shayibunda, on the road again towards Angola, suffered what appears to have been a massive heart attack. Fighting for his life in a Canadian Mennonite hospital along the border with Angola, he miraculously recovered after leaving the hospital and starting treatment with a local healer (even though he had become a Born Again Christian in the meantime). In 2005, however, he suddenly collapsed again and died while on the way to his office in Kulindji. Inevitably, it was whispered that his political adversaries had poisoned or bewitched him.

It can be argued that Shayibunda's or Kateend's sense of 'local' was firmly rooted in the Luunda village world and in the local politics of the royal lineage. Yet, their worlds were not confined to that reality alone. Throughout his life, Shayibunda struggled hard not to be totally swallowed up by that 'local' world, for example by refusing the role of paramount ruler for which he seemed to be predetermined long before his uncle's death. But in trying to broaden his horizon and break out of its confines, by moving between Angola, Brazzaville and Kinshasa, and getting involved in broader economic and political processes, by becoming a Born Again Christian and a state administrator, his life (which we would hardly think of as a 'cosmopolitan' one) also became so caught up in so many different trajectories, and between so many different codes, roles, moralities, or languages (in Shayibunda's case at least nine different ones), between war and peace, Congolese and Angolan politics, between local and translocal, or rural and urban worlds, between exogamous and endogamous marriages, between gift and money, between ethnic and other identities, between ancestors and Neo-Pentecostalists, traditions and modernities…, that his biography also reads, rather tragically, like an increasingly unsuccessful attempt to connect all of this, steer the course of his own life undamaged through it all, and fight the constant threat of dispersal.

Within the Congolese context, Shayibunda's life is not exceptional. Other people's lives are often even more complex than his was. Setting off from unexpected points of departure, the lines described in the course of such biographies connect figures of a praxis in their dimension of a negation of standard, straight lines. As 'an opening up to the unexpected', to use Mudimbe's expression (2008, 26), these lines often overrun all known boundaries (gender, belief systems, ethnicity, …), forcing people to live simultaneously in multiple territories, and making of each of them a community in itself. This is not so much to make the – by now overly familiar – point concerning the much celebrated capacity of post-colonial subjects strategically to use multiple identities in various contexts. It no longer comes as a surprise that one and the same person may live in a refugee camp outside Luanda, engage in worshipping ancestral Luunda shrines there, while also being a Muslim or a Neo-Pentecostal, be in contact with the London stock exchange by means of his cellular phone, go clubbing in a Kinshasa night-club, and visit prostitutes in Cape Town while on his way to Antwerp to sell diamonds on behalf of a trader based in Mumbai. The point I want to make, rather, is that all of this never seems to be carefully planned in advance. People are, of course, conscious actors and participants in their own lives, struggling to some extent to stay in control, and therefore continuously busy seizing and capturing the moment and the opportunity to reinvent and re-imagine their lives in different ways. But at the same time these processes of seizure remain highly unpredictable. In such lives there never is a straight line between today and tomorrow, or between here and there, between possibility and the impossible, success and failure, life and death. Rather than existing through habit and routine, or rather than being formatted by the temporalities of the static and the unchanging, post-colonial local lives are often shaped through movements of the unexpected, which constantly seem to be steering local actors off course, launching them into new orbits. Such lives, therefore, are never fully autonomous projects either. Rather, they seem to consist of constant stops and starts, directed by the tricky and unforeseeable processes of seizure and capture, which in turn are structured, not only by the spatialities of various networks, of shifting contexts and of connections, but also by the specific temporality of the *moment*, unpredictably caught between the immobility of endless waiting and the effervescence of sudden movement. Living in the local, which in itself has become increasingly unstable and nomadic, constantly generates new opportunities and openings, while simultaneously also causing sudden closures and producing a lot of fall out and collateral damage along the way (as illustrated, for example, by the dispersal of Shayibunda's children, or by the very fact that the act of migrating always entails a 'shedding of your body', and becoming a (legal) no-body, a *sans-papier*, someone without a true identity). Living and surviving in the moment of the local therefore often necessitates extreme (mental and physical) flexibility as well as mastery of the tricky skills of improvisation, a capacity that Kinois sometimes describe as *mathématiques* (a notion picked up and further developed by Jean Bofane in a recent novel, *mathématiques congolaises* (2008)). And indeed, to steer your life unharmed through all the pitfalls, all the possible parameters of your daily existence, seems to demand an advanced knowledge of higher mathematics and of topics such as chaos, fractals, and dynamics. Generated in the temporality of the now and therefore rarely knowing where they will end up, the meandering lines of local lives constantly generate conjunctures and conjectures of sudden action and passivity, power and powerlessness, expectation and disappointment, rise and fall, dream and nightmare.

In summary, because of the often instantaneous, spontaneous, improvised and random nature of the lines that unfold throughout individual biographies, and because of the equally unplanned ways in which these individual biographies get caught up and become entangled in other lines and networks of physical and mental contact with other people and other discourses, practices and ideas, the line of one's life is rarely a straight line forward. It is almost never uni-directional or teleological. Therefore, perhaps, lives lived locally remain difficult to capture within the historicist approaches of modernity and its accompanying ideologies of linear development, progress and accumulation. Living and surviving in the moment of the local, on the contrary, almost never is a project that one can plan ahead of time. To deal with the local is to deal with hazard. Prepared to open up to the unexpected, often because there is no other choice or option, local lives are profoundly marked by the dynamics of the hazardous and the accidental, and that is also why their memories often remain diffuse and opaque. In this way, as I stressed before, local popular cultures, as diverse theatres of dreams and of war, generate a world that continuously de- and reconstructs itself, continuously stops and starts, and keeps history, memory and questioning in motion.

Conclusion

Throughout this chapter I have, in various ways, been arguing that in order to understand worlds in movement, let alone intervene in them, we need to take into account the level of networking and the great mobility that characterize them. Taking all of these levels into account, the emerging figure of the city dweller transforms from poor and passive victim into active participant with his or her own social, economic, political and religious agendas, which are often situated far beyond the level of mere survival. All of that generates a specific 'agency' in a specific urban experience. It also creates the capacity or the ability to become a wilful actor in these urban networks. This may range from participating in smuggling rings, commercial networks or networks that channel the flow of remittances between the city and its diasporas, to membership of religious organizations, often with a strong trans-national character. In spite of all of the many marginalizing factors people have to face throughout their lives, people constantly generate (urban) life forms that are characterized by new modes of movement and migration, and new ways of positioning oneself within one's city and far beyond.

In order to capture and read the realities of these different trajectories, movements and migrations, I believe it is absolutely necessary to stay close to the actual lives of those who move through these various worlds, close to the specific lines these lives describe, the specific itineraries that unfold in the processes of living in contexts that are indeed often marked by a lack of opportunity, a lack that – paradoxically – often creates opportunities on others levels. All of the disabling factors that constantly punctuate the urban dwellers' lives also force them to excel in flexibility and improvisation, in the gymnastics and mathematics necessary to survive on a daily basis in Congo. Urban dwellers seem to be very good at doing exactly that: at opening up to this 'unexpected', that often reveals itself outside the known pathways constituting life as we know it. They are highly skilled at discovering itineraries beyond the obvious, at exploiting more invisible paths and clandestine possibilities that lie hidden in the folds of urban domains and experiences. Often, city dwellers have trained themselves to tap into this imbroglio successfully, and to exploit to the full the possibilities these juxtapositions offer. They are constantly busy designing new ways to escape from the economic impositions and excesses that urban life imposes on them. They often know where to look and what to look for in order to generate feasibility within what is seemingly unfeasible.

References

Archambault, Julie. 2010. *Cruising through Uncertainty: Mobile Phone Practices, Occulted Economies and the Politics of Respect in Southern Mozambique.* London: SOAS (Unpublished doctoral dissertation).

Bayart, Jean-François. 1994. *La reinvention du capitalisme.* Paris: Karthala.

Castells, Manuel. 1998. *The Information Age: Economy, Society and Culture. Vol 3: End of Millenium.* Oxford: Blackwell.

Bofane, Jean. 2008. *Mathématiques congolaises.* Paris: Actes Sud.

Christiansen, Catrine, Mats Utas and Henrik Vigh. 2006. *Navigating Youth, Generating Adulthood. Social Becoming in an African Context.* Uppsala: Nordiska Afrika Institutet.

Davis, Mike. 2006. *Planet of Slums.* London and New York: Verso.

De Boeck, Filip and Marie-Françoise Plissart. 2004. *Kinshasa. Tales of the Invisible City.* Ghent and Tervuren: Ludion and Royal Museum of Central Africa.

De Boeck, Filip. 1999. Domesticating Diamonds and Dollars: Identity, Expenditure and Sharing in Southwestern Zaire (1984-1997). In *Globalization and Identity. Dialectics of Flow and Closure*, ed. Birgit Meyer and Peter Geschiere, 177-209. Oxford: Blackwell.

De Boeck, Filip. 2004. On Being Shege in Kinshasa: Children, the Occult and the Street. In *Reinventing Order in the Congo. How People Respond to State Failure in Kinshasa*, ed. Theodore Trefon, 155-173. London: Zed Books.

De Boeck, Filip. 2005. The Divine Seed. Children, Gift and Witchcraft in the Democratic Republic of Congo. In *Makers and Breakers. Children and Youth in Postcolonial Africa*, ed. Alcinda Honwana and Filip De Boeck, 188-214. Oxford: James Currey.

De Boeck, F. 2008. 'Dead Society' in a 'Cemetery City'. The Transformation of Burial Rites in Kinshasa. In *Heterotopia and the City. Public Space in a Postcivil Society*, ed. Lieven De Cauter and Michiel Dehaene, 297-308. London: Routledge.

De Boeck, Filip. 2009. Death Matters: Intimacy, Violence and the Production of Social Knowledge by Urban Youth in the Democratic Republic of Congo. In *Can there be Life without the Other?*, ed. Antonio P. Ribeiro, 44-64. Manchester: Carcanet Press.

De Bruijn, Mirjam, Rijk Van Dijk and Dick Foeken, eds. 2001. *Mobile Africa: Changing Patterns of Movement in Africa and Beyond.* Leiden: Brill.

Devisch, René. 1995. Frenzy, Violence, and Ethical Renewal in Kinshasa. *Public Culture* 7 (3): 593-629.

Ferguson, James. 2006. *Global Shadows: Africa in the Neoliberal World Order*. Durham: Duke University Press.

Kopytoff, Igor. 1987. *The African Frontier: The Reproduction of Traditional African Societies*. Bloomington and Indianapolis: Indiana University Press.

La Fontaine, Jean, ed. 2009. *The Devil's Children. From Spirit Possession to Witchcraft: New Allegations that Affect Children*. Farnham, Surrey: Ashgate.

Lomomba Emongo, Jules. 1998. *Mwana-Mayi le Parisien*. St Léonard, Quebec: Editions 5 continents.

Malaquais, Dominique. 2006. Douala/Johannesburg/New York: Cityscapes Imagined. In *Cities in Contemporary Africa*, ed. Martin J. Murray and Garth A. Myers, 31-52. New York: Palgrave MacMillan.

Mayoyo Bitumba Tipo-Tipo, 1995. *Migration sud/nord, levier ou obstacle?: Les Zaïrois en Belgique*. Tervuren: Institut Africain.

Mbembe, Achille. 2001. Ways of Seeing: Beyond the New Nativism: Introduction. *African Studies Review* 44 (2): 1-14.

Mudimbe, Valentin Y. 2008. What is a Line? On Paradoxes about Allegories on Identity and Alterity. *Quest. An African Journal of Philosophy* XXI: 23-62.

Neuwirth, Robert. 2006. *Shadow Cities. A Billion Squatters. A New Urban World*. London: Routledge.

Piot, Charles. 1999. *Remotely Global. Village Modernity in West Africa*. Chicago and London: Chicago University Press.

Sene Mongala, Bienvenue. 2002. *Fwa-ku-Mputu.To lisolo ya moto oyo akanaka Poto pene akufa*. Brussels: Mabiki.

Simone, AbdouMaliq. 2001. On the Worlding of African Cities. *African Studies Review* 44 (2): 15-41.

Simone, AbdouMaliq. 2004. *For the City Yet to Come. Changing African Life in Four Cities*. Durham and London: Duke University Press.

Simone, AbdouMaliq. 2006. Some Reflections on Making the Popular in Urban Africa. Paper read at the *International Conference 'Making Sense in the City'* (Convener: Prof. R. Pinxten), University of Ghent, 19 December 2006.

Simone, AbdouMaliq. 2010. *City life from Jakarta to Dakar. Movements at the Crossroads*. London: Routledge.

Soromenho, Castro. 1956 [1941]. *Camaxilo [Terra Morta]*. Paris: Présence Africaine.

Vigh, Henrik. 2006. *Navigating Terrains of War. Youth and Soldiering in Guinea-Bissau*. Oxford: Berghahn Books.

Notes

1 A first draft of this chapter was presented at the ZMO International Seminar 'Migration at home: Migratory Imaginations and Imaginary Cosmopolitanisms in Africa and beyond', Zentrum Moderner Orient, Berlin, 11-13 March 2009.

2 *Fwa ku Mputu* is also the title of a 2002 novel written in Lingala by Bienvenue Sene Mongala, in which he tells the story of his own journey to Europe. The diaspora theme is a popular topic in Congolese literature, even though the journey towards Europe is realized only in one's imagination, as is the case in Lomomba Emongo's novel *Mwana-Mayi, le Parisien* (1998). The main character, Mwana-Mayi, refers to himself as 'the Parisian', even though he has never set foot outside Kinshasa.

3 Many classic songs of Congolese rumba deal with the issue of migration, either from the perspective of those who travel to Europe and address lovers and relatives at home, or from the perspective of the person (usually the wife or girlfriend) who remains behind and laments her partner's absence. The latter is the case in the classic Franco song *Makambo ezali minene* (The problems are huge), interpreted by male vocalist Madilu Système: *My husband has gone to Europe / He went away to study / He went away to a garden of pleasures / He went and did not come back / What's it all about? / In the fleshpots everyone usually has fun / In places of sorrow everyone usually cries / Me, I'm crying because my husband went away and did not come back / I found a spot in which the people were crying / And I started crying too / They are tears of sadness for my absent husband.*

4 The tape in question inspired a conference on 'Visualizing the Invisible', organized by Bogumil Jewsiewicki and Jean-Paul Colleyn at the Ecole des Hautes Etudes, Paris, May 10, 2005. See also De Boeck 2005.

5 For detailed examples see e.g. De Boeck and Plissart 2004, 183ff.

6 The whole informal economy which is generated around the evacuation of all these Congolese 'bodies' to *Mputuville* is called *système ngulu* in Kinshasa. *Ngulu* means 'pig' or 'pork'. *Système ngulu* refers to an older mythology that found its origin in colonial times, when it was believed that Congolese children who were 'invited' by missionaries to travel and study into Belgium were killed there, and subsequently returned to Congo processed as corned beef, which was sold to the local population by the colonizer.

7 Shayibunda is a fictitious name, as is Bibish earlier on in this text.

Spaces in movement: Town–village interconnections in West Africa[1]

Denise Dias Barros

Mobility in Africa is a field of study facilitating the interpretation of interconnection established through the action of people, groups and societies on the African continent. This field provides new leads both on the ties that have existed between women and men, between generations and between different age groups throughout history, and on social change in contemporary Africa. It also enables the controversy surrounding opposition between individuals and states, states and societies, individuals and communities, urban and rural life, town and village to be reconsidered. Authors such as De Bruijn, Van Dijk and Foeken (2001) from the African Studies Centre at the University of Leiden, basing their research on case studies on mobility in Sub-Saharan African societies, emphasize the centrality of movement in African life and its significance in understanding other social processes. They dismiss the notion that migration necessarily entails a break between the individual and his/her own society. One of the most suitable methods of understanding the local repercussions of globalization is to analyse cultural transformation at local level, as suggested by Hahn (2008). Considerable efforts have been made in the last few decades to encourage research on migration on the African continent. Institutional initiatives such the CODESRIA-SEPHIS[2] workshop *Historicizing Migrations* in 2007 and authors such as Touré and Fadayomi (1993), Koulibaly (2001) and Cissé (2004) provide examples of this.

One of the principal focuses of this research, conducted through a micro-local approach, concerns the ability to act, organize and coordinate collectives (with considerable personal investment) to maintain unity in a wide variety of situations accentuated by mobility.

My aim is to contribute to the understanding of the broad contours of a movement that has prevailed for many years in a specific region, namely between the village of Songho (Dogon Plateau) and Bamako, capital of the Republic of Mali. My initial purpose is therefore to demonstrate that, historically, Dogon territorialization was underpinned by mobility. This helped to build the foundations on which different forms of mobility have developed since 1940, and particularly since Mali's independence, leading to the current, more frequent movements back and forth between town and village according to the seasons – a phenomenon that began at the end of the 1980s.

The inhabitants' mobility in the Songho *ethos* was placed in the ethnographical and historical contexts based on specific bibliographical references and sought to describe certain characteristics, observed during seasonal migration to the capital. The organization, itineraries selected and preferred activities for men and women from different age groups were taken into consideration. Hazel (2006) demonstrates that a cyclical view of history is key to understanding the inter-generational and age group system. In the context of my fieldwork in Songho, this notion is also important in grasping the expansion of space and the formation of circularity in the Songho migration process.

In a different context, José Guilherme Mangani (2004, 2006a, 2006b) suggests the use of the concepts *pedaço*, literally piece or fragment, and *circuit*, when considering the analysis of constructions of sociability and identity in the metropolis of São Paulo, Brazil, by social groups on the margins of hegemonic experiences of sociability: believers, migrants, youth, etc. Magnani proposes to view social actors not as isolated and dispersed beings, but rather as agents who are able to develop survival strategies and work, to practise their religion, to establish emotional exchanges, to define specific ways of using the city such as public spaces, services and institutions, and able to maintain their manner of recreation and their culture. In this dynamic, the concept of *pedaço* focuses on the interactions established in a space, turning it into a reference point within a network of relationships, beyond the territorial limitations. Between their "pieces," journeys establish personal and collective circuits of belonging.

In West Africa, migration has long been characterized by people's seasonal movements in their own sub-regions of the continent. This, however, changed when mobility started to be directed to European destinations from the 1980s onwards. Nevertheless, it should be noted that considerable variations have been identified in relation to gender and the dynamics of migration. In the Sahel, seasonal migration is probably an important survival strategy and a way to strengthen domestic economy.

It implies the existence of trade and the possibility of developing an activity in a context of high agro-climatic risks and lack of social security. Migration can be a mechanism of diversification of possible economic activities and a way to reduce some inequalities (Hampshire, 2006; Konseiga, 2007). Finally, it provides insight into individual and group experiences in their adventures and quests to find spaces that connect their membership.

The back and forth movement of people in the context of migration studies is not a new issue; it is found already in Robert Montagne's (1954) investigation of the temporary migration of Algerian workers to the city. Gildas Simon (1979) referred to the building of a relational space through circulatory migration from Tunisia to France. According to Stéphane de Tapia (1998) migratory movements are widely taken up in the field of humanities and social sciences to analyse issues of international flows of people and labour, including different geographical and socio-logical concepts. The notion of circularity, used in this text, captures the movement of society and people in the direction of their individual and collective itineraries, their organizations, their challenges and motivations. This concept refers to the movement of the construction of spaces of meaning in different territories, despite their geographical remoteness, while pushing the boundaries of the village itself at the same time. It allows an approach to social dynamics in the city and in the village and takes into account the links between these two spaces.

In the framework of the fieldwork for this research, several questions arose in the initial stages of this study concerning the migrational patterns of the Songho population. Why do people leave Songho? Is this a recent phenomenon? What are its historical roots? How is departure from the village organized? Is the population's departure organized on an individual or on a collective basis? Which economic activities enter into the process? What motivations and dynamics underlie the de-parture of women? Did a weakening of social ties or sense of belonging occur? Does the implementation of collective migratory strategies form part of the experience as opposed to the alienation and weakening of social ties caused by distance? Would migration or mobility encompass the definition or redefinition of the expression 'se dire dogon' (to call oneself Dogon) (Bouju 1995; 2002) within a long-term per-spective?

My aim is to grasp the implications of these pendulum movements that gradually produce ramifications in time, the initial itinerary frequently generating others. Year after year, this (retroactive) action becomes self-inducing, thus deepening and modifying the intensity and quality of spaces charged with meaning. For example, the itineraries and circuits adopted by one age group are transformed into a reference point or standard which other, younger inhabitants tend to adopt at a later stage (Tilly 1990; Massey 1993; Martes 1999; Roussel 2003; Hily, Berthomiere and Mihaylova 2004). There are, however, changes caused by the new interactions created.

Migration as a historical Dogon identity

According to Walter Van Beek (2003; 2005), the Dogon region is formed of a network of autonomous villages, more or less connected through history, kinship, neighbouring territorial alliances and ritual ties.

Despite the development of multiple activities and jobs, the free market economy is limited in this agro-pastoral area founded on lineage as a socio-political unit, on patrilineage and the domestic group. Today, *se dire Dogon* still means that one is a farmer even if other activities carry some economic weight. Some 90% of the population is involved in agriculture, having to extract from the arid soil the food required for survival and exchange, whereas migration tends to foster and intensify trading activities (sale of fruit, vegetables and animals in the capital). Tourism has generated diverse activities such as the production of handicrafts for sale in the village or to meet city shopkeepers' demands, dance and theatre groups, tourist accommodation, and jobs as tour guides and cultural mediators within the scope of projects implemented by numerous organizations (NGOs) and associations.

In this context, Petit (1998) places special emphasis on migration as an integration phenomenon. Songho, like other Dogon localities, was formed from what is referred to as a 'movement of spaces.' The stages in the migration process are carefully transmitted from one generation to the next by each village unit (Degoga, Gindo, Karambe, Seiba and Yanoge). They recount their migration routes (Mande always being the point of departure) up to the time of establishment at the top of an abandoned rock called Songho-Kolo, at the beginning of the 20th century. There is apparent unity in the narration: all state that they dispersed in Segué.

The region sustained centuries of wars and raids. The population, split into small groups, found shelter and set up defence positions in the rocky mountains. But as soon as people settled (at the beginning of the 19th century, in all likelihood), they suffered from the slave trade, which led to raids, plundering by centralized states and political hegemonies in the Niger Valley (from the Mali Empire to the Peul Empire of Massina, in particular), Toucouleur domination and French colonialism.

In his work on social change in the Dogon region (Sangha and Ereli) during the colonial and post-colonial periods (1910–1980), Isaï Dougnon (2007) makes important observations on the migratory processes. According to Dougnon, the study of migration in Dogon territory, which underwent a transformation throughout the period researched, calls for an understanding of the society's imaginary dimension if the motivations for migration are to be fully comprehended; at the same time, mobility must be placed in its historical context. Corvee labour, imposed by the Toucouleurs, was one of the first forms of collective mobility in the 20th century to be experienced by the Dogon, in addition to military service (viewed as 'slavery') during the French occupation prior to World War I.

Other closely intertwined processes, unfolding particularly from the 1920s onwards, created a strong culture of mobility and travel. Target destinations included Ghana (up to 1980) and the Office du Niger, a major hydro-agricultural company that employed numerous men, women and children, for the rice harvest from the 1930s onwards. Large-scale colonial projects marked the lifestyle and history of the population in terms of mobility in the early 20th century.

Migrants' motivations have diverse, complementary sources. According to Dougnon (2007, 73), these include: tax liability, forced labour, abuse of power by the *Chef de canton*, hunger, and the desire to acquire new clothes, to learn languages (French, English and Bamanan) and to see the world. Dougnon quotes his interviewees as still making the distinction between travelling to acquire property and prestige on the one hand, and migration for love on the other, when relationships are met with resistance from family members and the larger community (2007, 58), as expressed in the popular song reproduced by the author in French (2007, 59):

> *Ce n'est rien que de se perdre en poursuivant le bien,*
> *Tel un beau sabre et une belle fille*
> *Ce n'est rien que de se perdre en suivant un homme d'un bon esprit,*
> *Même s'il faut traverser sept mers et sept fleuves.*
> *Migrer, c'est se perdre : les femmes, les chanteurs pleurent le migrant*
> *Ce n'est rien que de se perdre en cherchant des objets de valeurs.*

> (To get lost while seeking goods,
> a beautiful sword or a pretty girl
> or even while following an intelligent man means nothing,
> even if you have to cross seven seas and seven rivers.
> To migrate is to get lost: the migrant is wept by women and singers
> Getting lost when seeking precious objects means nothing.)

Véronique Petit (1998), head of research on Dogon migration (notably in the Sangha sub-region) sought to understand how the Dogon 'embed their identity in the collective imaginary encompassing massive social events such as migration' (1998: 9). Petit emphasizes the fact that population movement is not marginal behaviour and that mobility is strongly embedded in the Dogon identity. When in search of fertile land, migration destinations become transnational (particularly to Western and Central African countries), domestic (to urban areas such as Mopti, Ségou and Bamako) and regional (particularly the plain).

On the basis of their research conducted in 2002 and 2008, Sauvain-Dugerdil, Dougnon and Diop (2008) describe the temporary migration of youth from the Sarnyéré region, demonstrating how this now acts as a driver for cultural transformation and territorial expansion. Lastly, mobility is considered in the Dogon context (Petit 1998; Doumbia 2000; Thibaut 2005; Dougnon 2007; Sauvain-Dugerdil, Dougnon and Diop 2008) as not only an appropriate tool to manage family and community conflicts but also as an economic survival strategy. Local history is interspersed with intense population flows, forming a perpetual movement between Songho and Bamako.

Contemporary seasonal migration and the mobility of the Songho population

In daily parlance, the temporal dimension of mobility is often linked to specific events. History is seared into the collective memory, referring to different times of travel: the Ghana period, the Abidjan period and, lastly, the present Bamako period according to emic classification. Such periodical classification by the local populations highlights the importance of migration in Songho. No rift or linear approach to time is apparent, even in their discourse – quite the contrary. This periodicity facilitates the crisscrossing and overlapping of travel as a social practice: an individual may travel to Accra or to Abidjan, even in the Bamako era.

It is only in the Bamako period, however, that migration has become strongly tied to intensified age group mobility. During the Abidjan period, for example, familial and societal acceptance of the absence of certain members was not as tolerated as it became for the Bamako period. In many cases, the family went to fetch a member who had left when faced with social responsibilities such as marriage, settlement of land disputes or making commitments within a domestic group. In some cases, the individual who went to fetch a brother or a nephew took over the latter's job. The establishment of distance, even for periods of several years, was – and still is – not interpreted as definitive emigration and not accepted as such by the individuals who remained in the village. The emigrant was convinced to return in most cases, although a few families are now established in other towns in Mali such as Sikasso, Gao, Ségou and Mopti.

Pilgrimage to Mecca constitutes an important event that is defined as temporary movement, but in practice often becomes long-term. The Hajj has been a clear form of mobility, built up by generations of Songho pilgrims, since 1946. Many Songho pilgrims travelled across Africa, sometimes on foot. They often interrupted their journey to work at the stopping points in the journey created by generations of pilgrims in succession. Little by little, several settled in the different towns and countries along the route. Five families now reside in Mecca, providing support to Dogon pilgrims, especially those from Pignari.[3] The seasonal movement arose and developed as a result of the Office du Niger's rice-growing activity in Mali. Conversely, the current seasonal form of migration, which is the focus of this study, took shape 'after the arrival of Mali', according to our collaborators. The destination selected by most Songho migrants today is the capital.

Although, in the first decades, migration was essentially initiated by men, women contributed a great deal in the development of the movement to Bamako. Although it is true that several women 'experienced the exodus' as they say, they did not do so individually, however. If they migrated as adults, they were accompanied by their husbands (in increasing numbers once destinations gradually became further afield and the periods of migration longer), and if they migrated in their childhood they were following their parents.

Until the early 1980s, migration was not a back-and-forth movement and was not necessarily seasonal. Migration often took place in groups, with increasingly younger members. Once again, the phenomenon was initiated by men. In the Ghana and Ivory Coast periods, populations from different age groups migrated for relatively long periods, ranging from five to ten years. Mamadou Seiba, one of the first tourist guides in Songho, explains that he belongs to the period when the Ivory Coast was the preferred destination, and also that there was very little money circulating in Songho when he was young. In his and the following generations, the situation changed. Three members of the age group born in the period 1940-44 never returned to live in Songho (two live in Bamako, one in Abidjan). An increase in the number of migrants is recorded for the following age group (1946-48): 13 of the 36 members who travelled to Abidjan (1 individual), Sikasso (3 individuals) and Bamako (10 individuals) were classified as permanent emigrants in 2010. Some members of the preceding age groups, involved in this migration process, brought back knowledge and an array of initiatives including new economic projects (as for the development of local tourism or a health centre). The 1940-45 and 1946-48 age groups built the Songho encampment for tourists.[4] Access to schooling for men seems to have been an important factor for migration and social change. The first students were, in fact, recruited from the 1946-48 and 1949-51 age groups. It is important to note that only one of the men who finished his schooling during the colonial period remained in Songho. He played a major role in the village in terms of relations with government authorities and, at a later stage, with other foreigners or outsiders such as state representatives, NGO staff and tourists.

The mobility of African women and young people, according to many authors, was a striking phenomenon in the late nineteenth century. Lesclingand (2004) in his study of migratory strategies of the Bwa society, for example, relates this phenomenon to growing urbanization during the colonial period. Today, employees' exposure to physical and psychological violence beyond economic exploitation is analysed by Bouju (2008) in his work on the experience of young migrants from the Djenne region to different Malian cities. The author interprets the phenomenon as a form of structural violence of social relations and a sign of disagreement between different levels: community, village, city and public sphere. In the case of Songho one can see new strategies emerging for setting up collective norms to minimize difficulties and social violence resulting from mobility.

Corinne and Coquery-Vidrovitch (1995) note that the mobility of women for marriage purposes has long been practised in different societies, which rendered them capable of adapting to various environments. However, the post-World War II period witnessed an intensification of women´s mobility for other purposes, which was also encouraged for various reasons. In this regard, one can see similarities between this phenomenon and the mobility of young women in Songho.[5]

As in other parts of West Africa, as explained by Lesclingand (2004), the motive behind the first women's movement out of the Dogon country was mainly to join their husbands. However, pilgrimage to Mecca has also played a vital role in intensifying women's movement. In the early 1980s there were couples who lived in cities such as Abidjan and Bouake, Gao, Yaounde and even Mecca. From 1981 onwards, women began to travel with their husbands after marriage at the age of fourteen. Gradually, however, they began to migrate independently of their husbands and have created their own travel dynamics. The first groups were between the ages of fourteen and sixteen, the members of the age group of those born between 1965 and 1967, all of whom came from the *tóndó blanga*, one of Songo's section neighbourhood.

In Mali, young girls' mobility to the cities, starting as early as at twelve to fifteen years of age, has gradually become a considerable phenomenon over the past three decades. Jacky Bouju (2008: note 31) highlights: "There is no region of Mali that escaped the imperatives of urban migration to form the wedding trousseau." Nonetheless, at the beginning of the 1980s, women from Songho were not supposed to move away on their own. In this regard, Adama Karambe explains that at first, to go to Bamako, girls had to struggle hard. They decided to travel without their parents' approval or blessings as is required in the Dogon culture. This situation has changed today and girls now travel in an organized manner as groups. Data relating to a specific women's age group show that in January 2007, almost all of them were in Songho. Young women from Songho maintain constant mobility and return every year to the Malian capital.

As elsewhere, the motivation of these women to move is far more complex than the most immediate objective. Their mobility is aggravated by an urge to earn some money to buy all the necessary utensils for marriage.6 It is a long process, which is considered complete once a woman moves to the house of the husband's family. This, however, takes place, in most cases, after the bearing of two or three children. In general, women work in Bamako until they get the desired goods for their wedding trousseau, not only for the kitchen and the bedroom, but also the masher, pots and mosquito nets, all of which are materials to be used for the wedding ceremony. They are also responsible for purchasing salt and other seasonal products in sufficient quantities since they are obliged to prepare lunch for the husband's family (debu-bain) during the farming period which lasts about six months.

A female member of the age group of 1959-61, Korca Yacouba, who migrated to accompany her husband in the late 1980s, has become a benchmark for many women. She decided to seek work when her husband lost his job. After working as an employee, she became a trader in vegetables. Three years later, she started with her sisters to sell cooked rice. In 1995 she set up a restaurant in the market of Missira, with all its employees coming from Songho. She has six children, four of whom were born in Songho. The eldest daughter was 18 at the time of the interview (October 2001) and was going to marry a young man from a nearby village. From the age group of Korca Yacouba, there are only three women in Bamako who are settled with their husbands; all others repatriated to Songho. Many women stem from similar groupings of social networks, or, as mentioned earlier, they create or revive their pedaço. Once they arrive to Bamako, they leave their belongings with Korca, some begin working in her restaurant, and others devote themselves to their own activities in the fruit and vegetable trade, which is considered the main activity of the Songho women in Bamako.

In the case of young women's mobility, their social networks provide them with much needed support, especially upon their initial arrival in Bamako. A support network is generally established between women who stem from the same lineage whether it is paternal or maternal. Yet, support could also be provided by members of the same neighbourhood or the same age group.

Young women begin their movement to Bamako as early as possible. For example, during the course of this research, many young girls left home at the age of eleven. Upon their arrival in the city for the first time, they usually pay frequent visits to their relatives and friends of their parents to seek work or to participate in a small business. After a couple of endeavours, they become primarily engaged in the selling of fruit and vegetables. A lady from Songho explains that sometimes she has around twenty to twenty-five young women sleeping in her house. In this regard, her house acts as an important base for those who have just arrived in Bamako without their children in order to be able to look for work.

Fatmata arrived in Bamako for the first time at the age of thirteen with a friend of the same age group in late 2002. Fatmata sought support from a woman of her paternal family who managed to find her a job. She began selling water for a Bambara woman with whom she had many problems. In 2003, at the time of the interview, she worked as a maid and seemed to be satisfied with her job. She worked every single day of the week from the early morning till late at night earning a salary of 4,000 FCFA per month payable when she returns to Songho. She continued frequenting and constructing her own *pedaço* in Bamako in the following years which allowed her to move in a larger circle of spaces of belongings. During what she calls her fourth trip, Fatmata formed a group of young people to learn the Quran with a *marabout*. Later, Fatamata would become the first woman to adopt the contemporary reformist style of Islamic veiling in Songho. In this context, one can observe that new motives or projects can be added to the initial motives for the journey. It also shows that new meanings emerge, senses of belonging and networks of relationships can also be forged. We further observe how the boundaries of villages may change.

After Mali's independence in 1960, Bamako increasingly became the chosen destination, enabling seasonal migration to develop with growing circularity in the first 5-8 years of travel. After this experience, certain migrants tried to postpone their return further each time. Most migrants came back to settle in Songho once their children had grown up and, in turn, began to move. There is a new generation of young adults who grew up outside the village but still pay their taxes there[7] because their origin and place of residence of their families is officially Songho. They are, for the most part, employed in Bamako as servants, cooks, security guards for homes or businesses, small restaurant owners, or petrol vendors. Very few have access to schooling. There are two *marabouts,* and a significant number of young people resume their Qur'anic studies after several years in the capital. Populations of different ages and genders circulate between Bamako and Songho. From the age of 10 to 45-50, life is generally spent between Songho and Bamako.

The phenomenon of individual or group movements, leading to a culture of mobility, especially during the dry periods in the 1970s to the 1990s and during the annual dry season, is not new but deeply rooted far back in the history of Songho.

Nonetheless, the intensity, rapidity and the form of these movements have shifted in the last few years from a constant but individual occurrence to a routine activity for both men and women. In general, people live in Songho during the agricultural season (June to November) then move to Missira – the central district of Bamako – during the dry season (December to May). In the village, they undertake other commercial or tertiary activities. The establishment of collective services, tourism-related activities, school and health services (health and maternity centre) act as incentives for the young to remain in the village.

As an example of the scope of this phenomenon, in January 2007, only 11 of the 57 men in the 1971-73 age group had remained in Songho: 42 were in Bamako and 4 in other localities. At this age, 34-36 by 2007, they gradually no longer felt the urge to return regularly to the village. Seven individuals in this age group chose to live in the capital after going back and forth for several years. Of the youth, aged 13-15 by 2007, almost all the boys have at least one travel experience. This group is central to the case in point since these boys move regularly in both directions, travelling seasonally, generally after circumcision. In recent years, a few boys have travelled before this age but have had to return to the village to accomplish their initiation, which takes place in the dry season. Organization within each age group is based on small sub-groups with common interests, who preserve the continuity of their relationships and provide considerable mutual support. The family plays a complementary role during the initial years of mobility, but seeks to intervene only if the number of migrants hinders the smooth operation of the collective agricultural work or any other activities that may be crucial to its survival. Nonetheless, the family unit has an important role in settling disputes, in the event of sickness and when regulating marital alliances. When a younger member settles definitively in Bamako, the flow of older generations – who come to visit for several months – gives a new aspect to the movement already observed between Songho and Bamako. The circuits that develop and multiply accordingly are improved, certain circuits still originating from existing ties between close friends in a group, and others stemming from common religious activity, work, rituals (naming ceremonies and weddings) or festive occasions.

Social constructions in movement

Mobility in all forms fosters collective social constructions, the motivations of which, however, differ individually and change over time. Mobility is interspersed with more intimate microcosms, individual itineraries and narratives, perspectives on life and religious motivations.

What I want to highlight here is that in these processes we see the outlines of a redefinition of new memberships which are part of another form of territorial mobility based on a larger flexibility of lineage authority, rules of residence and by a wider differentiation of individual labour. Looking at the development of circular migrations over the decades, one can observe the emergence of new regulations that govern gender relations, between men as well as between women. These regulations also work to strengthen ties between members of the same group and between peers of the same age group. They reinforce the political and social authority of elders. They are meant to maintain the importance of landlords and to show the need for a new definition of domestic space and its dynamics. In this regard, transformations produce ties between the city and the village and become part of a transformed form of kinship.

The combination of different forms of power in Songho, based on a collective logic, guide the most important decisions. On one hand, we find the council of village elders, which lies at the top of a hierarchical authority. This hierarchical organization is connected not only to lineages, but also to each of the four sections of the village, to each age group of adults as well as to gender differentiation of social responsibilities. On the other hand, we can observe a different kind of subtle power that stems from Islam and the administrative structures of the Malian state, mainly those installled as part of the decentralization policy.

In the case of mobility, however, there is a set of rules that govern, at least in part, the relationships for both those who leave the village and those who remain. These rules are also used to transfer part of power relations dynamics to Bamako, for example to the oldest person in each lineage or age group. In these processes, interpersonal relationships are the most sensitive field of social reorganization. Therefore, maintaining cohesion within people's movements and their spaces of belonging is of a major concern. Norms that govern marital ties continue to be accepted and practised by most of the young people of new generations – even those who have been living for a long period in Bamako. Marital ties constitute the core of efforts relating to social regulations in Songho as well as in Bamako.

Women can achieve their travel plans only after the ritual of engagement. In the event of pregnancy, the family of the man asks both the woman and her fiancé if they 'know.' If the answer is 'yes,' in this regard the child belongs to the couple. If one of them says 'no,' it would be then considered the man's mistake and he must accept the child.

After marriage, some divorces take place during the time of migration. In this case, divorced women, being ashamed of returning to the village, may remain single in Bamako. In general, divorce is mostly a man's decision, although sometimes it could be initiated by women. In some cases, divorced women take another partner to remain in Bamako or leave for Abidjan. In such a situation, they risk facing new conflicts if, one day, they decide to return home and resume their life with their former husband and their children.

Some men divorce their wives who stem from Songho who are, originally, chosen for them by their parents for the sake of establishing a relationship with women from other Dogon villages whom they meet in Bamako. These situations do not imply transgression as would be the case in a relationship between a Dogon and a Fulani, for example. However, they create new processes of marriage since we find some of these women still not considered members of the husband's family even after five or six years of an established relationship because of not fulfilling the necessary ritual to conclude the marriage. Therefore, marriage with women from distant localities is viewed as a direct result of people's mobility.

Marriage, generally speaking, is a long process even in the ordinary conditions of Songho. Large-scale mobility; however, adds to this complexity and puts new challenges before the society. For example, marriages between children of migrants who grew up in Bamako and women or men from Songho are often a topic of discussion. This shows that migration, indeed, contributes a great deal to changes in village organizational dynamics, to rules that regulate relationships and to the power structure within households.

Mobility also exerts challenges to established and taken for granted marriage customs. Occasionally young people, after refusing to marry the person chosen by their parents, decide to marry someone from a different lineage. This is a significant transformation since it touches the limits of collective identity modelled on networks of alliances based on marriage.

Movements in both directions (from village to town and vice versa) cause a split in community boundaries and existential space. They lead to delocation, relocation and the construction of spaces along singular routes. The localities themselves are not just passive, empty spaces, but they provide a great many possibilities to organize, reorganize and to implement strategies to strengthen the population's social ties and collective identity.

Like all types of experiences and any kind of mobility, the itineraries sketched above are all unique and therefore difficult to generalize. For various historical reasons, some individuals and groups from different generations can be pushed to abandon their 'piece' or *pedaço* in order to define new paths and circuits of belonging (Magnani, 2004). In this sense, fear of moving from one's own place is a challenge because we must take into account individual experience and consider, at the same time, its importance as a historical phenomenon in the long run. The risk of omitting specific personal experience could thus render the phenomenon itself meaningless.

The continual movement between Songho and Bamako corroborates the concept of moving spaces so that these spaces can be expanded and affiliations redefined. This collective lifestyle triggers adjustments and negotiations for the purpose of social ties, which must be relevant to all spaces involved: the town, the village, or elsewhere.

Songho's case confirms the complexity of migration as a phenomenon, highlighting the shortcomings of the concept of migration within a static understanding of space. These dynamics provide us with insights to adopt a less simplistic vision of African history and social change. These phenomena follow a specific logic, incorporating, in turn, a wider, more diversified and complex movement of interactions.

Without creating rigid markings in the space frequented, generations of Songho inhabitants have developed territorialization (Taraf-Najib 1995) and therefore different circuits (Magnani 2004; 2006). In other words, groups appropriated space through different patterns of use (networks to support a job search, worship, meeting, trading in cereals, sale of fruit and vegetables, etc.) and by forming flexible ties of affiliation underpinned by socialization. The social interconnection thus produced is governed by a logic of origin (village, district), language, age group, kinship and relationship with the land. Once men's and women's movements are intertwined in time and over the years, town-village boundaries themselves become moving boundaries. This is made possible by individuals' repeated itineraries forming collective circuits. It is not only the people who seem to move; the spaces, too, are moving. These can be understood as processes of social construction, a type of territoriality developed on the basis of interconnections established elsewhere but able to give new meaning to the multiplicity of places occupied in a lifetime. They are linked organically, in the Gramscian sense, through the development of culture, and by the permanent construction of symbolic references and territorialization of scattered areas[8].

To conclude, the culture of mobility as clearly observed in Songho seems to constitute an expression of this society's extraversion (Bayart 2000) and its ability to allow diversity to coexist (Moraes Farias 2007) throughout its history. It also expresses the aspirations and capacity of human beings to overpass distances and reach out to other spaces in their dreams.

Migrant societies reorganize to face new situations and to preserve power and equilibrium in their endogenous (generational or gender), exogenous (tourism) or translocal (arising from extraversion, openness to others and interconnections) relations within a combination of different types of logic. I, therefore, consider it important to work on multifaceted combinations of phenomena and differentiate coexisting social practices (expressions of life) through different forms of extraversion or openness to others, through preservation and through individual or collective fractures: micro-ruptures, disorderly and chaotic situations and moments.

References

Bayart, Jean-François. 2000. Africa in the world: A history of extraversion. *African Affairs* 99 (395): 217-267.

Bouju, Jacky. 1995. Qu'est-ce que l'ethnie Dogon ? *Cahiers des Sciences Humaines* 31 (2): 329-363.

Bouju, Jacky. 2002. Se dire dogon. Usages et enjeux politiques de l'identité ethnique. *Ethnologies comparées* 5: http//www.alor.univ-montp3.fr/cerce/revue.htm. Retrieved 7 February 2009.

Cissé, Almahady. 2004. *Mali. An Ever-Growing Diaspora.* Bamako: Inter Press Service News Agency.

De Bruijn, Mirjam, Rijk Van Dijk and Dick Foeken, eds. 2001. *Mobile Africa: Changing Patterns of Movement in Africa and Beyond.* Leiden: Brill

Dougnon, Isaïe. 2007. *Travail de Blanc, travail de Noir—La migration des pays dogon vers l'Office du Niger et au Ghana (1910-1980).* Paris: Khartala.

Doumbia, A. K. 2000. *Migration et accès aux ressources. Le cas des Dogon à Sélingué.* Bamako: DEA de l'ISFRA.

Hahn, Hans P. 2008. Diffusionism, Appropriation, and Globalization. Some Remarks on Current Debates in Anthropology. *Anthropos* 103 (1): 191-202.

Hazel, Robert. 2006. Cyclicité, histoire et destin dans les systèmes de classes d'âge de l'Afrique de l'Est. *Anthropos* 101 (1): 81-98.

Hily, Marie-Antoinette, William Berthomière and Dimitrina Mihaylova. 2004. La notion de "réseaux sociaux" en migration. *Hommes & migrations* 1250: 6-12.

Koulibaly, Mamadou. 2001. *La pauvreté en Afrique de l´ouest.* Paris and Dakar: Karthala and CODESRIA.

Liberski-Bagnoud, Danouta. 2002. *Les dieux du territoire. Penser autrement la généalogie*. Paris: CNRS éditions.

Magnani, Jose G.C. 2004. Cultura Urbana: transformaciones de las grandes metrópoli. *Revista Esencia y Espacio*, Mexico, 19: 25-34.

Magnani, Jose G.C. 2006. Urban Youth Circuits in São Paulo. *Tempo Social. Revista de Sociologia da USP* 2 (1): 173-205.

Martes, Ana Cristina B. 1999. *Brasileiros nos Estados Unidos. Um estudo sobre imi- grantes em Massachusetts*. São Paulo: Paz e Terra.

Massey, Douglas S. et al. 1993. Theories of International Migration: A Review and Appraisal. *Population and Development Review* 19 (3): 431-466.

Moraes Farias, Paulo F. 2007. Au-delà de l'opposition coloniale entre authenticité africaine et identité musulmane. L'œuvre de Waa Kamisòkò, barde moderne et critique du Mali. In *Colonisations et héritages actuels au Sahara et au Sahel*, **dir.** Mariella V. Cervello, 271-308. Paris: L'Harmattan.

Petit, Véronique. 1998. *Migrations et société dogon*. Paris: Harmattan.

Roussel, Cyril. 2003. Désenclavement et mondialisation: les réseaux migratoires familiaux des druzes du sud syrien. *Moyen-Orient: mutations récentes d'un carrefour migratoire* 19 (3): 263-283.

Sauvain-Dugerdil, Claudine, Denis Dougnon and Samba Diop. 2008. *La mobilité est-elle le moteur de la transition culturelle? Etude micro démographique du Sarnyéré Dogon (Mali)*. International AIDELF Démographie et Cultures symposium: http://www-aidelf.ined.fr/colloques/Quebec/aidelf-2008/spip8d77.html?article88. Retrieved 13 January 2009.

Taraf-Najib, Souha. 1995. Territoires migratoires, territoires de familles chez le Libanais de Dakar: espace en mouvement et culture locale. In *Le territoire, lien ou frontière? Identité, conflits ethniques, enjeux et recompositions territoriales*, ed. Joël Bonnemaison, Luc Cabrézy and Laurence Quinty-Bourgeois. Paris: ORSTOM. http://www.documentation.ird.fr/fdi/notice.php?ninv=fdi:010014865-61. Retrieved 8 April 2009.

Thibaut, Bénédicte. 2005. Le pays Dogon au Mali: de l'enclavement à l'ouverture? *Espace, Populations et Sociétés* 4 (1): 45-56.

Tilly, Charles. 1990. Transplanted Networks. **In** *Immigration Reconsidered: History, Sociology, and Politics*, ed. Virginia Yans-McLaughlin, 79-95. New York: Oxford University Press.

Touré, Moriba and Theophilus O. Fadayomi, dir. 1993. *Migrations et urbanisation au sud du Sahara: Quels impacts sur les politiques de population et de développement?* Dakar: CODESRIA.

Van Beek, Walter. 2003. African Tourist Encounters: Effects of Tourism on two West African Societies. *Africa* 73 (2): **251-278**.

Van Beek, Walter. 2005. Walking wallets? Tourists at the Dogon Falaise. In *Wari Matters: Ethnographic Explorations of Money in the Mande World*, ed. Stephen Wooten, 191-216. Münster: LIT Verlag.

Notes

1 A more comprehensive version of this chapter was published in French as: Liens ville-village et changements sociaux face à la migration saisonnière. Le mouvement de personnes entre Songho (Région Dogon) et Bamako, Mali (Town-village interconnection and social change in the light of seasonal migration. Movements of persons between Songho (Dogon Region) and Bamako, Mali). *Anthropos* 105 (2010): 471-488. I would like to extend my warmest thanks to Marina Berthet and Fernando Rosa Ribeiro for their invaluable advice and comments.

2 Council for the Development of Social Science Research in Africa/South-South Exchange Programme for Research on the History of Development.

3 Research conducted with Mustafa Abdalla (Freie Universität Berlin).

4 Those groups are made up of girls and boys who were born within a period of 3 to 5 years. However, with higher birth rates per year, an age group could be made up of people born within a period of 2 to 3 years.

5 Because of virilocality, most families prefer to marry their daughters in their own village or in their immediate vicinity, which provides the conditions for women's associative groupings and collective agency also during their sojourn in Bamako.

6 The preferred marriage in Songho is between cross-cousins and is frequently discussed among women, just after the birth of a daughter. It is a patrilineal, exogamous system in which the father and brothers belong to a group and the mother's brother to another group.

7 In the Malian administrative system today, much as it used to be during the colonial period, each family pays taxes at their place of origin according to the number of people in that family.

8 For the way societies build their ties with their land and space, see Liberski-Bagnoud (2002).

Migration, identity and immobility in a Malian Soninke village

Gunvor Jónsson

Introduction

This chapter explores the local meaning of migration and experiences of immobility in a Soninke village in the Kayes region of Mali. In the village of Kounda, migration has for centuries been central to villagers' livelihoods. Household heads have a long tradition of working as labour migrants in France and through a regular flow of remittances and communication they have retained strong bonds with their families in Kounda. Meanwhile, many of the young Soninke men living in Kounda are expressing a sense of 'involuntary immobility', aspiring to migrate, but unable to do so (cf. Carling 2002). This chapter examines the social structures and meanings that shape young Soninke men's aspirations to migrate, and how their immobility affects their social interactions and social becoming, including their attempts to construct collective identities without migration.[1]

While globalization has made it easier for most people to get insight into what is happening around the world, the possibilities for travelling and settling in other parts of the world are restricted to a minority of the global population (Bauman 1998; cf. Alpes this volume). Contemporary globalization contributes to creating migration aspirations in the global South, but also impedes international migration and, generally, the socio-economic mobility of people in the South. The abjection and immobility of the global South are an aspect of globalization which tends to be overlooked, not only in studies of migration but generally in the social sciences (cf. Inda and Rosaldo 2002; Ferguson 2006).

Experiences of abjection may be widespread in the global South, but involuntary immobility tends to be particularly felt in communities which have had a long tradition of labour migration to the global North, and where such migration has become embedded in society's cultural values and meanings – sometimes referred to as 'cultures of migration' (Ali 2007; Kandel and Massey 2002; Cohen and Jónsson 2011; Carling 2002). Here, international migration is the norm and, usually for young men, a hegemonic ideal which puts them on the socially desired path to manhood and independence. Being unable to migrate in this context is often considered a social and existential problem.

Migration is the distinguishing feature of Kounda, as well as many of the surrounding villages in the Kayes region, where large proportions of the local population have migrated and generally maintain ties to the region via various forms of transnational exchange. In this part of Mali, migration is inscribed into the landscape. Coming to Kounda, you drive along a tarmac road that connects the northern rural areas to the regional capital of Kayes. This is one of the few metalled main roads in the entire country and it is partly funded by the migrants in France. From this road, if you peek out of the heart-shaped windows of the rusty taxi that drives past the village, you can spot the big water tower as well as the four minarets of the grand mosque of Kounda. These were built entirely with funding from '*les ressortisants*' – the migrants from the village. As such, they are the most significant monuments of the village, symbols of migration, which gives the village its *raison d'être*.

History of migration and change in Soninke society

In Mali, the Soninke people are popularly stereotyped as the country's '*ethnie migratrice*' – an ethnic group characterized by their culture of migration. There is a saying that 'the Soninke have migration in their blood'. The Soninke sometimes refer to themselves as '*commerçants*' (traders), since commerce is the economic activity with which they have been associated since the times of trans-Saharan trade. But since this occupation was always linked to migration, Soninke identity is inextricably associated with migration (cf. Whitehouse 2003, 19).

For nearly a millennium, people identifying themselves as Soninke have been settled in an area by the Senegal River near the south-western border of the Sahara desert, from where they initially conducted trading expeditions and fought wars, accumulating wealth and slaves whom they put to work on their farms. The beginnings of the modern migrations of the Soninke were linked to European commercial penetration in Africa in the 19th century. Already by the late 18th century, members of the Soninke aristocracy had started working as labour migrants, serving as indigenous sailors (*laptots*) for the French Navy on the Senegal River (Manchuelle 1997). In the mid-19th century, the Soninke also became involved in seasonal labour migration to peanut plantations in The Gambia (cf. Gaibazzi this volume) and, later, Senegal. This activity became known as the *navetanat* and was one of the most important migrations in the modern history of West Africa (Manchuelle

1997, 53). One of the reasons for this modern labour migration was the increasing need for money that was caused by colonial domination; many young Soninke men became *navetans* in order to raise the cash that their local economy could not generate (Kane and Lericollais 1975).[2]

With the abolition of slavery in the early 20th century, former slaves gradually got involved in temporary migration as *navetans* and later they presented themselves for military recruitment in French West Africa. As veterans returning from the First World War they refused to live in the same dependence on their former masters. As former slaves turned into labour migrants, so did a growing number of young males of the Soninke nobility. By the 1920s, patriarchal authority in the Soninke homeland was increasingly contested (Manchuelle 1997). During slavery, the young men had not owned slaves of their own and, therefore, had possessed no independent means of accumulating wealth and power. When patriarchal family heads lost power over the family's labour force (i.e. the slaves), they also lost their source of authority over the younger dependent males (Manchuelle 1989; Pollet and Winter 1971). This segment of society had for centuries been participants in seasonal migration, and when the slave trade ended they were ready to enter the West African labour market. Migration then in a sense became a declaration of independence, not just for former slaves, but for young males as well, who ensured their prestige and manhood by bringing back large sums of money that they presented as gifts to their families and clients, spent as bride wealth, invested in livestock, or used as capital to become traders (Manchuelle 1997).

With the completion of the Dakar-Bamako railway in 1923 the economic centre of Senegal moved entirely away from the Senegal River Valley into the peanut-producing regions, and commercial agriculture and river transport in the River Valley declined drastically (Manchuelle 1997). In the 1930s, Soninke migration lasted several continuous seasons or became permanent; flows shifted from rural-rural to rural-urban, and destinations covered a wider geographical area, including not only Mali and Senegal, but also the Ivory Coast, the Congos, and the ports of France. Former Soninke *laptots* were hired by French employers as sailors on international shipping lines and around 1930 many of these sailors started obtaining employment in the French port of Marseille.

After the Second World War, Soninke migration to France increased, as these unskilled labour migrants took part in post-war reconstruction. In 1960, this migration flow was spurred on significantly, both by the economic decline of the Soninke homeland and the need for manual labour in France. In 1960, France opened its borders to foreign labourers, which resulted in increased immigration, especially by sub-Saharan Africans. The acute labour shortage in France resulted in a complete breakdown of official immigration control, and French companies ran their own recruitment drives abroad. Employment of migrants from former French West Africa remained legally unrestricted until 1963, and since the French companies wanted to avoid recruiting 'illegal aliens' they preferred West African workers. The availability of unskilled jobs, especially in construction and industries in France, was coupled with the creation of migrant worker hostels (*foyers*) in French cities. Here, the Soninke migrants lived – and still do today – in a more or less parallel society. Older Soninke migrants organized the arrival, housing and employment of new immigrants, introducing new employees to the French firms, which recruited along ethnic lines. This system of inter-ethnic solidarity and mutual help in the Soninke migrant community was advantageous to French employers, leaving them fewer social obligations than with French labourers (Kane and Lericollais 1975).

The efficient and well-established Soninke migrant networks and the French employers' preference for these workers explain why, in 1968, the Soninke constituted 85 % of sub-Saharan immigrants in France (Manchuelle 1997, 2). Since the late 1960s, the Soninke homeland has experienced several severe droughts, particularly in the periods 1969-1974 and 1983-1985. Since then, the typical Soninke household has not been able to grow enough food to support itself and the remittances that families receive from their migrant relatives have become indispensable to the local household economy (Findley 1994; Whitehouse 2003). By 1975, about one third of the active male population in the Soninke homeland had emigrated to France (Kane and Lericollais 1975, 177).

In 1974, the French government took measures to stop the arrival of new foreign workers (Chastanet 1992; Quiminal 1994). The restrictions on immigration undermined the networks which had facilitated the replacement of older migrants by younger migrants within the same Soninke family; it lengthened migrants' stay abroad, and resulted in the development of family emigration with children and wives, which made return less likely (Chastanet 1992; Quiminal 1994). Illegal arrivals increased, and in 1976 the French State started to repatriate irregular immigrants, first by offering 'assisted return', which included an allowance and training for those who left voluntarily (Quiminal 1994). In recent times, more severe measures have been applied, such as arresting irregular immigrants, placing them on charter planes and sending them out of the country. Increased border controls since the 1990s, which have grown since the terrorist attacks of 9/11, and the policy of 'selective immigration' (*immigration choisie*) in France constitute further barriers to unskilled West African immigrants. The migratory system of the Soninke has therefore been largely disrupted and migration to France has largely changed from a viable liveli-hood strategy into a clandestine business.

'Stranger logic' and the imperative of migration

With its past history of migration, it is safe to say that geographic mobility has been both a stabilizing and a productive force in Soninke society. Migration has therefore, for generations, been an inherent feature of life for people in this region. Historically, the Soninke have imported their labour force in the form of slaves, while they themselves have migrated to supplement local production. Even today, Soninke migrants from Kounda and elsewhere employ labourers to farm their lands in their absence. These labourers are themselves migrants, who, like the Soninke, have left their native villages to achieve social and economic mobility.

Several authors have pointed out the important and ambiguous role that 'stran-gers' have played in West African societies (Fortes 1975; Skinner 1963; Shack and Skinner 1979; Whitehouse 2007). Georg Simmel defined the stranger's position as ambivalent, composed of certain measures of nearness and distance: "In spite of be-ing inorganically appended to it, the stranger is yet an organic member of the group" (Simmel 1950 [1908], 408). According to Shack (1979), strangers in the Simmelian sense were marginal as well as integral elements of African social and political sys-tems long before the beginning of colonial rule. In many African states, especially in West Africa, strangers as 'liminaries' often engaged in occupations disdained by the indigenous host societies in which they settled, temporarily or permanently.

In Kounda, strangers have an ambivalent position: They do not have the privileges and rights of locals; but this also means that strangers are not expected to adhere to the rules in the same way as locals, and this in itself becomes a privilege for the stran-ger. This is for example why foreigners in Kounda dominate local business, while the commercial activities of local entrepreneurs are impeded by an ethos of gift-giving. Virtually all the people who were earning money in the village were 'foreigners'[3] who were not born and raised in the village. Of the thirty-four registered shopkeepers in Kounda, only five were native to the village. Apart from shopkeepers, almost all the bakers, the mechanics, the tailors, and the builders were foreign.

To understand this situation, one needs to look at the type of exchange relations that are practised amongst locals and strangers in Kounda. In Kounda, most villagers stand in a close personal relationship, and favours and gift-giving are prominent. In contrast to this generalized reciprocity and emphasis on giving, the common form of exchange involved in commerce is payment, which is associated with immediate transaction and an impersonal contractual relationship between the partners exchanging (cf. Sahlins 1972). This type of exchange does not harmonize with the system of generalized reciprocity that defines local exchange relations in Kounda. Accepting payment from one's kin is nearly taboo and, therefore, native villagers avoid conducting commerce in Kounda. Local Soninke informants held the common view that, 'you cannot succeed in your father's village'. In fact, making a local income was considered unappealing, even shameful, because it signified that you profited at the expense of your relatives.

Local Soninke traders in Kounda felt they could not refuse to give credit to their relatives because, 'if relatives demand something from you, you are morally obliged to help'. But if the trader was a foreigner, the rules of balanced reciprocity came into force and at some point the creditor would demand repayment. But while their business was relatively profitable, foreigners in Kounda were marginalized from local infrastructure and decision-making. Affection and familiarity, more than wealth, determined whether the local Soninke villagers accepted a newcomer. Villagers who were not born and raised in Kounda were not considered part of local webs of solidarity and kinship.

According to my Soninke informants, this stranger logic that makes foreigners integral to yet marginalized from their host society applies not only to strangers within Kounda, but also to the Soninke themselves when they go abroad to work. When a Soninke man migrates, he himself becomes a stranger in another society and he adopts the ambivalent position that he associated with the strangers within his own society. As an immigrant, you become unfamiliar – something which my Soninke informants seemed acutely aware of. It should be noted here that since the fieldwork was not multi-sited, the focus of this analysis is on the perception of migration from the villagers' perspective; I cannot elaborate on the actual extent to which Soninke migrants retain their 'strangerhood' in their host society. To the Soninke in Kounda, when a man migrates he does so in order to become a 'stranger'. Moving to places where one has a strong social network does not constitute an 'aventure'. On the contrary, the point of migrating is exactly to profit from one's status as a stranger. Although the marginal position of the stranger may appear to be a negative factor, this is exactly what the aspiring Soninke migrant strives towards.

Abroad, the migrant is a stranger who has 'no shame and no obligations'. This enables him to conduct the kind of economic activities that are not socially acceptable in his familiar, local society. My informants considered the hardship and low status associated with certain jobs easier to endure in a foreign environment where people's opinion did not matter as much as the profit one could make performing these jobs. The endurance of migrant labour is thus conceptualized as a necessary liminal phase in the lives of Soninke men. When leaving his familiar place, the Soninke migrant enters a place where he has 'no social obligations' and therefore, he is free to take part in commercial activities and accumulate wealth. On a symbolic level, the migrant who goes abroad exits the sphere of familiarity and affection, and enters one of interest.

The notions that informed the villagers' 'stranger logic' were also invoked by the villagers to justify the presence of Soninke migrants in French society. This first of all meant that their only purpose as immigrants there was to earn money and later return to their place of origin. Aspiring migrants in Kounda emphasized the fact that they had no intentions of 'bothering' the French by staying there permanently. They just wanted to go there temporarily and later return to the village. Moreover, according to villagers' stranger logic, France, like any society, needs strangers. Informants referred to the fact that immigrant workers helped to reconstruct France after the war and make it what it is today, and referred to the welcoming of guest workers in the 1960s; and especially the young men argued that there was a continued availability of unskilled jobs in service and construction. Informed by this logic, young men could not see why they should not be allowed to enter France: they needed to go there temporarily in order to generate what they could not obtain locally, and France needed its strangers and, therefore, the obvious thing to do would be to welcome the Soninke immigrants.

The local meaning of migration

The economy of the village of Kounda can be described as 'assisted self-sufficiency', as farming is complemented by migrants' remittances (Quiminal 1991). The money migrants send to their relatives in Kounda is indispensable to the survival of most households in the village; migrant remittances cover half of the annual consumption of an average local household. Moreover, the communal projects funded by migrants have done much to develop the local infrastructure, including the digging of wells, construction of schools, a health clinic, town hall, a water tower and water canalization system, a communal system of electricity, and a local soccer stadium. The Malian government and NGOs are conspicuously absent in Kayes, where most development projects are partially or entirely funded by emigrants (Daum 1995; Gauvrit and Le Bahers 2004). Many of the villagers were resentful of the State, which they felt had abandoned them. In Kayes, the migrants act as substitutes for the State.

The young men in Kounda wanted to follow the migrants' example by financing projects in the village. As migrants, they wanted to '*realiser quelques choses*', that is, achieve something in the village, by starting a project or constructing something. Generally, migrants' communal projects in the village were not just white elephants; they had significantly increased the living standards and welfare of local villagers. Without their migrants' money, the Kayes region would be as destitute as the rest of Mali, since the weak Malian State – one of the poorest countries in the world – has little capacity to make a difference for its rural inhabitants. In an analytical sense, the migrants in France could be considered Homerian heroes, who venture off to sacrifice themselves on behalf of their communities, as they accept the risks and hardships of migrant life. Migration is therefore related to a sense of moral responsibility towards the community where a young Soninke man grows up.

However, presiding over the means and the authority to define local development also endows migrants with significant local power. Migrants' money transfers to Kounda were therefore perceived by some villagers as symbolic acts demonstrating the migrants' wealth and power. Generally, the migrants preferred to determine themselves what they would finance. The division of responsibility was reflected in a local expression, where villagers said, "The migrants are the head, we are the arms". This implied that the migrants would come up with the ideas and the financing, while the villagers supplied the necessary manual labour to carry out a project. This division of roles was not always beneficial. For example, although the villagers' main priority remained the acute need for drinking water, the migrants were more interested in funding the construction of a new mosque. Migrants' donations towards communal projects in Kounda thus contain the central paradox of gift-giving as both altruistic and interested (Levi-Strauss 1969; Bourdieu 1996; 1997; Sahlins 1972).

Villagers' relations to the charitable migrants somewhat resembled a system of clientage. But even if some villagers saw migrants as sorts of dictators, who unilaterally determined local development, most villagers certainly benefitted economically from their position of dependency. Yet, as elderly informants pointed out, this dependency was not necessarily for 'the greater good' of the local society, especially in the current context of immobility. To the elderly men, migrants' apparent disregard for the authority and self-determination of local villagers threatened to destabilize the power balance between the local community and migrants, giving migrants the upper hand in the management of village affairs. With increasing numbers of men who are unable to migrate to France, Kounda's symbolic status in the transnational exchange relations with migrants in France might change from that of an authoritarian elderly to a dependent minor. They will be alienated from local decision-making, which is relegated to the diaspora in France. Most of the young men in the village therefore maintained the hope of being able to emigrate, aspiring to attain this position of authority and becoming 'community patrons'.

As a form of livelihood, migration is not just a matter of earning the daily bread, but relates broadly to the social construction of the ideal life (cf. Olwig and Sørensen 2002). Migration is considered to be central to the process of 'social becoming' of a young Soninke man, defined by Vigh as 'a movement along an expected and desired life trajectory' (Vigh 2006). In Kounda, migration has traditionally facilitated this process of social becoming and the village has constituted the centre around which the ideal life cycle of a Soninke man revolves. This ideal life trajectory can be illustrated with the following model:

TIME	Childhood	Youth	Adulthood	Old age
PLACE	Village	Abroad	Village/Abroad	Village

Ideally, the oldest migrated son of a household is supposed to return to the village in old age and take over the position of household head from his father. In turn, the younger brothers in the village are then expected to leave on *aventure*, representing a new generation of migrant breadwinners to the local household. However, this system of replacement is disintegrating. A group of young men explained that their brothers in France were unable to return to the village, either because they had no money or because they were residing illegally in France: "Our brothers in Paris are so tired. They say we must come and replace them there; but we can't go!". But despite their physical absence, migrants were conceived of as full members of the local family: Through their remittances, phone calls or visits, they maintained a social and economic presence, and by maintaining an active exchange relation with their family they remained members of it (cf. Olwig 1999). In the words of one villager, "The migrants complete us".

In Kounda, migration is a socially sanctioned strategy, whereby a young man can detach himself from his family and become an independent, mature individual. Hence, to the Soninke villagers, being on *aventure* implies being on the path to adulthood, and migration can therefore be considered similar to a rite of passage for young men. Migrants residing in France overcome the liminal phase of youth as they 're-attach' themselves to the local families in Kounda, making their presence felt through transnational bonds. Even if a Soninke migrant does not physically return to the village in his own life-time, the ideal life cycle may still be completed when the corpse of the dead migrant is transported from France back to the village.

Migration and, generally, mobility are integral to 'hegemonic masculinity' in Kounda – the form of masculinity dominant in society, and which bestows power and privilege on men who espouse it (Morrell 1998, 607-608). In Kounda, hegemonic masculinity entails the freedom of mobility, and this is one of the distinguishing features between the two genders in the village. Soninke women are to a large extent fixed inside the household, while men are outside moving between the fields and other tasks, both within and beyond the village, and taking part in public life. Men who do not migrate and remain economically dependent on their kin are generally considered immature youngsters. Women expressed great contempt for non-migrants and referred to them by a derogatory term, *tenes*, which literally means 'being stuck like glue, unable to move'. In the mid-1990s, two women from Kounda broadcast a song about the *Tenesy*, denouncing non-migrants as parasites with nothing to offer their families and undesirable to women. By characterizing non-migrants as immature, cowardly, lazy and selfish, the song reproduced the conceptual link between migration and status as an adult male, and construed non-migration as an immoral choice. Today, *tenes* has become a vernacular term denoting non-migrants, and its connotation is more joking than humiliating. The perception of non-migrants in the village has changed in the past ten years. When I asked women about their views on immobile men, they saw their situation as pitiful rather than immoral. Hence, non-migration is now conceptualized as an involuntary, forced condition. This however, does not make it more attractive.

Being and becoming in the context of immobility

The young men in Kounda apply various strategies to make meaning out of non-migration and to construct their identities without migration. On the one hand, they appear to be creating their own 'spaces of freedom' and trying to introduce new values by developing their own particular 'youth culture'. Yet from another perspective, the activities of the youth seem to be mainly about imagining – imagining that one can afford the luxuries of a life with money, imagining a life in the city or abroad (on migration as an imaginary trajectory cf. chapters by de Boeck and Schielke this volume). But experiencing such imaginary connectedness is not necessarily very fulfilling for these young villagers.

Schulz (2002) refers to urban Malian youth as a 'generation-in-waiting', observing that, 'they wait not only for achieving a status of adulthood, but for parental support and for the state's creation of the very conditions that would enable them to become full grown members of the social and political community' (Schulz 2002, 806). Arguably, male youth in the village of Kounda also constitutes a 'generation-in-waiting' – some literally waiting to obtain a visa to go abroad, but also awaiting the passage to adulthood and economic security that was traditionally secured by migration. As these young men sit and wait, they socialize in groups that resemble traditional age sets.

Institutionalized age sets for adolescents (*īre*) have existed since pre-colonial times. They have always had their own quarters apart from their families, where the members would sleep. One of their main purposes, which is still relevant, was that the groups could be mobilized by the village chief for communal purposes, for example to dig a well, construct buildings or roads, or put out fires (Pollet and Winter 1971). The increasing migration to France since the 1960s probably reduced the significance of the *īre*. However, in the late '80s, Kounda witnessed a revival of the *īre* and of youth culture. The first sign of this change was the introduction of a group (or *grin*) called 'Mickey Black Paul' in 1989. This date is not arbitrary, and was probably related to certain political events at the time: visa restrictions imposed by France in 1986 made it even more difficult for young Soninke men legally to pursue the path of migration; moreover, the political atmosphere in the wake of the transition to democracy in Mali in the early 1990s may have inspired village youth to contest the traditional authorities.

Mickey Black Paul was founded by young villagers who had spent time in urban milieus and who were inspired by the kind of male socializing known today all over Mali as the *grin* (cf. Schulz 2002). The *grin* refers to a group of male friends who meet regularly to socialize, often in a particular location, where they drink tea, listen to music, play cards, or discuss. The *grin* in Kounda is in many ways a re-invention of the *īre*. Right from its inception, the *grin* culture in Kounda was in opposition to the local authorities and older generations. Three of the founders described their introduction of the new practices in the conservative village:

> In 1989 we put up a flag to announce the *grin*. There was the name
> [Mickey Black Paul] and messages written on it like, 'all we want is peace'
> and 'foreigners and villagers are all equal'. The old complained that the

flag should be pulled down. ... The old were constantly complaining about us. We started out being eight people in the *grin*, but with all the trouble there were eventually only four of us left. Every two weeks we used to be taken to the *chefferie* [chief's council]. ... Our group was the first one that had a name. We were the first who held really big parties, where all the youth from the surrounding villages paid to get in. *Moghole* was the traditional way of dancing at the time, but our *grin* was the first to introduce the reggae and rap dance. We were also the only ones in the village who used to go to Kayes and Bamako. ... Our girlfriends were the daughters of civil servants, so they also knew more about the urban life.

The *grins* that I observed would regularly throw parties and play music at night. On such occasions, young women frequently showed up and sneaked into one of the bedrooms with a *grin* member, to have a quick intimate moment. Most girls had a secret boyfriend, but these relationships became very complicated when the young girls were married, usually around the age of fourteen. The prominence of such intimate pre-marital relations was new to Kounda, and a modern discourse of romance set the youth apart from senior generations in the village. Young men's rivalries over girlfriends often became violent and, moreover, an increasing number of young, unmarried girls had recently become pregnant.

The village chief was concerned about this situation, and as he took office in 2006 he therefore decided to ban *all* music in the village. The youth would normally organize to protest at such outrageous decisions by the chief; but the youth of Kounda were not mobilized. It was more friction than collaboration that marked the relations between the different *grins* in the village. While the youth generally blamed this tension on the negative influence of conservative villagers, some villagers saw the problem as due to boredom and a lack of cohesion. Towards the end of my fieldwork, a returned migrant in his thirties managed to mobilize the village youth and led a procession to the village chief, demanding the un-banning of music, referring to the law and democratic principles that overrode the chief's decisions. This returned migrant was then elected the 'chief of the youth'.

The *grins* had the capacity to provoke the necessary social transformation of youth into a consolidated social category with potential to develop agency. Here, young men practised their own version of youth culture and this set them apart from the surrounding local community. They often listened to hip hop and reggae music and the walls of their bedrooms were plastered with posters of Afro-American music and film stars. Some of the young men had nicknames that they had taken from famous rap stars, such as 2 Pac, Snoop Dogg or Puff Daddy, and at parties they often performed with innovative dance moves or self-composed rap music.

The space of the *grin*, the local youth parties, the practice of rap music and dance, the young men's romances, and their appeals for democratic principles in the conservative village society are examples of what anthropologist Michael Barrett calls 'spaces of freedom': moments of freedom from the constraints of their elders, and places where young people can exercise certain types of agency that are at odds with, or lead to alternative versions of, personhood as understood by their elders (Barrett 2004, 32).

Yet, parallel to this portrayal of a brewing modern youth rebellion in Kounda, the local practice of youth culture might conversely be considered as an imaginary substitute for migration – a sort of 'mental mobility' towards the global horizon (see Graw & Schielke's introduction to this volume). From this perspective, the young men's involvement with Afro-American popular culture reflected their aspiration for community in an imagined world (cf. Appadurai 1996; Frederiksen 2002). Consumption, especially of products and styles related to urban life, was a prominent way in which young involuntarily immobile men took part in an imagined global community. The aspiration to consume above the local means was expressed in many ways, including a conspicuous form of consumption, where the display of consumer objects was valued just as much as the actual consumption of these objects.

Consumption may be an attempt to 'hook on' to the global community; but being part of an imagined community of global consumers is not necessarily the form of global connection these involuntarily immobile young men aspire to. In line with James Ferguson (2006), it could be argued that their 'longing for goods' signals a longing for membership of an imagined global community, where capital, people, goods and information flow freely and instantly across borders. As immobile villagers, they were cut off from the global community to which they aspired and their experience of globalization was confined to a local appropriation of urban and Western forms and practices (cf. Ferguson 2006). These cultural dimensions of globalization may not lead to the form of globalization that the young men most desire: to be unimpeded by international borders, to take advantage of the global economic market and, basically, to have the chance to create a livelihood that is not confined to a local subsistence life.

References

Ali, Syed. 2007. 'Go West Young Man': The Culture of Migration among Muslims in Hyderabad, India. *Journal of Ethnic and Migration Studies* 33 (1): 37-58.

Appadurai, Arjun. 1996. *Modernity At Large: Cultural Dimensions of Globalization*. Minneapolis and London: University of Minnesota Press.

Barrett, Michael. 2004. *Paths To Adulthood. Freedom, Belonging and Temporalities in Mbunda Biographies from Western Zambia*. Sweden: Uppsala University Library.

Bauman, Zygmunt. 1998. *Globalization – The Human Consequences*. Cambridge: Polity Press.

Bourdieu, Pierre. 1996. The Work of Time. In *The Gift: An Interdisciplinary Perspective*, ed. Aafke E. Komter. The Netherlands: Amsterdam University Press.

Bourdieu, Pierre. 1997. Marginalia – Some Additional Notes on The Gift. In *The Logic of the Gift*, ed. Alan D. Schrift. New York, London: Routledge.

Carling, Jørgen. 2002. Migration in the age of involuntary immobility. *Journal of Ethnic and Migration Studies* 28 (1): 5-42.

Chastanet, Monique. 1992. Survival Strategies of a Sahelian Society: The Case of the Soninke in Senegal from the Middle of the Nineteenth Century to the Present. *Food and Foodways* 5 (2): 127-149.

Cohen, Robin and Gunvor Jónsson. 2011. Connecting Culture and Migration. In *Migration and Culture*, ed. Robin Cohen and Gunvor Jónsson. Cheltenham: Edward Elgar.

Daum, Christophe. 1995. Les migrants, partenaires de la coopération internationale: Le cas des Maliens en France. In *Programme du recherche "Migrations internationales et développement"*.

Ferguson, James. 2006. *Global Shadows: Africa in the neo-liberal world order*. US: Duke University Press.

Findley, Sally. 1994. Does Drought Increase Migration? A Study of Migration from Rural Mali during the 1983-1985 Drought. *International Migration Review* 28 (3): 539-553.

Fortes, Meyer. 1975. Strangers. In *Studies in African Social Anthropology*, ed. Meyer Fortes and Sheila Patterson, 229-253. London, New York, San Francisco: Academic Press.

Frederiksen, Bodil Folke. 2002. Mobile minds and socio-economic barriers: Livelihoods and African-American identifications among youth in Nairobi. In *Work and Migration. Life and Livelihoods in a globalizing world*, ed. Karen F. Olwig and Ninna N. Sørensen, 45-60. London and New York: Routledge.

Gauvrit, Lisa and Goulven Le Bahers. 2004. *FSP Codéveloppement Mali. Practiques associatives des migrants pour le développement de leur pays d'origine: le cas des migrants maliens de France originaires de la Région de Kayes*. Mali: Cellule Technique du FSP Codéveloppement Mali.

Inda, Jonathan Xavier and Renato Rosaldo. 2002. Introduction: A World in Motion. In *The Anthropology of Globalization – A Reader*, ed. Jonathan X. Inda and Renato Rosaldo, 1-34. USA: Blackwell Publishers.

Jónsson, Gunvor. 2007. The Mirage of Migration. Migration Aspirations and Immobility in a Malian Soninke Village, Master thesis. Copenhagen, Denmark: Institute for Anthropology, University of Copenhagen.

Kandel, William, and Douglas Massey. 2002. The Culture of Mexican Migration: A Theoretical and Empirical Analysis. *Social Forces* 80 (3): 981-1004.

Kane, Francine and André Lericollais. 1975. L'Émigration en Pays Soninké. *Cahiers ORSTOM* 12 (2): 177-187.

Levi-Strauss, Claude. 1969. The Principles of Reciprocity. In *The Elementary Structures of Kinship*, ed. Claude Levi-Strauss. London: Eyre & Spottiswoode.

Manchuelle, François. 1989. Slavery, Emancipation and Labour Migration in West Africa: The Case of the Soninke. *Journal of African History* 30: 89-106.

Manchuelle, François. 1997. *Willing Migrants: Soninké Labour Diasporas 1848-1960*. USA: Ohio University Press.

Morrell, Robert. 1998. Of Boys and Men: Masculinity and Gender in Southern African Studies. *Journal of Southern African Studies* 24 (4): 605-630.

Olwig, Karen Fog. 1999. Narratives of the Children Left Behind: Home and identity in globalized Caribbean families. *Journal of Ethnic and Migration Studies* 25 (2): 267-284.

Olwig, Karen Fog and Ninna Nyberg Sørensen. 2002. Mobile Livelihoods: Making a living in the world. In *Work and Migration. Life and Livelihoods in a globalizing world*, edited by Karen F. Olwig and Ninna N. Sørensen. London and New York: Routledge.

Pollet, Eric and Grace Winter. 1971. *La Société Soninké*. Brussels: Editions de l'Institut de Sociologie, Université Libre de Bruxelles.

Quiminal, Catherine. 1991. *Gens d'Ici, Gens d'Ailleurs. Migrations Soninké et transformations villageoises*. France: Christian Bourgois Editeur.

Quiminal, Catherine. 1994. The Changes in the French Migratory Policy and Their Consequences Upon West Africa. *The Journal of Social Studies* 66: 59-74.

Sahlins, Marshall. 1972. On the sociology of Primitive Exchange. In *Stone Age Economics*, ed. Marshall Sahlins, 185-230. London: Tavistock Publications.

Schulz, Dorothea. 2002. 'The World is Made by Talk'. Female Fans, Popular Music, and New Forms of Public Sociality in Urban Mali. *Cahiers d'Etudes Africaines* 168 (XLII-4): 797-829.

Shack, William A. 1979. Introduction. In *Strangers in African Societies*, ed. William A. Shack and Elliott P. Skinner, 1-17. Berkeley, Los Angeles, London: University of California Press.

Shack, William A. and Elliott P. Skinner, eds. 1979. *Strangers in African Societies*. Berkeley, Los Angeles, London: University of California Press.

Simmel, Georg. 1950 [1908]. The Stranger. In *The Sociology of Georg Simmel*, ed. K. H. Wolff. London: The Free Press of Glencoe.

Skinner, Elliott P. 1963. Strangers in West African Societies. *Africa* 33 (4): 307-320.

Vigh, Henrik E. 2006. Social Death and Violent Life Chances. In *Navigating Youth Generating Adulthood: Social Becoming in an African context*, ed. C. Christiansen, M. Utas and Henrik E. Vigh. Uppsala, Sweden: Nordiska Afrikainstitutet.

Whitehouse, Bruce. 2003. *Staying Soninke*. Providence, Rhode Island: Brown University.

Whitehouse, Bruce. 2007. Exile Knows No Dignity: African Transnational Migrants and the Anchoring of Identity, PhD. Providence, Rhode Island: Anthropology, Brown University.

Notes

1 This chapter draws on my Master's thesis (Jónsson 2007).

2 However, Manchuelle's (1997) detailed historical research disputes many of the conventional assumptions regarding the link between colonialism and migration in West Africa, including the need to pay colonial taxes, which he claims was a far less significant impetus for migration than was the attraction of high wages and incomes, which provided a potential for social promotion within Soninke society (Manchuelle 1997, 91-92).

3 Villagers referred to them as *étrangers*, lit. foreigners – even if they originated from a neighbouring village.

"God's time is the best":
Religious imagination and the wait for emigration in The Gambia

Paolo Gaibazzi

Following the boom in undocumented boat migration to the Canary Islands (2006-9), Sub-Saharan African youth have received a lot of public attention. Most local and European media have featured dramatized stories of shipwrecks, rescue operations on the high seas and arrivals of exhausted young men on the islands. Journalists eventually made the opposite journey, seeking to report on the reasons for such a hazardous undertaking in countries of origin. A market for vivid stories of young men emerged. For instance, Emmanuelle Bouilly has mentioned that the *Collectif pour la lutte contre l'immigration clandestine de Thiaroye-sur-Mer* (a group of women fighting against illegal migration) takes European journalists on a tour of the town, where they can meet local young men[1] and listen to their despair, dreams and misadventures: the 'candidate for emigration', the 'repatriated', the 'friend of the migrant', etc. As one of Bouilly's informants boasted, "Me, I've helped the journalists a lot, I've done about ten reportages." (Bouilly 2008, 24-26, my translation)

Youths' hardship and despair are real enough not to be dismissed as mere media constructions, however morbid and ideological these representations may be. For many young men in the region, migrating is not just a well-entrenched livelihood strategy; in places where the usual avenues to social adulthood (marriage, work, etc.) are closed, migration seems to have become a way, or even the only way, out of misery and social invisibility (e.g. Mbodji 2008, 308; cf. Vigh 2009). I myself have documented the migratory aspirations of Gambian young men and their frustrations at being forced into a perpetual wait for emigration by restrictive migration policies (Gaibazzi 2010a). However, even when narratives of potential emigration are nuanced by ethnography, an exclusive focus on migratory aspirations may cloud African youths' relationship with emigration and home, thus reproducing tropes of representation that conceal as much as they reveal. Without neglecting the poignant experiences of hardship and compelling presence of travel in young men's lives, a critical anthropological reflection on youths should deal with the complexity of young men's understandings of home and travel.

This chapter concentrates on religious imagination as an under-researched, and yet central, aspect of discourses of (im)mobility among Gambian youth. It shows that aspirant migrants' horizon of experience and expectation (cf. Introduction) is not simply dominated by an 'elsewhere', but it is also overlaid with moral concerns and discourses about staying and managing the appropriate timing of emigration. While, on the one hand, youths feel impatient to leave the country, on the other they maintain that the lure of emigration can be fraught with perils. Too much haste can lead to dangerous and religiously illicit behaviours. Youths may thus praise waiting as a virtue, an appropriate pacing of opportunities in life, delivery from temptations, while at the same time showing readiness to seize whatever opportunity may be offered by the vagaries of destiny.

In the Gambia, a predominantly Muslim society, encouragement to wait for 'God's time' – the right timing established by divine will – generates new hope and prompts young men to regain agency. Hope reveals not only a fatalistic attitude and a future-oriented projection, but also an active mode of engaging with the present (Zigon 2009). By referring to 'God's time', youths call for proper timing and patience: they articulate a moralizing discourse that addresses the sense of urgency and despair in their lives and suggests ways in which they can live a moral life at a time of hardship and uncertainty (cf. Kleinman 2006).

Alternative discourses of migration and immobility are not necessarily verbalized as coherent narratives suitable for journalistic reporting. Moreover, youths do not envisage pious conduct as the sole solution to prolonged abeyance, nor do they talk about waiting for the divine schedule solely in doctrinal and erudite terms. Rather, references to religion surface in everyday conversations and narratives. I thus use 'God's time is the best' as an index to discourses on emigration and immobility which draw on, and yet go beyond, the religious domain in the strict sense. I am interested in how young men's use of Islamic concepts in narratives and discussions about migration sheds light on the complex and at times contradictory predicament of going and staying through which they view and attempt to repossess the wait for emigration as a purposeful social time (cf. Pandolfo 2007).

It is impossible to speak in generalizing terms about Gambian youths' religious imaginations. Although Gambia is a small country, it is a very diverse setting, one where different currents and practices of Islamic thought coexist and are quickly changing. The chapter is thus best seen as an attempt to show the complexity and diversity of discursive articulation. Its objective is to describe how specific individuals construct themselves in relation to the temporality of (im)mobility and how their imaginations are grounded in social interactions. Such narratives were collected in 2006-8 in rural and urban Gambia,[2] mostly within the Soninke speaking milieu, an ethnic group known in the region for its long history of mobility and Islamic scholarship (see Jónsson, this volume). When I followed Soninke young men from the village to the city during the dry season,[3] I also had the opportunity to interact with a more diverse group of youths, as my interlocutors often participated in ethnically mixed youth gatherings in their neighbourhoods. While the essay is heavily influenced by a rural Soninke perspective, this experience proved that the concerns and discourses described in what follows are highly relevant to many other Gambian youths.

"God's time is the best"

Since the 1980s, international migration has become a key livelihood strategy across all segments of Gambian society. Over the last three decades, employment and subsistence opportunities in The Gambia have shrunk as a consequence of declining agriculture, rising inflation, neoliberal restructuring and, at least for some, the deterioration of political liberties, all of which have contributed to making international migration a dominant model of success (Gaibazzi and Bellagamba 2009). Although women's presence in migratory flows is by now solid, in most (rural) Gambian families it is still young men who must take up migration in order to provide for their households. In a context in which success stories are increasingly migrants' stories (cf. Riccio 2005), young men thus imagine their future lives in another country, searching for means to maintain their families and to carve out a personal trajectory of emancipation and success.

Restrictive immigration policies in popular American, European and African destinations are, however, such that most Gambian young men must often put their plans to emigrate in abeyance (cf. Carling 2002). Gambian youths who wait impatiently for an opportunity to leave the country often experience mounting frustration at the impossibility of fulfilling their aspiration. To use a local expression, youths are *nerves* to travel. Elsewhere (Gaibazzi 2010a), I have described this feeling *nerves* as a double edged phenomenon: on the one hand, it is an embodied longing for travel, an urge and a determination that young men perceive to be fundamental in order to emerge from hardship and succeed; on the other hand, being *nerves* can easily become an overwhelming burden of concerns and frustrations about the inability to travel *and* the uncertainty about performing as householders and farmers, activities that ought to give respectability to 'stay-at-homes' within migrant households, but ones which are overshadowed by the achievements of the migrants. It is as if youths are called to a state of alertness, showing their readiness to travel and to be hard working, while at the same time the absence of meaningful income opportunities in the Gambia and the deferral of emigration progressively wear out their hope. As youths cultivate an aspiration to travel, these contrasting experiences eventually lead to a degeneration of self-confidence, loss of focus in the everyday struggle for subsistence and even despair.

Given that aspirations and preoccupations relating to migration are central in young men's lives, it is perhaps no surprise that religious-moral matters play an important part in their discourses. It is impossible to underestimate the significance of religion (Islam in particular) and religiosity in Gambian society, politics and everyday moral life (Darboe 2007). References to God are ubiquitous in verbal and non-verbal forms of expressions, including popular music and the visual arts (cf. McLaughlin 1997). Sometimes religious references are, however, more implicit and demand some decoding of the commonsense knowledge that lies behind them. The following story, which I collected in one youth gathering in Serekunda (Gambia's metropolitan area along the Atlantic coast), provides us with an example of such implicit references as well as with a starting point to discuss religious imagination in young men's understanding of emigration and its temporality:

> A young man from the rural areas, from the very 'deep rural areas', comes to Serekunda in order to look for a visa. He barely speaks any Mandinka and speaks no Wolof at all; and obviously he does not speak English, the official language. Nevertheless, thanks to some good contacts, he manages to file an application at the American Embassy. At the Embassy, after having checked all the paperwork, the receptionist tries to notify the next appointment to him; he tells him in Mandinka: 'Ta, *sama* yen na' ('Go, come back tomorrow morning'). The young man stands still for a moment, nods and goes back to his host's house. In the evening, his host calls him into his room and asks for news about his application.

'Everything was fine', the young man replies, 'I've handed in my papers. I just have to go to *Soma* [a town a couple of hours' drive from Serekunda] tomorrow morning. So I'm going to bed now'. The host frowns at the young man's plans but does not enquire further, and lets his young guest go to bed. After morning prayers, the young man goes to the station and waits for a vehicle heading to Soma. Meanwhile, at the Embassy the clerk, not seeing the young man coming, rings the telephone number on the application form. The landlord picks up the phone and, after crafting an excuse, rushes to the station. He finds the young man already seated on the vehicle and yells at him: 'What are you doing here!? The Embassy is looking for you'. 'But', he replies, 'they said: ta *Soma*, yen na' ('go to Soma, and come back'). The landlord shakes his head, grabs his arm and drives him to the Embassy, reaching there just before the clerk stamps 'rejected' on the young man's form. The young man is then issued with a five year permit.

This story theatrically rehearses several common tropes of migration in Gambian young men's discourses. Even the 'remotest' areas of rural Gambia – usually associated by urbanites with backwardness and ignorance – have been reached by the 'fever' of migration, the *nerves syndrome*. The young protagonist is not educated and has not even mastered the country's most widespread vernaculars – Mandinka and Wolof – and yet he harbours a greater goal in his mind. He is determined to emigrate to America, where many Gambians are working hard to support their families back home and saving money to marry, to build good houses and live a good life. He thus ventures into the maze of visa applications, reference letters and bank statements. When he is so close to securing a visa for himself, his lack of awareness of the 'modern world', epitomized by his lack of familiarity with national languages, nearly jeopardizes his opportunity.

Narrated with much irony and mimicry, the story caused hearty laughter among the young men in the audience. Some of the young men sitting around me could readily connect to the experiences of the protagonist. Like him, they were from the rural areas and had spent a few dry seasons in Serekunda. Unlike the young man, however, they had become acquainted with Wolof and English (most already spoke Mandinka), and most of them were very familiar with the daunting bureaucratic procedures involved in visa applications, either by direct experience or through friends and relatives who had gone through the process. Due to the very restrictive conditions of migration policies in European, American and some African countries (e.g. Angola), they had failed to obtain travel papers. Some had tried to circumvent the legal barriers to emigration but lost their money to canny visa dealers or their counterfeit papers were discovered during ordinary airport checks. Others still wished to travel but did not have either the money to apply for a visa or a relative in Europe or America who could help them do so. For all these reasons, I felt that the story had a bittersweet epilogue for them. In spite of all their attempts and impatience to leave the country, they were – unlike the naïve protagonist of the story – still waiting for their opportunity to go. The young unemployed often sat jobless in groups, brewing green tea, pondering on their situation and nourishing a dream to be in Europe or America one day.

What I had not realized was that for many of them the story contained a deeply moral and hopeful message. At the end of the story, seeing that I hesitated as if looking for an explanation, a friend commented: "God is great, you see…God's time is the best". This expression 'God's time is the best' is a common reply or consolation phrase for someone who is overwhelmed by concerns about a goal the realization of which depends on several, often uncontrollable, variables. Emigration appears to be a perfect example of this: while someone may strive to migrate as soon as he can, due to the difficulties and vagaries in acquiring rights to travel, it is only in due time, God's time, that this will happen. When this time arrives, no matter how inexperienced and clumsy the aspirant traveller may be, he will realize whatever his destiny has in store for him. As my friend added, by obtaining the visa the protagonist "got his 'luck': nothing could stop him from getting it. If God decides something for you, you will not die until you get it."

'Luck' (Soninke: *warijaxe*) is not a chance event as commonly understood in English. In Gambian English, it refers to the lot – or bounty, benefit, sustenance or providence – decreed by God as a part of one's own destiny, along with one's lifespan and the fruits of individual effort.[4] 'Luck' can manifest itself in many ways, though the term is usually employed to talk about begetting children and acquiring material wealth (see also Bledsoe 2002, 164ff; Whitehouse 2003, 25-27). 'Luck' is a central element in life, and partly accounts for personal success. Although several 'worldly' elements certainly affect progress, differences and uneven distribution of resources between individuals may be accounted for in terms of 'luck'.[5] God's will may be especially invoked in situations of unpredictable happenings, windfall gains, or sudden economic losses.

Given their complexity and unpredictable course, visa applications thus fall into this category of 'luck'. Indeed, my informants would often conceptualize migration as a quest fraught with incognita and unforeseen twists. It should be noted that the commentary on the 'visa story' subscribes to a fatalistic view of Islamic predestination. Yet Muslim Gambians' understandings of destiny are often more nuanced and ambivalent (cf. Acevedo 2008; Hamdy 2009). Interpretations that emphasize a predetermined course of events comparable to the 'visa story' often offer an *ex post facto* rationalization of outcomes over which little or no control can be exercised (Horst 2006, 45). In other circumstances, my interlocutors highlighted self-determination and free will. If God ultimately sets the limits of what one can and cannot have, the young men I worked with held that they had actively to search for the means to sustain their families and themselves. After all, visas must be applied for.

One may wonder whether there is any consistency in views on destiny and self-determination in the Gambia, and it may well be that there is little.[6] As Fortes (1983 [1959]) pointed out more than half a century ago, West African religious systems often juxtapose views of unchanging and inexorable predestination with views that allow space for individual agency. What matters for the present discussion is less accounting for diverging views than highlighting the ways in which young men mobilize them to frame migration and immobility. Invoking 'God's time' youths position their desires and concerns about emigration in a multidimensional horizon. In sight is not simply a spatially removed place – a country of destination – but also a temporality of actions and steps that lead to that place. This has a religious significance. In many ways, it is precisely the mutlivocality of religious concepts such as destiny and 'luck' that allows youth to appropriate them, but also poses fundamental questions: if a person must actively create his 'time', how far can he shape the course of his life? Does he have to migrate at any cost and as soon as he can? And if not, what should he do in the meantime?

A matter of life or death? Undocumented boat migration and (im)proper timing

If the bureaucratic uncertainty of visa applications appears to constitute fertile ground for religious discourses to proliferate, undocumented routes make the religious stakes of migration even more evident. When boats full of migrants began to depart from the Senegambian coastline around 2005 (Tall 2008, 47), the debate on migration in the region became heated. In spite of the limited number of youths who actually left, the Senegalese media covered this phenomenon extensively and depicted candidates of the *voie piroguière* as people gambling with their very lives (Bouilly 2008; Hernàndez-Carretero 2008, 45ff; Willems 2008). Journalists gave echo to the sentence 'Barça ou Barzak' (Barcelona/success or Hereafter/death), which became a symbol of the combination of bravery, despair and risk associated with the journey at sea.[7] In Gambia, the coverage of illegal migration was much less abundant and sensationalist. In addition, few youths with whom I spoke would depict themselves as either completely hopeless and destitute or reckless aspirant migrants. Nevertheless, discussions about the virtues and vices of boat migration eventually penetrated informal circles of sociality, triggering some young men's imaginations and prompting them to position themselves vis-à-vis questions of life and death raised by the availability of the 'water path' to Europe. This is where the trope of divine temporality and destiny emerged most poignantly.

During my fieldwork, I often had the opportunity to discuss boat migration with H., a man in his late twenties from the Upper River Region. H. often said that this was a route for people like him who have no 'supporter' or sponsor, that is, no close relative willing to help with the paperwork and the finances needed to apply for, let alone obtain, a visa. Some of H.'s friends who were in a similar situation had taken boats to Spain. They had raised the money for the journey (in the range of 800-1200 Euros in early 2008) by doing odd jobs and engaging in petty trade in Serekunda, and probably by borrowing money from a number of friends and other relatives. Once they reached Spain, some of them called H., so he had concrete evidence that journeys by sea were often successful. H. too migrated seasonally to the city after the harvest season was over (November-December). He went "to find money – but money is too small", as he often remarked. "If I have a good chance", he often said to me, "I will go [by boat]". In response to my counter-argument that such routes proved fatal to many, he often rebuffed by saying: "If your day has come, you'll die anyway, whether you take a boat or not."[8]

H.'s reference to death is directly linked to destiny, for lifespan is an element of it. His statement would seem to subscribe to a static, fatalistic view of predestination, as if the occurrence of death lay beyond people's control, and they had to accept it for what it is. However, when H. made such statements in the company of his friends, some of them firmly rejected his interpretation. Like many other informants, they likened gambling one's life on migrant boats to suicide, which is a forbidden act in Islam precisely because it defies God's timing and power over life and death. They proposed a more nuanced interpretation of destiny, one which left room for human agency and co-responsibility in causing death. Often, even H. was much more ambivalent about his real intentions to board a boat, and seemed to resort to statements like the one above as a mantra borrowed from other people during discussions on that topic. As I pointed out, attributing agency to a predetermined course of events can be a way of rationalizing (possible) outcomes over which people have little control. Yet, H. turned down the charge of suicide because, "If I go on the boat, I don't go because I want to die; I'm going to hustle abroad." In his view, encountering death during such an undertaking would thus be regarded as honourable and just (Hernàndez-Carretero 2008, 46-47).

Clearly, the timing of death is only one instance of 'God's time', an extreme example of the moral significance of discourses about leaving and staying. The urge to emigrate, fomented by the glimmer of migrants' successes, created slippery ground for H. and other Gambian young men like him. Looking, so to speak, at the horizon at the end of the sea allowed them to see themselves beyond the impasse of their everyday livelihoods and potentially having achieved honour in their attempt to secure a living. At the same time, religious concerns fogged the horizon, casting doubts on the religious legitimacy of boat migration as a path leading to success.

Haste and patience

The moral hazards of improper temporality of migration emerge not only in relation to (il)licit routes of emigration, but also in relation to one's conduct during other phases of the migratory process, including the stay in the Gambia. The story of another young man in his late twenties, A., illustrates this point well. One night, I was spending time with some acquaintances in a neighbourhood that I often visited in Serekunda. A. arrived at the crowded youth gathering and, noticing the presence of a European, he introduced himself. He greeted me in German – which I did not speak – even though he had heard me speak Soninke with other youths. His introduction immediately bespoke his migratory past and, as I soon realized, A. was eager to talk about it.

A. began his story by listing in rapid succession his movements to and within Europe. It had all started when a relative entrusted him with a considerable amount of money. The money was to be delivered to A.'s father. With this wad of cash in his hands, A. instead rushed to Bamako, where he knew that some visa dealers were issuing original documents to go to France. He paid for and obtained his visa, and flew to Paris. In the French capital, he managed to find a job, yet overstayed his permit. However, anxious to make money, *fast money*, as he described it, he moved to Germany, where some of his acquaintances introduced him to drug dealing. He made money, fast money; but after a year the police caught him. He was detained in a camp, and before the German authorities flew him back to Gambia a drug was injected into his left arm to sedate him. A. showed me his arm: it had not yet recovered its full mobility. A. concluded his story by turning to the young men around him, and citing a Soninke proverb: "all these boys are in a hurry to travel, but 'if you speed up the horse of the world, one day you'll be walking like a chameleon [Soninke: *an ga na duna si wurundi, kota yogo an na ri tera xoyi nyange*]'."

A. used the story of his failed migration as a moral lesson, ending his narration with a proverb to warn other young men: 'more haste, less speed'. The way he narrated the stages of his migration conveyed the sense of a rushed trajectory, each stage underpinned by an excess of haste that caused mistakes and sins, from stealing his father's money, to dealing in drugs, and thence to detention and harassment by the German police. After all that travelling and hustling, A. was nonetheless back to square one. He was, so to speak, an immobile man with an immobile arm. His reputation was now more compromised than ever. As he himself acknowledged, it was very unlikely that his senior relatives would trust him if he ever tried to find support to leave the country again.

A. was acutely aware of the social and political determinants of his failure. He said that he had realized 'many things' during his journey. He lived in the *banlieux* during the riots in 2005; he supported the grievances of the *banlieusards* and criticized Sarkozy – the then Minister of the Interior. It did not escape his mind that the injection he received in Germany was a blatant violation of human rights, and he lamented that African immigrants in Europe can be abused and kicked out of the continent. And yet he ultimately imputed his arm injury to the fact that he had hastened his quest for money abroad. One may even say that his public self-reproach was an attempt to express repentance and show that he had grown wiser now. Nevertheless, at least for that night at the youth gathering, his audience were young men who were in haste to leave the country and make *fast money*.

Although not all youths were as forthcoming as A. about their failures, their stories were often narrated in their absence. When youths engaged in discussions anticipating what they would do and how they would behave when they went abroad, referring to known examples was a common way of substantiating the points one made. In some cases, these stories had a social life of their own, passing from mouth to mouth, from gathering to gathering, until they became almost allegories, many of which had a religious, pedagogical overtone, like the 'visa story'. In truth, that night it was sufficient for youths to look about fifty metres down the road from where A. was telling his story to realize that his adventure could have had a different outcome. There stands a fine four-storey building which, according to the youths, was built by a Gambian drug dealer in the US. Although they praised the building, the youths speculated that this man's wealth would wither sooner or later because it was acquired through illicit means. Such money was not blessed, the precondition for wealth to stay and proliferate.[9]

A.'s hastened quest for money was interpreted along similar lines. On the way back to my house after speaking with A., my friend Baba and I continued to talk about him. As Baba tried to explain the meaning of the Soninke proverb A. had cited, he insisted that A. had not made real progress despite all his efforts to make money. A. was in the same situation as he was before he had left the Gambia. Baba thus concluded that 'God's time is the best'. By invoking a divinely sanctioned temporality not only did Baba frame A.'s impatience and hastened life trajectory in religious and moral terms, but he also highlighted A.'s individual responsibility. A. was held responsible for 'causing' his fate. His current situation was the result of illicit conduct before and during migration.[10]

Baba proposed patience and endurance (*sabari*, from the Arabic: *sabr*) as an antidote to haste. Acceptance of the divine schedule and patience did not necessarily mean fatalistic resignation to him; rather, he commended engagement with affliction, which in theological terms can be framed as a trial to test people's reliance on God and perseverance (Mahmood 2001, 220). As Hamdy (2009) has shown in relation to Muslim medical patients in Egypt, acceptance of affliction requires continuous alignment and the cultivation of forbearance and faith through work on the self and prayer. Having tried and failed several times to emigrate to Europe, Baba was not exactly the kind of person who passively waited for his turn to travel. Yet he also represented himself as a person who, in contrast to A., knew that 'things come little by little'. For him, 'managing little by little' did not imply forgoing aspirations to emigrate; nor was it simply a way of making ends meet. It was a proper way to wait for emigration, choosing pace over haste, and showing his readiness to look for money abroad. Not only did he show this by being a pious Muslim, but also especially by engaging in more mundane local activities, he traded in second-hand mobiles, and supervised the construction of his migrant brother's building.

I do not wish to construct people like Baba as heroes who resist the call for migration. If, on the one hand, by trying hard at home, young men may eventually find a good business opportunity in Gambia and forget about travel, on the other, finding a stable and well-paid job is extremely hard for young men, especially for the rural and uneducated ones with whom I conducted my fieldwork. Accumulating or accessing enough start-up capital to do business at home is difficult and depends on one having good contacts among well-established kin in Gambia or abroad. Enduring market and income uncertainty may heighten the young men's sense of being stuck in a loop.

As one acquaintance put it, it is to remain in a 'world of management', where one can make do on the brink of survival, but where money goes from hand to mouth, with no possibility of saving and financing long-term security and investment plans.

Concluding remarks

A number of scholars have rightly pointed out that African youths live in a state of abjection, and have interpreted their aspiration to mobility as a response to, and an expression of, it (Jónsson 2008; Mbodji 2008; Bordonaro 2009; Vigh 2009). Gambian young men's expectations of leaving the country are rooted in similar experiences and make manifest a wish to accelerate their social emancipation. This makes the wait for emigration an inchoate time fraught with concerns and mounting impatience. However, exploring the way in which young men discuss the temporality of (im)mobility, this chapter has revealed surprisingly tenacious hopes and discourses that defy the simplistic categorization of youth as abject and desperate candidates for (illegal) emigration. I have highlighted religious imagination as a central element in these discourses. Stories and debates about the wait for 'God's time' provide a window onto their diverging, and often contradictory, understandings of travelling and staying put as well as on to the ways in which youths moralize and inhabit their immobile present.

It may be countered that faith is a last resort in desperate situations, or that emphasizing moral conduct and reliance on God inhibits the full expression of young people's grievances, and produces God-fearing, docile subjects who dare not challenge the status quo. It is nonetheless necessary to underline that subordination and agency seem to coexist in young men's religious imagination of timing, patience and forbearance (cf. Mahmood 2001). While religiosity is important to young men, by moralizing spatial and temporal moves, people like Baba are also concerned with reconfiguring their options at home in practical, economic terms. Rather than allowing themselves to be overwhelmed by the lure of migration, their engagement with local employment and business may be thought of as an active, meaningful mode of occupying the time-space of immobility, and thus a way of expressing forbearance and maturity.

References

Acevedo, Gabriel A. 2008. Islamic Fatalism and the Clash of Civilizations: An Appraisal of a Contentious and Dubious Theory. *Social Forces* 86 (4): 1711-1752.

Bledsoe, Caroline H. 2002. *Contingent lives: Fertility, time, and aging in West Africa – with a contribution of Fatoumatta Banja*. Chicago: University of Chicago Press.

Bordonaro, Lorenzo. 2009. Sai fora: Youth, disconnectedness and aspiration to mobility in the Bijagó Islands (Guinea-Bissau). *Etnográfica* 13 (1): 125-144.

Bosworth, C.E. and Jane D. McAuliffe. 2009. Rizk. In *Encyclopaedia of Islam, Second Edition*, ed. P. Bearman et al. Brill Online, Harvard University: http://www.brillonline.nl/subscriber/entry?entry=islam_COM-0931. Retrieved 5 March 2009.

Bouilly, Emmanuelle. 2008. Les enjeux féminins de la migration masculine: le Collectif des femmes pour la lutte contre l'immigration clandestine de Thiaroye-sur-Mer. *Politique Africaine* 109: 16-31.

Carling, Jørgen. 2002. Migration in the age of involuntary immobility: Theoretical reflections and Cape Verdean experiences. *Journal of Ethnic and Migration Studies* 28 (1): 5-42.

Cohen, Ronald. 1966. Power, authority and personal success in Islam and Bornu. In *Political anthropology*, ed. Marc J. Swartz, Victor Witter Turner and Arthur Tuden, 129-140. New Brunswick: Aldine Transaction.

Darboe, Momodou N. 2007. The Gambia: Islam and Politics. In *Political Islam in West Africa: State-society relations transformed*, ed. William F. S. Miles, 129-160. Boulder: Lynne Rienner Publishers.

Fortes, Meyer. 1983 [1959]. Oedipus and Job in West African religion. In *Oedipus and Job in West African religion*, ed. Meyer Fortes and Robin Horton, ix, 92 p. Cambridge [Cambridgeshire] and New York: Cambridge University Press.

Gaibazzi, Paolo and Alice Bellagamba. 2009. 'Babilonia', oppure? Mobilità internazionale e logiche d'appartenenza nella Repubblica del Gambia. In *Inclusi/Esclusi: prospettive africane sulla cittadinanza*, ed. Alice Bellagamba, 86-115. Novara: Utet.

Gaibazzi, Paolo. 2010a. "I'm nerves!": Struggling with immobility in a Soninke village (The Gambia). In *Mobility, transnationalism and contemporary African societies*, ed. Tilo Grätz, 106-129. Cambridge: Cambridge Scholars Publishing.

Gaibazzi, Paolo. 2010b. Migration, Soninke Young Men and the Dynamics of Staying Behind (The Gambia), PhD diss. University of Milano-Bicocca.

Hamdy, Sherine F. 2009. Islam, Fatalism, and Medical Intervention: Lessons from Egypt on the Cultivation of Forbearance (*Sabr*) and Reliance on God (*Tawakkul*). *Anthropological Quarterly* 82 (1): 173-196.

Hernàndez-Carretero, Maria. 2008. Risk-taking in unauthorized migration, MA diss. University of Tromsø.

Horst, Cindy. 2006. *Transnational nomads: How Somalis cope with refugee life in the Dadaab camps of Kenya*. New York: Berghahn Books.

Jónsson, Gunvor. 2008. Migration aspirations and immobility in a Malian Soninke village. *IMI Working Paper* no. 10. Oxford: International Migration Institute, University of Oxford.

Kleinman, Arthur. 2006. *What really matters: Living a moral life amidst uncertainty and danger*. New York: Oxford University Press.

Mahmood, Saba. 2001. Feminist theory, embodiment, and the docile agent: Some reflections on the Egyptian Islamic revival. *Cultural Anthropology* 16 (2): 202-236.

Mbodji, Mamadou. 2008. Imaginaires et migrations. Le cas du Sénégal. In *Le Sénégal des migrations: mobilités, identités et sociétés*, ed. Momar Coumba Diop, 305-320. Paris, Dakar, Nairobi: Karthala, CREPOS, ONU-habitat.

McLaughlin, Fiona. 1997. Islam and popular music in Senegal: The emergence of a 'new tradition'. *Africa* 67 (4): 560-81.

Pandolfo, Stefania. 2007. 'The burning': Finitude and the politico-theological imagination of illegal migration. *Anthropological Theory* 7 (3): 329-63.

Rabbani, Faraz. 2005. Moral Responsibility and Divine Will. Re: Blaming Destiny? *SunniPath – The Online Islamic Academy*: http://qa.sunnipath.com/issue_view.asp?HD=1&ID =131&CATE=24. Retrieved 11 September 2009.

Riccio, Bruno. 2005. Talkin' about migration – Some ethnographic notes on the ambivalent representation of migrants in contemporary Senegal. *Stichproben – Vienna Journal of African Studies* 8 (5): 99-118.

Tall, Serigne Mansour. 2008. La migration internationale sénégalaise: des recrutements de main-d'oeuvre aux pirogues. In *Le Sénégal des migrations: mobilités, identités et sociétés*, ed. Momar Coumba Diop, 37-68. Paris, Dakar, Nairobi: Karthala, CREPOS, ONU-habitat.

Vigh, Henrik. 2009. Wayward Migration: On Imagined Futures and Technological Voids. *Ethnos: Journal of Anthropology* 74 (1): 91-109.

Watt, W. Montgomery. 1948. *Free will and predestination in early Islam*. London: Luzac.

Whitehouse, Bruce. 2003. Staying Soninké: Migration, Multilocality and Identity in a Community of the West African Sahel, MA diss. Brown University.

Willems, Roos. 2008. Les 'fous de la mer'. Les migrants clandestins du Sénégal aux Îles Canaires en 2006. In *Le Sénégal des migrations: mobilités, identités et sociétés*, ed. Momar Coumba Diop, 277-304. Paris, Dakar, Nairobi: Karthala, CREPOS, ONU-habitat.

Zigon, Jarrett. 2009. Hope dies last: Two aspects of hope in contemporary Moscow. *Anthropological Theory* 9 (3): 253-271.

Notes

1 Although women migrate too, young men are still the main migrant group, and the exclusive one in hazardous routes like boat migration. 'Young men' broadly refers to men aged between the late teens and mid-forties, the age group which normally expresses a desire to migrate.

2   Funds for field research and writing up were generously provided by: University of Milano-Bicocca, Unicredit Foundation, Italian Ministry of Foreign Affairs via Ethnological Mission in Benin and West Africa (MEBAO), and Germany's Federal Ministry of Education and Research (BMBF) via the research project 'Muslim World – Worlds of Islam?' hosted at the Zentrum Moderner Orient (Berlin). I thank Knut Graw, Samuli Schielke, Alice Bellagamba, Jonah Wedekind and an anonymous reviewer for their comments on previous versions of this chapter.

3   Labour migration to urban areas on the Atlantic coast is seasonal (December-June). Despite rural-urban mobility, for young men 'travelling' in the true sense means emigrating to a foreign country.

4   The act of decreeing refers to the existential determination of destiny, or predestination (Arabic: *kadar*). 'Luck' corresponds to the Arabic *rizk*: lot, sustenance, provision (Bosworth and McAuliffe 2009).

5   In a seminal essay on the topic Fortes (1983 [1959], 7-10) found that concepts similar to 'luck' are widespread in West Africa. Ronald Cohen (1966, 134ff) found that among the Muslim Kanuri of Bornu a similar concept (*arziyi*) is used to account for personal success and an uneven distribution of power. Somali Muslims refer to *nasiib* (chance, fortune, destiny) to explain the vagaries of events and fortunes (Horst 2006, 38ff).

6   Destiny is one of the most debated concepts in Islamic theology, particularly regarding the role of human free will in the course of achievements and actions as determined by God (see Watt 1948). In some places in the Quran, free will is accorded to human beings: to obey or disobey, to discern the right or wrong path (e.g. Quran 7:43, 18:29, 76:3); nevertheless, according to a Sunni interpretation, God's power and knowledge are unconditioned by time and space, so that He will know in advance the outcomes of human choice (Rabbani 2005). This view is especially popular among Gambians with a formal Islamic education.

7   Barça can refer to the city and stand for reaching Spain, but it is also a reference to the Spanish football team, and thus a sign of success (Tall 2008, 47).

8   In her interviews with Senegalese candidates for boat migration, Hernàndez-Carretero (2008, 46) has found similar statements.

9   Blessing (*baraka*) is the state of grace one earns through material support and devotion to parents and family elders (and towards charismatic religious figures). In some cases, parents do not spend the money received from their migrant sons if they suspect it was obtained illicitly (e.g. by drug dealing).

10 People generally tend to attribute misfortune to misconduct (hence the teaching of free will), whereas positive achievements are rhetorically attributed to God's benevolence.

The Eiffel Tower and the eye: Actualizing modernity between Paris and Ghana

Ann Cassiman[1]

Tu es tout
Tour
Dieu antique
Bête moderne
Spectre solaire
Sujet de mon poème
Tour

Blaise Cendrars (1969)

Introduction

In mainstream development ideologies, a great deal of attention is paid to the evolution promised by the passage from past to future, from 'tradition' to the 'modern', or from rural to urban, oral to written, gift to commodity. As already noted by Mudimbe (1988:4) and many others since (Comaroff & Comaroff 1993, Miller 1995, Piot 1999, Ferguson 1999), this presupposed jump from one pole to the other is in fact misleading. In this chapter, which deals with rural life among the Kasena in Northern Ghana, I will illustrate how the two temporalities inherent in the paradigms of tradition and modernity do not obliterate one another, or logically follow each other on a linear historical line (as if the introduction of modernity in Africa is *delayed*), but rather collide to construct a future for autochthonous worlds in which renewal and change are embedded in an ongoing *continuity*.[2] In this sense, the case I will present in this chapter is more about a local actualization of historical modernity than about a modernizing of tradition.

It intends to illustrate how the resemblances between modernity and tradition are in fact as important as the differences between them. In my view, the way in which the Kasena people merge their own world with that of Western modernity is analogous to the African artist's fundamental attitude described by Mudimbe in 'Reprendre', a seminal article on the nature of contemporary African art. According to Mudimbe, for the African artist, *reprendre* signifies three things: first, it means taking up an interrupted tradition, not out of a desire for purity, which would testify only to the imagination of dead ancestors, but in a way that reflects the conditions of today. Secondly, *reprendre* suggests a methodological assessment through which the artist evaluates his tools, means and projects of art within a social context transformed by colonialism and later influences from abroad. Finally, *reprendre* implies a meditation on the meaning of the two preceding exercises (Mudimbe 1991). What I propose here also comes close to the stance taken by Geschiere, Meyer and Pels in their introduction to a reader on the genealogies of modernity in Africa (Geschiere, Meyer & Pels 2008). In their argument, modernity is a relational concept, which "starts from the assumption that the extraordinary effectiveness and spread of notions of the modern in Africa have to be understood as an effect of the illusory unity of modernity, as it is supposed to manifest itself some time in the future" (ibid. 2008:5). In their view, the power of these notions lies in their capacity to articulate temporal inequalities, classifying some as modern and others as 'not yet modern'. For them, modernity is 'not a package deal, but a set of powerful practices and ideas held together by "family resemblances"' (Geschiere, Meyer and Pels 2008:2). This chapter focuses precisely on these family resemblances between the paradigms that structure both rural Kasena worlds and modern urban landscapes.

Starting from the example of a young man's movement between his village and Europe, I will show how this increased mobility contributes to the reinterpretation and strengthening of the meanings of village life. At first sight, the introduction of new mentalities and commodities seems to introduce a material and moral rupture with existing forms of rural living. In reality, however, people incorporate newer mental and material infrastructures in such a way that these actually sustain, rather than disrupt, autochthonous values and meanings. In this chapter I will show that the meanings which are generated in the mediation between western modernity and Kasena village life are shaped by key metaphors of *seeing* that are shared by both worlds. The next sections will explore the meanings embedded within the notions of seeing, concealing and revealing in the context of rural Ghana. I will compare those to the centrality of perception and display in the construction of urban public space in the West. In my conclusion, I will build on this comparative exercise to question the validity of the notions of 'alternative modernity', 'multiple modernities' and 'delayed modernity'.

Kobenah in Paris

Some time ago, one of my Kasena friends from Navrongo, a small town in the rural North of Ghana, came to visit Europe for the first time in his life for a short course programme at one of Belgium's universities. He visited Antwerp, Brussels, Amsterdam and Paris. Before returning home, he bought presents for his wife and children, as well as his brothers, as any self-respecting Ghanaian man would: Nike shoes, clothes, an umbrella, a backpack, a cell phone, and... the Eiffel tower, the ultimate trophy which signified his capturing of Europe. The small glass souvenir of the tower stood on a plastic base, in which four colour LED lights alternately lit up the tower in green, red, blue and purple at high speed, thereby evoking the flickering effect of its nightly illumination.

A couple of days after his return, Kobenah called me on his newly acquired cell phone from the small town of Navrongo, located near the border with Burkina Faso. He was drinking Star beer with his friends on the garden terrace of Navrongo's only hotel, a modest local interpretation of the Holiday Inn. He told me –not without pride– that, in the opinion of his friends, he was now 'behaving as a white man' (*n kè fella*, lit. 'doing white' or 'going white'). The expression is used to qualify those who return home after having travelled to the 'white men's world' *(fello logo),* also denoted as 'today's world' *(zim logo)* or 'the modern world' *(lele logo,* lit. 'the now world'). A person who has made such a journey to the Western world is referred to as someone 'whose eyes have opened' *(o yia puuri).* A new world has been revealed to him or her.[3] The same is said of a villager who returns after having spent some time in the urban worlds of the Ghanaian Southern belt. Cities such as Accra and Kumasi are considered to be both the tentacles of and the first gateways to the Western world. One's eyes have opened when one has proved to be capable of capturing, accumulating and consuming particular commodities belonging to that world, such as beer, cell phones, cars and motorbikes. The conspicuous consumption and the masterful display of these iconic items signify one's successful participation in a western defined modernity. They turn one into a 'big man' *(nonkamunno),* locally known as a 'guru' *(nadum, 'a heavy man').* Acquiring this label obviously adds to one's status and prestige.

Kasena notions of seeing

The expression 'one's eyes have opened' emphasizes the centrality of visual metaphors in the construction and development of Self and society in Northern Ghana. More generally, Kasena notions of seeing are crucial for defining, regulating and guarding boundaries between different social worlds and the specific ways in which these worlds are kept separate or made to interact. For Kasena, accessing and controlling knowledge is produced through specific modes of concealment and revelation. There is something very empowering in disclosure. By lifting the taboo and seeing what was secret and hidden, one acquires knowledge about and control over previously inaccessible or forbidden worlds and forms of knowledge. In many contexts, the gaze implies a transgression of boundaries.

An ethnography of the gaze among the Kasena illustrates to what extent the interplay of seeing and not seeing is very central in daily life. For example, the differentiation between men's and women's worlds, or between elders and youngsters is regulated by (the denial of) visual access. In some clans, for example, in the first days following a child's birth, the newborn child and a specific relative (this can be the father, the grandfather, the maternal grandmother, or the brother and sister) are not allowed to see one another. When the relative and the child (represented by the mother) finally meet, they will blow ashes towards one another to lift the taboo, while whispering 'I have disclosed you' *(a piire mo)*. The same ritual of disclosure is performed at the discovery of a young woman's first pregnancy, or at the end of a parturient's period of seclusion, when she 'comes outside' *(o nongi poone)*. In the early morning of the day of 'coming outside', the grandmother fetches ashes, takes a broom and a broken earthenware pot and guides the mother to the main gate of the house. The grandmother covers the mother's eyes with her hand and places the ashes in the mother's left hand. When guided outside the gate, the mother blows the ashes away while saying *a poone, a poone*, meaning 'I am outside, I am outside', until she has crossed the front yard of the house. Her eyes are now uncovered. This practice is referred to as blowing *(fiiru)*. The grandmother then goes to the path leading to the mother's parental house; she puts down a broom in the form of a cross, covers it with the ashes and tops it with the broken pot on which she stamps very hard so that it breaks. It is a sign that the womb of the house has broken, the house has given birth (Cassiman 2007a: 239-242). Leaving the room of seclusion and opening her eyes to face the outside world ritually introduces a parturient to her new status of mother and her new relation to the world inherent in this status.

Similarly, the relationship between a father and his first-born son is regulated through strategies of concealment and disclosure. For example, a man's first-born son is not allowed to look into his father's granary, where the latter stocks his harvest. The granary is the ultimate symbol of the accumulative capacities of the father. Likewise, a first-born daughter cannot look into her mother's pot, the *punga*,[4] a red spherical pot with a square lid. Symbolically, in both cases, one is not allowed to look into one's own source of life. The Kasena say that if the daughter looks into her mother's *punga* 'she will see her own mother there'. The same holds true for the senior son who looks into his father's barn (*tiu*), since 'he will see his own father there'. What is meant here is that the barn and the *punga* contain the essence of fatherhood and motherhood respectively. Looking into them would untimely reveal these parental essences (Cassiman 2007a: 283). It is only at the death of the genitor or genitrix that the senior son or daughter is ritually made to look into the father's granary or the mother's pot. Not respecting this rule would violate the succession of generations.

Passage through a Kasena house is another way to play with notions of (not) seeing and being seen. When one enters the house through its only small entrance, the immediate impression is one of visual fragmentation, and of an elaborate or-chestration of different larger and smaller constructions, such as granaries, walls, rooms and animal coops, scattered around the central kraal. The house's architecture obstructs the gaze by means of obstacles to the visitor's view, preventing him or her from observing the multiple daily activities in the yards surrounding the kraal. Ar-chitecturally and materially, the house creates phased access to increasingly intimate spaces, and this phasing is spatially imposed on the visitor by playing on contrasts between light and dark, high and low, and narrowness and openness. In this way, the inhabitants of the house remain largely invisible to the visitor, whereas the visitor himself can immediately be spotted by all. Thus, the house structures the relation-ship between insider and outsider, stranger and kin, visitor and inhabitant, and those who know and those who are ignorant, those who belong and those who do not, through a complex interplay between concealment and revelation or visibility and invisibility. The more one penetrates the hidden insides of the house, and the more one accesses its secrets, the more one is empowered. These almost sensuous geographies shape the degree of one's belonging to the house.

The ultimate example of this spatially imposed phased intimacy is the interior of a woman's rooms. Inside these rooms, which can be entered only by female relatives and children, a woman exhibits her belongings and through them proclaims her place in the world. An elderly woman carefully keeps her belongings inside a double or two-lobed room, called the twin-room (*di-nia*). Upon entering the dimly lit first room through the narrow doorway, one is confronted with impressive shining piles of pots, carefully arranged against the wall of the room. The pots are piled in a remarkably orderly fashion, the larger ones at the bottom and the smaller ones on top, all sitting on the rim of a specially designed storage place (*chirayiga,* lit. 'the face of the ancestors') (see figure 1). The pots and calabashes testify to a never-ending accumulation of belongings by the woman, her mother, and her grandmothers. They bear witness to the women's accomplishments and skills and represent the core of female power and knowledge.

Figure 1: The interior space of the twin-room with 'the face of the ancestors', a storage place for pots and calabashes. (Photo by the author. Chiana, Ghana, 2011)

All of these examples illustrate how a transition from one world to another, a transformation in the construction of social identity, or a shift in the rhythms of intergenerational succession is generated through the playful manipulation of secrecy and revelation, of hiding, seeing and displaying.

Whereas female power is constructed through forms of concealment, the power of men reveals itself in the public domain. The public realm is referred to as *poone,* meaning 'outside, open, luminous or illuminated space', 'where the wind blows'.[5] This space stands in stark contrast to the darkness of the house's female inner spaces. In various ritual contexts, people are brought out of seclusion into the open, an act which is referred to as *nongi poone* (lit. 'to come outside, to appear in the public space'). This indicates a person's successful transition into a new identity or self. When, for example, a newly appointed chief is brought out of seclusion, he goes to the public front yard of the house, climbs the rubbish heap (*puuri*)[6] which is located there, and proclaims he has 'seen the future'. This visionary act bestows power upon him and signifies the beginning of his reign.

Etymologically, *poone* is related to the verb *pòòre*, which means 'to open, to be wise, to be enlightened'. Daybreak is referred to as the opening of the earth (*tiga poore*, lit. 'the land opens') and announces a new day, a new start, or the opening up of a new world yet to come. Questions about engagements or activities in the very near future are often answered with '*tiga na poore de ni*' (lit. 'when the earth opens we will see', i.e. let us first wait until the day breaks before we decide), for human beings cannot spell out what tomorrow will bring.

Opening up to new worlds and knowing how to navigate between various realms gives one power, knowledge and wisdom. A person who is not capable of doing so is considered, in a way, to be 'blind' (see also Liberski 2002:289). Those who consult diviners are also called 'blind': their eyes are 'lost' (*ba yia jei-mo*) or they have lost their 'front' (*yiga*) and they need the diviner's intervention to open their eyes and reorient themselves in the order of the world. Since a diviner is able to see into other realms (*yinèère*, lit. 'the act of being able to see'),[7] he can reveal the world order *(logo wonno)* to those who consult him. Through the divinatory oracle, the blind client is made to see again, 'his eyes are opened'.[8] After a successful divinatory session, a client has 'found his front' or sees his ways clearly and is able to reshape his future aspirations in line with the outcome of the divinatory session. In a similar vein, Graw, in his analysis of Senegambian divination, elucidates how the divinatory encounter opens up a cultural space that allows the subject to realize and confront the issues which are at the core of his concern or affliction: "[i]n an attempt to spell out the possible developments of the client's future, divination is in itself 'chrono-poetic', time-making, i.e. shaping and re-shaping the subject's consciousness of the future with every consultation. ... The divinatory encounter produces prospects for the future and enables the subject to develop new hope" (Graw 2005: 28-29).

A witch (*chiru*, pl. *chira*) too is said to have the ability to see different worlds and to transgress the boundaries between the realms of the visible and the invisible. As elsewhere throughout Africa, a witch is considered to have four eyes. Witchcraft is believed to be transmitted in the maternal line through the ritual practice of force-feeding (*nyii*) or opening the eyes (*su yia*, literally 'washing/opening the eyes') with the water derived from boiling a victim's bones. A witch is referred to as someone 'who sees' *(nae)* or 'whose eyes can see' (*o yia nae*).[9] Sometimes the expression 'having opened the eyes' can also be used for someone who is initiated into witchcraft *(yi-puuri* or *yi-su)*.

Finally, in the same way as the diviner and the witch make various simultaneous worlds through their visionary capacity, the Kasena also use the notion of vision to denote movements of colonizing and appropriating unknown spaces.

Today, the Kasena emphasize how a man needs to have *seen* or *entered* the bush in order to become a real man *(baaro)*: an able suitor during the preamble to marriage, a respected man, a good family head and a strong farmer. To leave one's house and hazard into the unknown, i.e. into dangerous or hostile places (the bush, *gaao*), is part and parcel of a man's maturing into adulthood. Formerly, this movement from boyhood to manhood was punctuated by a specific rite of passage named 'they enter the water' *(ba zo na)*, which consisted of a collective journey and seclusion in the bush, a ritual killing and the sharing of particular food, drinks and bathing liquids. This ritual initiated young men into adulthood and prepared them for marriage and the office of family head. Today, for many youngsters, the journey to a large urban centre in the south has replaced this rite of passage. The migratory movement towards towns is now considered the ultimate penetration of the 'bush' (cities are also called *gaao*, bush). As in former times, *seeing* the bush implied gaining knowledge about it. It is an act that is perceived to be the entry into what people consider 'modernity' to stand for (see also Cassiman 2007b).

All of these examples illustrate the multiple meanings of complex Kasena semantic networks surrounding notions of vision, revelation and concealment. The metaphors of seeing and of 'opening the eyes' relate to the ability to cross or even transgress boundaries (between men and women, between public and private, between open and closed, between what is concealed and what is revealed, between the living and the dead). These metaphors also signify the capacity to access and navigate between various worlds and to colonize the unknown, whether it is the natural space of the bush, the metaphorical bush which is the city, or the invisible realm of the occult. So metaphors of seeing pertain to notions of light, enlightenment, opening up, expanding one's life into different worlds, travelling, moving forward, developing, appropriating knowledge and acquiring wisdom. Seeing relates the past to the present, while also connoting one's visionary powers to foresee the future, as in the case of the chief, or to reveal the order of the world, as in the case of the diviner. The very act of seeing is empowering and helps to construct the world anew, by appropriating new knowledge that was previously unknown. Both temporally and spatially, it propels one forward by indicating new paths into the future or into the space of distant worlds.

In conclusion, what seems to be suggested here is that, in principle, the autochthonous notions of seeing in Kasenaland lend themselves well to covering the forward looking developmental dynamics of a western (neo)liberal modernity. Moving forward, or seeing and knowing one's front and ways orients one in the different worlds one inhabits. The further or more alien these worlds, the larger the power of the insider. Similarly, the Ashanti living in the Southern part of Ghana have a common expression 'your eye is opened' *(wa nii a bue!* in Twi*)* which refers to one's achievements in terms of having entered a western, 'developed' world and an 'enlightened' way of life. The semantics of local meanings of seeing, concealing and revealing thus blend well with the dynamics and key issues of what is at the heart of colonialist modernity: enlightenment, development, progress, colonization, and an orientation towards the future.

All of these themes are often sung about, as the following excerpt of a Kasena song by Nyangano Wodabala (a musician from Chiana Asunia) illustrates. The metaphor of opening one's eyes in this and similar songs appears to be a powerful strategy for inserting oneself into a more global oecumene.

> *"Let us be together because the world's people's eyes have opened.*
>
> ...
>
> *I told you, let us hold one another because the world is wise.*
> *Human beings, let us hold one another because the world is wise.*
> *The people's eyes are opened* (noona bam yia puuri ne mo).*"*[10]

Beyond the Kasena world: seeing and the archaeology of modernity

As Berman pointed out in *All that is Solid Melts into Air,* his ground-breaking work about the experience of rising modernity in Europe, the magic realms of the invisible and the occult have been at the heart of modernity's realities from the very beginning (Berman 1988). He convincingly argues, for example, that the figure of Faustus is crucial to understanding what the rise of enlightenment and the subsequent notion of the 'modern' in the West was all about. The link between magic and development is always present (Berman 1988: 71-86).

Geographically shifting this argument from the historical heartlands of modernity to its (post)colonial peripheries, the ever growing literature on the introduction of modernity/modernities and on the simultaneous rise of accompanying occult economies throughout Africa has paid detailed attention not only to the witchcraft of western modernity, its specific multiple links between material realities and magical interpretations, but also to the modernity of witchcraft itself. Not surprisingly, in Africa, far from being mutually exclusive, it is argued that both realms are intimately linked and produced in and through each other (Comaroff & Comaroff 1998, Geschiere 1997,

Moore & Sanders 2001). In this by now significant body of literature, modernity as defined in the West and local practices and discourses concerning the occult and the realms of the invisible are understood to go hand in hand. Both strengthen each other where they meet, whether in rural areas or in the urban setting (De Boeck & Plissart 2004), where the distinction between the West and the rest has actually collapsed to form one commonly shared new global urban culture (cf. Pile 2005).

In both local African interpretations and western ideologies of modernity and progress, the very act of 'seeing', the capacity to see 'with four eyes' and open up the realm of the invisible, seems to be the central issue. The parallels between local discourses concerning visibility and invisibility and the imported ideologies of modernity that are locally appropriated, transformed and redirected are thus by no means restricted to the Kasena world alone, but concern a much wider context of interpretation that has developed in large parts of Africa. A recent example of the multiple links between witchcraft and modernity in Africa was provided by Harry West in his rich analysis of witchcraft in Mozambique. According to West, Muedan witchcraft practices and discourses may be perceived not only as acts of destruction, but also as constructive acts, expressed through the powerful key notion of *kupilikula* (lit. 'to undo the effects of sorcery', to turn it around on those who seek to harm others). Thus, local Muedan concepts of sorcery become a means to formulate and shape ideas about new economic orders, about new political forms and new engagements with the level of the state and beyond. These give form to alternative views of what development might mean in the North of Mozambique (West 2005). Similarly, James H. Smith, in his recent book 'Bewitching Development' (2008) on witchcraft and the reinvention of development among people in the Taita Hills of contemporary Kenya, offers a careful analysis of the parallels and links between a western, neoliberal notion of development on the one hand, and local understandings of the occult on the other. His ethnography illustrates how Wataita capture and appropriate the western notion of development, and make sense of it by connecting this to their own changing understandings of witchcraft.

Long before these recent monographs, however, John Peel (1978) devoted an article to Yoruba concepts of development which, perhaps, provides an even more useful parallel with the processes which I have observed amongst the Kasena of Northern Ghana and have tried to outline here. In this insightful text he analyses the autochthonous Yoruba notion of *olaju* which, in its most general meaning, signifies 'enlightenment'. However, he also shows how *olaju* is a central notion in a much broader metaphorical field, a local 'traditional' Yoruba philosophy concerning the sources of power and the relationship between power and knowledge. *Olaju*, he argues, also relates to education, religion, commerce, and travel, and as a concept it gradually became associated with access to western ways of schooling. More broadly, the term is used by the Yoruba to denote 'modern' processes of development and social change. Again, the notion of seeing is crucial here: the stem *laju* literally means: 'to open one's eyes'. *La*, Peel explains, connotes the idea of distribution (of knowledge, for example) and the notion of drawing borders. *Aala*, is the border indicating the property right over a certain piece of land; *ila* is an ethnic marker, indicating one's social identity; *la* also means 'to clarify'. The term *olaju* is more metaphorical than these related words: it indicates a state of enlightenment, a social process of heightened knowledge and insight, knowledge that is necessary to obtain a greater common good. In the same way as an individual is enlightened by opening his eyes, a societal constellation is enlightened by opening itself to the outside world, to new (western) technologies and educational insights. Therefore *ilosiwaju*, literally 'to go ahead', indicates progress, and is considered to be a positive quality, in the same way as *itesiwaju*, (to step forward') or *idagbasoke*, 'to grow up', 'to become mature'. The *idagbasoke* of a village is the acquiring of an asphalt road, for example, a dispensary, a court house, i.e. things that will draw more people to one's village and make it grow.

From a totally different perspective, Peel notes, missionaries and colonizers talked about the 'opening of Africa', and ideologically constructed their actions as 'the bringing of light into the darkness' or 'the opening of the blind's eyes' (1978:144). Peel convincingly illustrates that these metaphors were not only western imports but strongly resonated with the already existing Yoruba metaphors mentioned above.

The same, I would argue, can be demonstrated with regard to specific Kasena notions and modes of seeing, which are used as autochthonous forms of empowering, of crossing borders into unknown lands, of capturing and bringing back home the world beyond the Kasena houses' horizons, thereby remaking that local world. It is no coincidence, for example, that Kobenah brought back the flickering Eiffel tower, itself an iconic object of modern urbanity.

Modernity and the image of the Tower

In this section, I would like to dwell at greater length on the icon of the Eiffel tower and what it might represent for Kobenah. From Walter Benjamin to Roland Barthes, the Tower has been proclaimed the symbol of industrial and artistic progress, of modernity and utopia, the colossal golden *Phare* of industry and capital (Thompson 2000:1133). In the face of the grand itineraries of dreams, the Eiffel tower is the inevitable symbol.

Barthes invokes the Tower in a mutual encounter of looking: "[l]a tour est un objet qui voit, un regard qui est vu." (Barthes 1964:27-28). In other words, modernity reached its apotheosis as a phantasmogoria of display, epitomized in the International Exposition of 1889 which also produced the Eiffel Tower itself. Through the Tower, a new kind of leisure-oriented, spectacular urban culture was created, transforming Paris into a 'Ville Lumière'. Electric lighting familiarized urban dwellers with new sources of modern stimulation, with an emphasis on vision and motion. The Eiffel Tower, literally a beacon of light in the Parisian night, but more broadly also a beacon in the history of modernity itself, epitomized this modern stimulation to the full. "The Tower, like Parisian modernity itself, is deeply implicated in the project of modern urbanism and its connection to commercial visual culture, to which its nightly illumination has contributed in significant ways" (Schwartz 'The Eiffel Tower', online document). It is precisely this 19th Century industrial culture as it took form in Paris which Walter Benjamin described in his famous, but unfinished and posthumously published Arcade Project (*Passagen-Werk*) (Benjamin 1982). In this work, he uses the central image of the 'passage' as an architectural image to talk about urban dream worlds, the modern city as a looking-glass city, and the spectacle of Paris as a magic-lantern show of optical illusions. The passage here becomes the original temple of commodity capitalism, which is privately owned but publicly traversed, where the fetish-like character of commodities is underscored by putting them on display. For Benjamin, the construction of modernity hinged not so much on the notion of commodities-in-the-market, but rather on the notion of commodities-on-display. Paris as the City of Light dazzled the crowd, and in the Passage, the showcase of an urban economy of desire, the crowd itself became a spectacle (Buck-Morss 1989: 82-83). In the modern urban city, the urbanite was redefined as a consumer rather than a producer.

Similarly, the boulevards of Haussman's Paris created a new primal scene of display for the *flâneur*, who strolled along these new public spaces to see and to be seen, engulfed by its immense and endless flux: "[t]he vision, the epiphany, flows both ways. In the midst of the great spaces, under the bright lights, there is no way to look away" (Berman 1988:153). In short, the new setting of modern city life makes all urban humanity a great extended 'family of eyes' (Berman 1988: 153) propelling it forward on the waves of progress.

The glitter of the Eiffel Tower as a new architecture of vision and an icon of enlightenment 'illuminates the dark lives of people at whose expense the bright lights shine' (Berman 1988:153). Meaningfully, Balzac compares the old and unenlightened working class neighbourhoods of Paris to the darkest jungles of Africa (Berman 1988:153). Here, the Parisian working class collides in a very real sense with the African Other, put on display at the foot of the Eiffel Tower during the international exhibitions that were held between 1889 and 1931 and that functioned as real 'theatres of alterity' (Bancel et. al. 2002). It is no coincidence that today's largest European collection of African objects is housed in the shadow of the Eiffel Tower, in the Musée du Quai Branly. The museum thus incorporates the primitive into the heart of urbanity, turning Paris into *Paris primitive* (Price 2007), in a movement that, I would argue, ironically mirrors African migrants' triumphant appropriating and taking home of the Eiffel Tower and other trophies iconizing modernity.

Modern displays inside the house

The playful manipulation of secrecy and revelation, of hiding, seeing and displaying, that takes place in the Arcades and in the iconic construction of the Eiffel Tower is not worlds apart from the long-standing notions of revelation and visualization existing in Kasenaland. In my opinion, it was not by chance that Kobenah carried home the Eiffel Tower to symbolize his successful journey and the 'opening of his eyes'. In the same way as Kobenah brought home Paris (the Tower as *pars pro toto* of modernity) others return with similar trophies, as tangible proof of the fact that 'their eyes have opened'. In their case, the flickering Tower often takes the shape of glistening corrugated iron sheets or other items that signify one's successful capturing of the modern world.[11]

For young men and, to an increasing extent, young women, leaving for metropolitan or faraway places has become a major part of passing into adulthood. Tokens of these journeys are brought home and explicitly exposed in the realms of the house. Other emblems of 'having seen the bush' are implicitly reworked in mutations of domestic architecture. The biographies of these rooms and materials on display are testimony to the occupants' ventures into new lands and their initiation into adulthood. The houses are increasingly transformed by an intensified borrowing of and 'adding on' of urban and 'western' housing styles, whether in design, ground maps or materials and objects used.

If the display of commodities is at the heart of what modernity is about, then this modernity also finds its unproblematic expression in the way Kasena returnees ostentatiously display these commodities. The social body of the house and the physical body of the returnee become the stages upon which the capturing and spending of modernity is performed.

At the same time, the rhythms of showing and showing off, which hyphenate the spaces of both the Parisian Arcades and the Kasena house, are reformulated and reframed in terms of their complement, namely the practices and discourses on secrecy, hiding and concealing that surround local forms of accumulation and are central to the Kasena construction of power and knowledge. This becomes clear in the following example of the interior of the female rooms.

The interior arrangement and decoration of the rooms make the modern worlds metonymically present through a display of fashionable objects and consumer goods which women have brought home from their journeys. Nevertheless, and in spite of these stylistic ruptures, autochthonous meanings and values continue to be respected in the selection, features and arrangement of such new commodities. The new items are manipulated in ways that reshape and re-articulate female patterns of ordering and furnishing, thereby incorporating these objects' biographies into the culturally meaningful architecture of women's rooms and lives. Earthenware pots are substituted by silver bowls (*siliba* in Kasem), made-in-China plastics and ceramics, receptacles and cups. A showcase or small table serves to exhibit these items, thereby replacing the 'ancestor's face', (the *chirayiga*), and the rows of earthenware. Piles of iron kitchenware are displayed in the rooms, rehearsing and reformulating the rhythmical motifs of the rooms' interiors. Neatly accumulated rows of bowls of different sizes, from large to small, are the hidden testimonies to the different worlds a woman oversees, be it urban or rural, her mother's world, her migrant son's worlds or her own cultural orderings (see Figure 2).

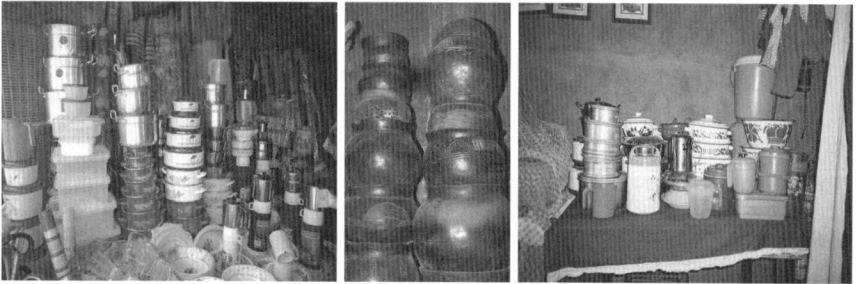

Figure 2: *The interior arrangement of the women's rooms shows new objects and commodities that they, or their migrant children, brought home. Despite these new 'modern' objects, the autochthonous features are continued in the selection and arrangement of the new commodities. (Photo by the author. Chiana & Navrongo, Ghana, 2006)*

The journey beyond one's cultural horizon and the objects that are brought back from that journey do not uproot female modes of (semi-secret) display, but actually strengthen them, creating a symbolic *surplus* value, added to existing forms of female power and expanding the scope of that power.

Reprendre and actualizing modernity

The foregoing fully illustrates this chapter's point of departure, namely Mudimbe's observation that tradition and modernity do not succeed one another on a linear teleological path of 'progress'. What I have tried to demonstrate, on the contrary, is how the modes of empowerment produced by modernity are not necessarily or fundamentally different from those which are common in Kasenaland. In both worlds, the production of self and the accompanying logic of commodification, consumption and desire hinge on shared notions of display and empowerment. At the same time, modernity's showcase is effortlessly rearticulated in terms of specific Kasena notions of secrecy and concealing. This shows how modernity does not necessarily introduce a rupture or breach, but can sometimes also be understood as a strengthening of local continuities. The modern appendix which is added to the Kasena house does not destroy its traditional architecture. It rather signifies a *surplus* or added value. Not only does it reinforce the durability and flexibility of local architectural forms, it is rather effortlessly re-inscribed in the specific terms of local moralities, ethics and modes of self-making as well.

This chapter shows how the traditional modernity of the 19th Century Paris of Benjamin not only modernizes tradition, but is itself modernized, to become a modernized modernity in rural Ghana. This brings us back to a fundamental idea underpinning Benjamin's Passagen-Werk, namely his attack on the myth of automatic historical progress. As Benjamin himself states in the Arcades project, his main objective was to drive out any trace of 'development' from the image of history and 'to overcome the ideology of progress in all its aspects' (quoted in Buck-Morss 1989: 79). In the Arcades project he attacks the premise of progressive development. For him, the basic principle of history is not progress, but actualization (Benjamin, 1982, in Buck-Morss 1989:79).

This is precisely what the Kasena incorporation of modernity is about: it is not (just) about the introduction of progress and development, or about a 'delayed introduction of modernity', or the creation of 'alternative traditions', but above all about a local *actualization* – a specific form of *reprendre* – of 19th Century modernity, rendering it significant for a Kasena in today's global world. Metaphors of concealment and disclosure, of shielding the eyes and opening them, not only provide the Kasena with a powerful cultural tool with which to think and reflect upon their own history as it unfolds in the succession of generations (for example the disclosing of the granary), but it also provides them with the ability to reposition this history in the light of a wider and more Western world.

References

Adler, Alfred and Andras Zempléni. 1972. *Le bâton d'aveugle: divination, maladie et pouvoir chez les Moundang du Tchad*. Paris: Hermann.

Bancel, Nicolas, Pascal Blanchard, Gilles Boetsch, Éric Deroo and Sandrine Lemaire, eds. 2002. *Zoos Humains: de la vénus hottentote aux reality shows*. Paris: Editions la Découverte.

Barthes, Roland. 1964. *La Tour Eiffel*. Paris: Delpire.

Benjamin, Walter. 1982. *Gesammelte Schriften, Vol V: Das Passagen-Werk*. Ed. by Rolk Tiedemann. Frankfurt am Main: Suhrkamp Verlag.

Berman, Marshall. 1988. *All That Is Solid Melts Into Air: The Experience of Modernity*. London: Verso.

Buck-Morss, Susan. 1989. *The Dialectics of Seeing: Walter Benjamin and the Arcades Project*. Cambridge: MIT Press.

Cassiman, Ann. 2006. *Stirring Life: Women's paths and places among the Kasena of Northern Ghana*. Uppsala: Uppsala studies in Cultural Anthropology.

Cassiman, Ann. 2007. Home and Away: Mental geographies of young migrant workers and their belonging to the family house in northern Ghana. *Housing, theory and society* 25 (1): 14-30.

Cendrars, Blaise. 1969. La Tour Eiffel: A Madame Sonia Delaunay. In *Oeuvres complètes*, Blaise Cendrars. Paris: Editions Denoël.

Comaroff, Jean and John L. Comaroff, eds. 1993. *Modernity and its Malcontents: Ritual and Power in Postcolonial Africa*. Chicago: University of Chicago Press.

De Boeck, Filip and Marie-Françoise Plissart. 2004. *Kinshasa: Tales of the Invisible City*. Ghent: Ludion.

Fainzang, Sylvie. 1986. *«L'intérieur des choses»: maladie, divination et reproduction sociale chez les Bisa du Burkina*. Paris: L'Harmattan.

Ferguson, James. 1999. *Expectations of Modernity. Myths and Meanings of Urban Life on the Zambian Copperbelt*. Berkeley: University of California Press.

Geschiere, Peter. 1997. *The Modernity of Witchcraft: Politics and the Occult in Postcolonial Africa*. Charlottesville: University of Virginia Press.

Geschiere, Peter, Birgit Meyer and Peter Pels, eds. 2008. *Readings in Modernity in Africa*. Bloomington: Indiana University Press.

Graw, Knut. 2005. Culture of Hope in West Africa. *ISIM Review* 16: 28-29.

Liberski-Bagnoud, Danouta. 2002. *Les Dieux du Territoire: Penser autrement la Généalogie*. Paris: CNRS Editions: Editions de la Maison des Sciences de l'Homme.

Miller, Daniel, ed. 1995. *Worlds Apart: Modernity through the Prism of the Local*. London: Routledge.

Moore, Henrietta L. and Todd Sanders, eds. 2001. *Magical Interpretations, Material Realities: Modernity, Witchcraft and the Occult in Post Colonial Africa*. London: Routledge.

Mudimbe, Valentin Y. 1991 [1988]. 'Reprendre'. Enunciations and strategies in contemporary African Arts. In *Africa Explores: 20ᵗʰ Century African Art*, ed. Susan Vogel. New York and Munich: The Center for African Art/Prestel.

Peel, John. 1978. Olaju: A Yoruba Concept of Development. *The Journal of Development Studies* 14 (2): 139-165.

Pile, Steve. 2005. *Real Cities. Modernity, Space and the Phantasmagorias of City Life*. London: Sage.

Piot, Charles. 1999. *Remotely Global: Village Modernity in West Africa*. Chicago: Chicago University Press.

Price, Sally. 2007. *Paris Primitive. Jacques Chirac's Museum on the Quai Branly*. Chicago: University of Chicago Press.

Smith, James H. 2008. *Bewitching Development: Witchcraft and the Reinvention of Development in Neoliberal Kenya*. Chicago: University of Chicago Press.

Schwartz, Vanessa. 2006. *Eiffel Tower*. Atlas Entry on the 'Atlas of Urban Icons.' Online Document: http://www.usc.edu/dept/LAS/history/urbanicons/urban_icons_companion/index.htm.

Thompson, William. 2000. 'The Symbol of Paris': Writing the Eiffel Tower. *The French Review* 73 (6): 1130-1140.

West, Harry. 2005. *Kupilikula: Governance and the Invisible Realm in Mozambique*. Chicago: University of Chicago Press.

Notes

1   Ann Cassiman is an associate professor at the Institute for Anthropological Research in Africa, Katholieke Universiteit Leuven, Belgium. The research was funded by the Flemish Fund for Scientific Research FWO. I thank Filip De Boeck for the useful suggestions and editorial comments.

2   This chapter is based on fieldwork that was carried out in Northern Ghana, in the Kasena-Nankana District, in June and July 2007 and again in April 2008. Earlier fieldwork on Kasena architecture has been published in *Stirring Life: Women's paths and places among the Kasena of Norhtern Ghana* (2006).

3   The expression 'one's eyes have opened' *(yia-puuri)* not only has positive connotations, but can also refer to qualities of cunning and deceit. These negative connotations find their roots in past experiences, where the so-called 'enlightened' people were said to deceive ordinary man, treating the latter as stupid and dull. It is also believed that someone whose eyes have opened *widely (yia-poro)* is a proud or arrogant and unreliable person, who does not respect elderly people (also referred to as *yi-nèèri)*. The same holds true for young women who have been brought up in the city: they are said to have 'opened their eyes', which equally can have negative connotations. Such women are believed to be spoilt by western ideas and influences

and are therefore no longer considered good spouses, in contrast to young women who grew up in the village (*diga-kaane*, lit. room-women).

4   The *punga's* peculiarity does not result primarily from its red colour and unusual shape but from the symbolic value it exemplifies. The *punga* is always covered by a small pot turned upside down, as if to emphasize its concealing qualities.

5   Someone who is referred to as a *nonpoona* (lit. 'an outside-person') is someone who does not hide things for others, someone who is certainly not a witch.

6   The *puuri* or remnant heap contains all the waste produce of the house and thus forms a measure of the productivity of the house. It is the paradoxical symbol of the age, power and vitality of the house. In various ritual contexts (war dances, funeral celebrations), climbing the *puuri* indicates the appropriation of the house and its power and productivity.

7   Note however that the seeing of a diviner *(yinèère)* is considered to be very different from the seeing *(nae)* of a witch. Usually the diviner's capacity to see is situated in the divination bag *(lòò kom o nia*, lit. 'the diviner's bag sees'*)*: it is the diviner's bag that sees and shows the order of things in a divinatory session.

8   Compare with Fainzang for similar connotations of blindness in a divinatory context among the Bisa of Burkina Faso. She stresses however that it is not only the client who is considered to be blind, but also the diviner himself: "Le bâton du devin donne à l'aveugle le moyen de s'orienter et de connaître le monde qui l'entoure de même que c'est lui qui donne au devin (aveugle) le pouvoir de connaître 'le fond des choses'" (Fainzang 1986:130). Similarly, in Adler and Zempléni's account of divination among the Moundang of Tchad, the diviner appears as the blind person who is guided by the stone he throws during the divinatory session (Adler & Zempléni, 1972:40).

9   Witchcraft in Kasenaland is commonly considered to be transmitted through matrilineal ties. Hence, relationships between members of the matriclan are defined by metaphors of seeing: a woman's children are called her 'eyes-followers' *(yii-kam)*; children from two sisters are referred to as 'eyes can deny' *(yi-fura)*: this means that only relatives in the female line can confirm or deny that they are witches.

10   Recorded by Ann Cassiman in January 1997, Asunia, Nyangano Songo.

11   There is an interesting correlation to make between the Eiffel Tower, as a hyphen between two different worlds, and the ritual object of the horn, the Kasena symbol of power, which is domesticated by the matrimonial relationship between the figure of the wandering hunter and the head of the sedentary house. The hunter is the 'feeder' who provides the meat, the flesh of exchange, and the horn, a power object from the bush, to those 'seated' and settled, who are to be fed. An exchange is established, and that is a vital prerequisite for the settled house to be able to regenerate life (see Cassiman 2007b).

Literacy, locality, and mobility:
Writing practices and 'cultural extraversion' in rural Mali

Aïssatou Mbodj-Pouye

Global cultural flows and their local appropriations have come to attract a growing interest in anthropology, and Africa counts as one of the areas where such approaches have been widely developed.[1] At the same time, the issue of migration has been brought dramatically to the foreground, both as a political matter and as something that fuels local discourses and imaginations, be it in the form of actual practices of mobility or of constrained 'immobility'. How do these two lines of investigation intersect? A common view of migration easily attributes the motivation for migrating to a fascination (a 'mirage') with the wonders of the North, as displayed by the glittering images offered on TV, in a contemporary version of the colonial 'bright lights theory' (Manchuelle 1997, 4). Such a simplistic view can be readily dismissed, in that it neglects the socioeconomic situations and historical processes that provide the basis for emigration in most countries, thus overemphasizing the cultural terrain of emigration. Furthermore, the way it portrays the migrant as a passive consumer of these flows of images is unsatisfactory. However naïve, it does point to the difficulty of understanding the interplay of global cultural flows penetrating the continent and fluxes of people migrating from Africa to the North.

This problem can be reformulated as a question about the link between 'cultural extraversion' and migration. The notion of extraversion was coined by Jean-François Bayart to mean what provides the substratum for the insertion of Africa in world history in the *longue durée* (Bayart 2000). It reconceptualizes the dependence that is viewed as characterizing the African continent as a 'mode of action', meaning that African actors have been deliberately using extraversion strategies for their own projects, rather than being forcibly drawn into a globalized world. This perspective illuminates how ways of life, material culture, and cultural practices have been creatively borrowed and appropriated.

Studies of migrants and would-be migrants mobilize the concept of extraversion to address the predicament of African urban youth (see notably Fouquet 2007; 2008). This perspective aims at 'locat[ing] African practices of the self and migratory aspirations on a common scheme of intelligibility: that of extraversion as a mode of subjectivation' (Fouquet 2007, 104, my translation). In the dialectics between 'here' and 'there', comparison to an often idealized 'elsewhere' is also a way to relate critically to one's own society.

In this chapter I want to make two points. Firstly, I wish to insist on the practices and technologies which mediate imaginations and expectations; this is a methodological point (discourses alone tell only part of the story) as much as a theoretical point (images by themselves rarely make people act and take decisions). Secondly, I attempt to offer some historical depth to the question of the global horizon by suggesting that the same practices may open distinct horizons at different moments.

Given the focus of recent studies on would-be migrants among the urban youth (Fouquet, 2007 and 2008, Vigh 2009), the point of view I adopt here – which is that of villagers in a region characterized until recently by its low international emigration rates – is a way to take a step back. My perspective is thus in line with the purpose of this book as advocated by Graw and Schielke in the introduction, which aims at understanding migration 'as being part of the larger sociocultural horizon of a given society or person', rooting these reflections in a social, cultural, economic, and historical context. In this respect, my purpose is to understand how extraversion only partly accounts for the way people deal with global cultural flows. I will develop this line of investigation by turning to data from a previous work on literacy practices in a rural area of Mali.

I focus on personal practices that I consider to be practices of cultural production even though they are undertaken by low-literate writers and rarely display much textual continuity. Among these practices, one is of particular interest: keeping a personal notebook. As I have developed elsewhere (Mbodj-Pouye 2009; forthcoming), this practice derives from the habit of writing a farm notebook, initially sponsored in post-literacy training. It evolved into a more personal practice, outside any institutional setting, giving way to the emergence of individual *compendia* where farming data and family events, as well as personal and secret information, are written down.

In approaching these practices, I will not attempt to disentangle what strictly counts as 'cultural' (notably what pertains to a youth culture identified as urban) from the rest. Rather, the intricacy of what our analytical categories would easily distinguish as local and global is integral to the data. I will stick to the paths the writers themselves use to introduce some order into this material. I will deal with these literacy practices as instances, among others, of the cultural practices the villagers engage in. I will associate them in the analysis with other domains of cultural practices, such as listening to the radio or watching TV.

This material will firstly be approached as a cultural site where we can point to phenomena of cultural extraversion. Then, the investigation on the process of subjectivation at work will help broaden the perspective to the socio-historical context where literacy provides – or fails to provide – opportunities at home or elsewhere. Finally, returning to a more literal view on mobility, I will interrogate the way some practices of literacy may actually sustain certain forms of migration.

The cultural dimensions of literacy: extraversion in question

The local currency of global forms

I begin with an ethnographic vignette that helps to dismiss a superficial understanding of extraversion.

In the personal notebooks kept by young male villagers, aged approximately 15 to 25, records of international competitions and lists of names of famous football players is one of the favourite topics.[2] At first glance, recording sports results or players' names seems to testify to an insertion into wider cultural circulations. To what extent is the logic of extraversion central in the practices analysed here? The double-page on Figure 1, from Somassa Coulibaly's notebook displays the usual heterogeneity of 'personal' notebooks. The left-hand page is the continuation of notes copied during an information campaign on HIV, in Bamanan, that occupied the first eight pages of the notebook. This page is the point where the copying ends and the notebook is turned into a personal object. The end of the page is devoted to a list of dated events, essentially family events recorded in French from 1997 to 2003: deaths and births, as well as one marriage, his father's departure to Mecca, and one notation concerning a television bought for the Africa Cup of Nations football competition organized in Mali in 2002. This list was copied from an earlier version in another notebook.

The right-hand page is devoted almost entirely to the results of the following Africa Cup in Tunis in 2004 (some figures relating to a weight of cotton appear on the right). This page details, in French, the results of the first round of the competi-

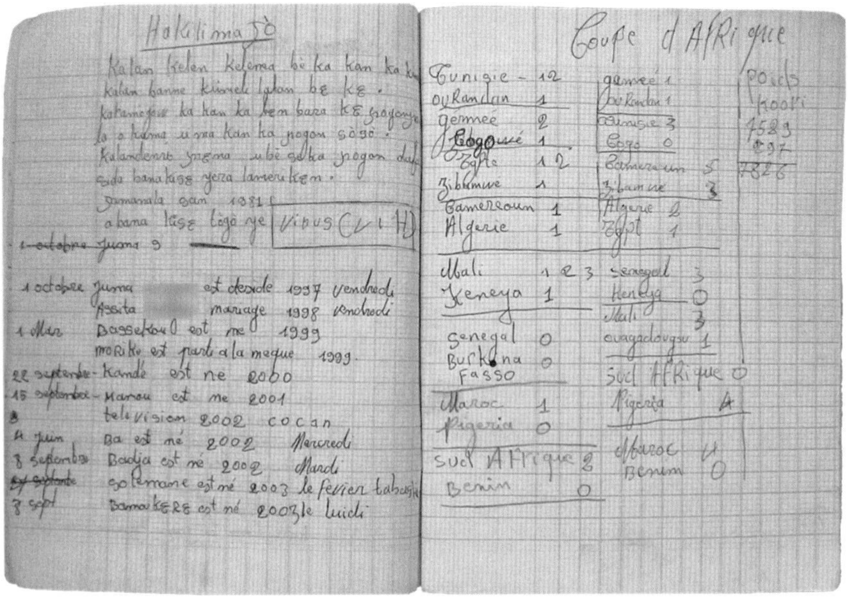

Figure 1: 'Coupe d'Afrique[3].

tion. Changes in ink suggest that the writing took place at different moments, maybe after each match. The writing is organized in columns displaying the results by pools.

The matches are listened to on the radio or, more recently, watched on the very few televisions present in the village. The results are written down in French, which may be the language the match was reported in, but not necessarily, as local radios also provide comments on the matches broadcast on TV in Bamanan. This choice of French is not specific to these kinds of notations. Somassa Coulibaly, born in 1975, went to the bilingual school, where he acquired the writing skills in Bamanan and French evidenced on this double page. He prefers French for his more personal writings, as appears in his notebooks and as he himself declares during the interview.

Writing down the results of international competitions pertains to a larger set of practices associated with international football, supported by different commodities, such as stickers, that sometimes make their way into the village environment. What does keeping a record of detailed information on this topic mean?

It seems obvious that football culture is a way of cultivating a sense of belonging to a wider environment and inscribing oneself in a global culture (for a range of studies on football in contemporary Africa see Baller and Saavedra 2010). But what are the actual uses of these records? First of all, they provide topics of discussion with friends in the village, in the neighbouring town of Fana, or elsewhere. The notes are described as providing pieces of evidence in the arguments that inevitably arise. Another very often quoted use of the personal record of results is to answer radio-show quizzes. These contests organized by local radio stations ask questions on football, sometimes on past competitions, such as where and when the first Africa Cup was organized. Some notebooks keep records of this past information when it is provided by the radio.[4]

When referring to these notations, the writers insist on the actual sociability and exchanges permitted by this knowledge. Those exchanges exceed the village boundaries and delineate specific groups of sociability between young men sharing the same preferences. Being competent in football provides some kind of local authority.

This initial approach compels us to be cautious, as obviously interest in global forms can meet local ends. As Richard Hoggart aptly demonstrated in *The Uses of Literacy*, exposure to and consumption of cultural products do not in itself imply adhesion to the values promoted in this production, and the repertoire of attitudes of keeping a distance and being only partially involved should not be underestimated (Hoggart 1957). Even when pieces of information are borrowed, they may be appropriated to local ends in unexpected ways. Thus, the link between the presence of global forms and cultural extraversion demands every time to be empirically established, as by itself this presence does not imply much.

In that sense, I would argue that through cultural work such as the writing of a personal notebook, global cultural products and expressive forms gain local currency. Personal writings appear to be a privileged site for cultural translation.

The open-ended work of translation

Translation is an effective way of articulating not only languages but also cultural systems of reference. For instance, to record dates, many writers adopt a double notation of the date in the two calendars in use in the region: the Gregorian calendar, which is the civil calendar officially used in Mali, and the lunar calendar with Bamanan names, which nowadays follows the Islamic calendar and is used as the shared reference at village level.

Moreover, concurringly to extraversion as making 'global' forms meeting 'local' ends, the writers also proceed the other way round, in providing new forms for 'local' bodies of knowledge.[5] Magical formulas or spells (*kilisiw*) are one of the main genres in the notebooks, practised by men and women. The process of 'entextualization' of this orally transmitted body of knowledge shows that writers borrow from the model of the recipe: the text of the formula is quoted, accompanied by indications for use. Interestingly, the main channel for becoming acquainted with this model is again the local radio, where broadcasts devoted to local medicinal knowledge bring in analytical forms of describing the uses of herbs. Writing down a formula implies borrowing some of these forms to re-contextualize knowledge acquired in a specific setting in order to provide it with a written form that is more sharable.

Islamic knowledge is also reworked in the notebooks. The writers draw from print booklets in Bamanan, French and Arabic, radio broadcasts, and cassettes. The wider transformations of religious knowledge associated with the uses of new media, and the changing forms of transmission are well documented (Schulz 2003). Writing down prayers or numbers of benedictions to say, collected from different sources, in order to make one's own compendium is part of these dynamics, as careful attention to the uses of language and the modalities of quotation shows.[6]

Thus, the idea of extraversion seems too unidirectional to account for these dynamics. Some texts testify to a renewed attention to local culture, reshaped throughout processes of transcription, adaptation to new media and new uses. The logic of extraversion is but one of the cultural processes at work, in a larger dynamic of cultural translation, providing equivalences for meanings, combining distinct sources and appropriating global contents and forms in creative ways.

Since focusing on the content of the writing as testimony to extraversion proves deceptive, I will turn to a more pragmatic perspective on this material, interrogating the significance of the practices rather than engaging in content analysis. In so doing, I share with the studies quoted above an interest in African modes of subjectivation, or 'African modes of self-writing', to quote from Mbembe (2002). Approached as a 'technique of the self', this practice needs to be set in a wider context where literacy has become a major feature of rural life in the cotton-growing area.

Literacy, locality, and mobility: socio-historical variations

Literacy and mobility as common experiences

In the cotton-growing region of Southern Mali, a conjunction of educative enterprises, notably adult literacy classes in Bamanan conducted by the CMDT (Compagnie Malienne pour le Développement des Textiles), has rooted literacy practices in ordinary experience.[7] My main fieldwork site was a village situated near Fana, a small Malian town.

In the Mande area, as throughout West Africa, Islamic uses of literacy in Arabic have entailed the development of written and graphic traditions. More recently, colonial imposition of writing has also fostered specific uses of writing in French.[8] However, the massive diffusion of writing in the cotton-growing area dates back to the mid-1970s. Functional literacy campaigns in Bamanan, initially organized by the governmental organization in charge of literacy programmes, the DNAFLA (Direction Nationale de l'Alphabétisation Fonctionnelle et de la Linguistique Appliquée), were taken up and broadened in the 1980s by the CMDT. The Company had its own interests in developing literacy classes as it was implementing a major organizational change, which implied delegating many tasks to local villager associations. This process required that some villagers would be literate in Bamanan, and able to keep records and perform a series of accounting, measurements, reading and writing tasks. In the village I worked in, a literacy centre was opened in 1971.

Schooling is the other main channel for acquiring literacy skills. Since the colonial period schooling has affected the village irregularly: during the interwar period two children were recruited for a newly opened school in Fana where they learned to read and write in French, and became the first literates in French in the village. In 1974, a school was opened in a neighbouring village, and in 1979 the village gained its own school, which was one of the first bilingual schools in the country.[9]

These different ways of acquiring literacy involve three languages: adult literacy classes organised by the CMDT are in Bamanan, written in a modified Latin-based alphabet; schooling combines two languages, Bamanan and French; Islamic learning implies the use of Arabic, oral and written.[10] Ethnographic interviews provide a view of the process of becoming literate, which implies studying in one or more of the educational institutional settings, but also learning through informal experiences, such as migrating in urban places where the scope of literacy experiences is wider. I have investigated literacy practices in the village in a wide range of contexts, institutional and professional (the practices linked to the production of cotton organized by the CMDT), private and informal.[11]

In this village, two generations of literates can be identified: during the 1970s, literacy classes in Bamanan were directed at men, mainly householders. After their training, most of them gained access to positions within the association of cotton-producers sponsored by the CMDT. Schooling extended literacy skills to wider segments of the population, with a number of young men and women having access to the sixth grade in the primary school and sometime the seventh grade in Fana (for those who passed the exam to pursue their studies in the town, the drop-out rate during the first year was very high). The few who succeeded in further studies did not come back to live in the village: most of them obtained informal occupations in the cities; some volunteered as community teachers (with very low status). Many young adults with an intermediary level (having more or less completed primary schooling) of education live in the village. Only a few of them have been co-opted by the village association of cotton-producers. Even without any regular post-literacy training and professional encouragement, some of the others have developed their own uses of literacy.

I will now turn to experiences of mobility in order to articulate dynamics around literacy and migration.

The village I worked in is located 10 kilometres from Fana, where many villagers spend the day on Wednesdays for the weekly market. In that way, mobility characterizes the life of the villagers on a routine basis. More generally, villagers are part of what has been described as a 'culture of mobility' characterizing West Africa (De Bruijn, Van Dijk and Foeken 2001; Jónsson, this volume). The present focus on international migrations might lead us to overlook regional migrations, especially rural-urban mobility which constitutes a prominent feature of Malian societies (see Dias Barros, this volume).

To provide an overview of migration habits in the village, I rely on data collected through a survey conducted in the village (cf. table 1[12]). This broad approach indicates firstly that most villagers are mobile: only 26% of the adult population has never left the village for a month or more. This global figure masks an important gender disparity as it represents 36 % of women and 10% of men.

As for the destinations, Bamako and other locations in Mali have attracted respectively 31% and 35% of the villagers. 25% of them have been outside Mali, in the surrounding African countries (mainly the Ivory Coast, more rarely Guinea, Senegal, and Morocco once). Migration to Europe is basically not practised – until 2004, only one villager was reported to have been to Europe (to Belgium for the second-hand car trade on a short trip). Since then, two young men have left for Spain, starting a new kind of migration.[13]

Age affects the migration rate very little, testifying to the fact that spending some time out of the village is an experience historically rooted in the village (cf. table 2[14]). Yet destinations and conditions for migration have varied throughout history:[15] older villagers went to Senegal and Gambia in the 1930s. The Ivory Coast became more attractive for the following generation. In the 1950s and 1960s, migration to other rural zones was also practised, especially in those areas already involved in cash-crop production and colonial and postcolonial agronomical experiments.

In recent times, migration has tended to focus on urban centres, sometimes as a follow-up to student mobility, sometimes competing with schooling. This is especially the case for young girls migrating to Bamako in search of domestic employment, which has become more and more attractive in recent times (Lesclingand 2004, 32).[16] More recently, migration patterns have changed with the crisis in the Ivory Coast, and the return of some villagers settled there. Former pupils of the village school interviewed as young adults (25 to 30 years old) often had a rich migration record, including in several locations, mostly urban. This mobility involves periods where migration is limited to the dry season (which is tolerated by the elders) and longer periods (most often disapproved of by the elders).[17] Many expressed their wish to find a way out of the village in order to settle permanently in towns.

I will now attempt to bring together these two experiences of literacy and mobility that, each in its own way, shape villagers' lives, both of which could count in a broad sense as extraversion. When trying to articulate the reflection on literacy to the common experience of mobility, we encounter a classical line of investigation, as migration has been identified as one of the social correlates to literacy (Scribner and Cole 1981). This association between literacy and migration in West Africa has recently been reasserted (Schmitz and Humery 2008). The direction of the correlation is not always clear, however: does migratory experience foster the acquisition of literacy skills and practices or is it literacy which helps the migratory project and its effective realization? Another set of questions arises when one considers the level at which the causality would operate; if migration and singularly urban experiences facilitated the acquisition of literacy: is it as a place where specific skills and knowledge are acquired and experimented with, or as a site where literacy appears valuable? Among the range of literacy practices migrants engage in, the role of letter-writing in maintaining ties with their place of origin and in sustaining diasporic networks is well-known, though sometimes also carried out through brokers when people lack literacy or language skills (Charpy and Hassane 2004). As we shall see, the local practices described here also bear an imprint of the culture of mobility that characterizes this area.

Writing in a notebook and the 'production of locality'[18]

Keeping a personal notebook as Somassa Coulibaly does, is a common practice for literate individuals of different ages and backgrounds in the village. Very often the notebook is not initially dedicated to personal writing. It may have been received during an agricultural training course run by the CMDT or an NGO. On such occasions, the organizer gives out blank exercise-books to the audience. At the end of the training, each participant will have conscientiously filled in a part of the notebook by copying down the statements written on the blackboard by the teacher. This notebook will then be taken home and be used for one's own purposes. Some intensive writers end up buying notebooks for their own use.

I will consider here the notebook kept by Makan Camara, born in 1967. He was one of the first pupils to complete primary schooling in the bilingual school. He passed the exam to pursue his schooling in Fana, but left after a few months. He went to the Ivory Coast for several months, and then settled in the village, where he was recruited by the village association as a monitor for the literacy classes in Bamanan.[19]

During our discussion, he went over his notebook for me, and allowed me to photograph most of the pages. On six pages, he had recorded different kinds of events dating from 1996 to 2001. The notebook displays a specific form of organization, with the following topics being covered on distinct pages:

– page 1: record of the death of his father in 1996 (reproducing the form of the obituary notice addressed to the radio), and table of the donations for the funeral;
– page 2: agricultural notations, and again the death of his father, 1996;
– page 3: other family events (four births and one marriage, 1996 to 2001);
– page 4: distant events (the death of Pepe Callé, a Congolese musician; the death of a Malian Islamic preacher; 1998; see Figure 2);
– page 5: village events (the death of the village chief; the inauguration of a mosque; 1998);
– page 6: personal notations (the day when he bought a radio and other personal items; an unidentified death notation).

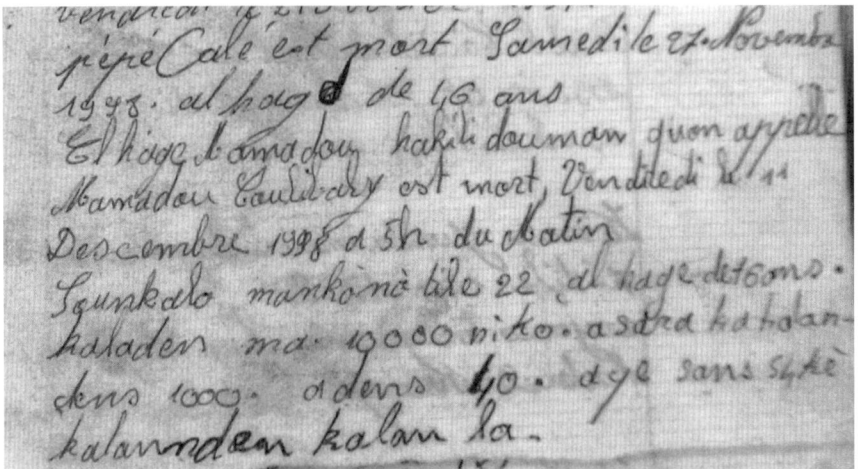

Figure 2: Recording distant events.

This overview reflects the general topics in the notebooks: domestic and farming notes form the main bulk of the writing (here farming appears marginally, but domestic records are dominant). The use of languages in this notebook gives a good idea of the way personal writings mix different languages and scripts. Though code-switching is pervasive and precludes any easy assignation of language, French dominates. This is a common feature of the notebooks kept by biliterates, where a strong preference for French is obvious, as I have already mentioned in the case of Somassa.[20] Again, the importance of the radio is notable.

Makan Camara's practice is remarkable for the way he manages time and space. He makes his notes in a strikingly organized manner, considering that the writing spans more than six years. He has 'opened' several pages at the same time, and written down each event on the relevant page, following an order he himself has determined. This order corresponds to the distinction between the three social spaces to which he belongs: the household, the village, a wider public space.

The other point which this case highlights is that the writing of events is often mediated, notably by the radio: not just the distant events of page 4, but also the death of his father which appears in the solemn form of the obituary as sent to the local radio. For one of the village events (the inauguration of the mosque), the presence of a radio reporter from Fana is recorded, as if the importance of the event – locally self-evident – could be enhanced by its recognition as an event for a wider audience.

Family events are recorded in a sober and matter-of-fact manner, which roughly follows the model of the official births register. The fact that personal writing borrows from institutional models is congruent with a forging of the self that follows the lines of the assigned identities, mainly that of a household head (*dutigi*) and a member of the agricultural association. Both the CMDT and the administration direct most of their injunctions to these male individuals, and in a way their domestic writings bring home and extend the written devices deployed by these institutions into their management of their own farms, families, and lives.

Yet, this form of writing is supplemented by records of other events: from the village, and even outside. This testifies that he uses the notebook to sketch out a wider chronical of the different arenas he inscribes himself in. But domestic events constitute the core of this notebook, and give this spatial sense of belonging a local centre.

Being literate in the village: changing patterns of social opportunities

Obviously, this form of writing relies on effective participation in local life, and depends on the status of household head, or at least requires that the writer have some responsibilities in family and farming. As I mentioned earlier, the first literates in the village were often household heads and became involved in the management of the village association. For them, the double dimension of professional use of writing at the village level and domestic use provides a space to display and exercise their skills. Even those who were not in this position gained specific power from being the first literates in their families. They belong to a generation that clearly took advantage of the organizational changes in the CMDT in the mid-1970s and early 1980s. Literacy proved to be a way to gain access to valued forms of mobility, such as when being chosen by the village as a representative for training sessions held by the CMDT in Fana or other locations. Perspectives of return were opened, and these first literates developed strategies which gave value to the experience gained in the cities, as several narratives of migration and successful return and insertion reveal.

Those who became literate in the mid-1980s and early 1990s (the first promotions of villagers who had been to school) had some local opportunities. Some of them gained positions in the village association, taking over from the first literates. With the development of syndicates, NGOs and other forms of civil associations in the 1990s, others got a chance to value their literacy skills in French and Bamanan as local representative of these projects. Since the late 1990s the crisis in cotton production has limited economic possibilities, and the perspective of privatizing the CMDT has accelerated its disinvestment in 'non-productive' activities, such as literacy and post-literacy training. For the younger literates, there are very few opportunities to value these skills in the village, and often their literacy practices are not even used at the family level, as there are older literate family members who are already in charge of domestic writing. Local narratives tend to highlight the successes of those who manage to settle in Fana or Bamako and send money home regularly.

Thus, literacy takes on new meanings in a socioeconomic context where its localizing potential has eroded.

Mobile objects and practices of mobility

Literacy has always been associated with mobility. In the village, early records of migration mention letters sent to and from the village (for instance a villager who went to The Gambia for further Islamic studies in the 1930s was called back home by a letter in Arabic). Letters may be sent in advance to prepare for the departure, and they, along with personal messages, are one of the main vectors of communication between villagers and their relatives established elsewhere.[21]

When focusing on writing in the village, we can identify specific practices associated with mobility, such as recording addresses in notebooks or keeping handwritten travel indications and maps. Indeed, the city is often described as a 'graphic' environment: villagers stress the importance of graphic artefacts, such as signs and numbers, for self-orientation while travelling. Urban life also fosters important changes in the literacy practices, with a development in the use of French (in writing as well as in oral communication), and above all a diversification of literacy uses and commodities.

As mobile objects, notebooks might be taken by the villagers on their journeys, and some of them bear witness to the mobility of the writers and the literacy experiences provided by urban life. This can be seen from the small notebook belonging to Moussa Coulibaly during his stays in Bamako and Ségou. Born in 1977, he completed primary school in the village. After leaving school, he practised seasonal migration for some years. His marriage was not approved of by his family, and he lived for some years in Koutiala with his wife where he worked in a truck-repairing garage. Finally he was called home by his father, and he returned to the village in 2001.

As the youngest son of an important family, he suffers from control by his numerous older brothers. As he is not the first literate in the family, he is not in charge of important family records, though he sometimes contributes; for instance he records the weight of cotton collected individually by family members, so that each member can earn his portion of the cash. He also writes a weekly shopping-list of goods he is asked to buy at the market in Fana for other family members. He writes down the credits taken for the little shop he manages on behalf of one of his brothers. He keeps several notebooks where these notations (credits, family cotton records) are mixed with prayers copied in Arabic, incantations collected from friends, and football results. Since he returned, he has moved several times for a couple of months. On his journeys, he takes two small notebooks with him.

Some notations are directly associated with the migratory process: addresses and phone numbers give a view of his journeys. In this case, as has been pointed out in recent studies, the migratory process diverges from older networks of solidarity (Boesen and Marfaing 2007, 14). Recording phone numbers and addresses is part of a process to prepare for migration, but also functions as a personal *aide-mémoire* for future mobility. In this vein, Moussa also records in a personal way itineraries for shorter journeys to specific places (in a form close to oral forms and reminiscent of classical itineraries in Arabic: 'from this place to this other, and then from this place to this other'). A handwritten copy of his birth certificate also appears, as a replica of the identification papers he also carries with him when travelling.

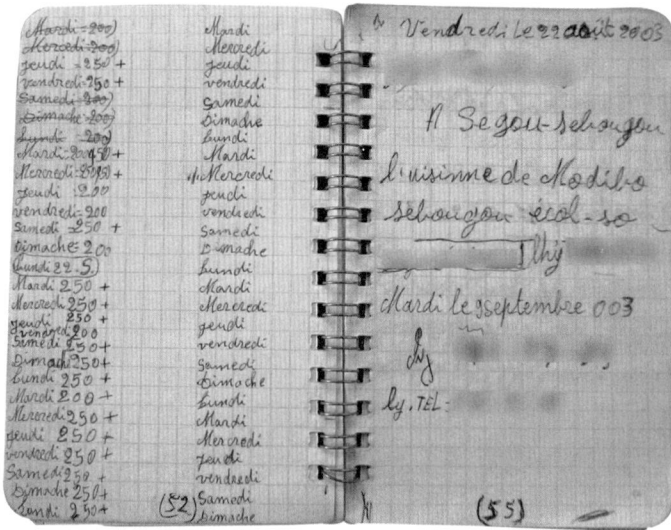

Figure 3: A travel notebook.

But this practice is not only an actual support for geographical mobility; it also serves as a record of the experience of migration. On one page, he records his daily earnings as a manual labourer in Ségou, in a factory (see figure 3). Recording the losses and gains was quoted by other migrants as a way to make sense of the adventure. Other notes give a sense of migration as a much wider cultural experience. During his trip to Ségou, he also wrote down the titles of songs he wanted to put together on a cassette, a radio show on child education that he particularly appreciated and other souvenirs.

Conclusion

A set of local literacy practices has emerged since the 1970s in the CMDT region. At the outset, these personal and domestic practices, as well as the status of being literate, were distinctive. They provided opportunities for the first generations of literates to gain positions of power and authority at the village level. For some, they enhanced specific and valued forms of mobility. They provided opportunities for return for migrants who valued both their skills and their experience. For the following generations, social opportunities associated with literacy declined. They developed practices that were both more self-oriented and open to arenas wider than the village level and the locally supported network of literacy activities. Their mobility appears to be less controlled by older generations, and perspectives of return more volatile. In this context, the same array of literacy practices is developed to support individual trajectories involving migration and to enhance possible insertions into wider arenas.

Keeping a personal notebook, considered as a practice of the self, provides a view on a variety of attitudes to locality and mobility. The logic of extraversion appears to be only one of the dimensions of processes of cultural translation that can also be directed to better insertion in changing local economies of knowledge. If the practice cannot as such be identified as something that triggers migration, when the project emerges, notebooks and booklets may become a space where the aspirations take form, provide actual support to mobility, and even offer a record of this experience.

Table 1   Past migrations (Residents over 15)

Migration and destination		%
None	163	26
Bamako	193	31
Other locations, Mali	219	35
Outside Mali	156	25

Surveyed: 631 / No reply= 47 / Respondents: 584 / Answers: 731
Percentages are calculated on the basis of surveyed population.

Table 2   Variation of destinations over the time (Residents over 15)

% Lines

Migrations / Age (years)	None	Bamako	Other locations, Mali	Outside Mali	Total
15-19	*38*	49	*12*		100
20-29	17	44	32	*7*	100
30-39	*19*	28	30	23	100
40-49	24	*9*	32	34	100
50-59	*23*	*11*	32	34	100
60-69	*26*	*13*	32	29	100
70 et plus	*17*	*11*	*36*	*36*	100
Total	22	26	30	21	100

Italics indicate that the statistics rests on number inferior to 30.

References

Appadurai, Arjun. 1996. *Modernity at large: Cultural dimensions of globalization*. Minneapolis: University of Minnesota Press.

Barber, Karin, ed. 2006. *Africa's Hidden Histories: Everyday Literacy and Making the Self*, Bloomington: Indiana University Press.

Bayart, Jean-François. 2000. Africa in the world: A history of extraversion. *African Affairs* 99 (395): 217-267.

Baller, Susann and Saavedra, Martha. 2010. *La politique du football en Afrique: mobilisations et trajectoires*, special issue of *Politique Africaine*, n° 118.

Boesen, Elisabeth and Laurence Marfaing. 2007. *Les nouveaux urbains dans l'espace Sahara-Sahel. Un cosmopolitisme par le bas*. Paris: Karthala, Berlin : ZMO.

Charpy, Manuel and Hassane Souley. 2004. *Lettres d'émigrés. Africains d'ici et d'ailleurs, 1960-1995*. Paris: Nicolas Philippe.

De Bruijn, Mirjam, Rijk Van Dijk and Dick Foeken, eds. 2001. *Mobile Africa: Changing patterns of movement in Africa and beyond*. Leiden: Brill.

Dombrowsky, Klaudia, Dumestre Gérard and Simonis Francis. 1993. *L'alphabétisation fonctionnelle en bambara dans une dynamique de développement. Le cas de la zone cotonnière (Mali-Sud)*. Paris: diffusion Didier Erudition.

Fouquet, Thomas. 2007. De la prostitution clandestine aux désirs de l'Ailleurs: une « ethnographie de l'extraversion » à Dakar. *Politique africaine* 107 (octobre 2007): 102-123.

Fouquet, Thomas. 2008. Migrations et «glocalisation» dakaroises. In *Le Sénégal des migrations: Mobilités, identités et sociétés*, dir. Momar-Coumba Diop, 241-273. Paris and Dakar: Karthala, Onu habitat and Crespos.

Hawkins, Sean. 2002 *Writing and colonialism in northern Ghana: The encounter between the LoDagaa and "The world on paper", 1892-1991*. Toronto: University of Toronto Press.

Hoggart, Richard. 1957. *The Uses of literacy, aspects of working-class life with special reference to publications and entertainments*. London: Chatto & Windus.

Lambert, Michael. 2007. Politics, Patriarchy, and New Tradition: Understanding Female Migration among the Jola (Senegal, West Africa). In *Cultures of Migration: African Perspectives*, ed. Hans Peter Hahn and Georg Klute, 129-148. Berlin: Lit Verlag.

Lesclingand, Marie. 2004. Nouvelles stratégies migratoires des jeunes femmes rurales au Mali: de la valorisation individuelle à une reconnaissance sociale. *Sociétés Contemporaines* 55: 21-42.

Manchuelle, François. 1997. *Willing migrants: Soninke labor diasporas, 1848-1960*. Athens, Ohio: Ohio University Press.

Mbembe, Achille. 2002. African Modes of Self-Writing. Transl. Steven Rendall. *Public Culture* 14 (1): 239-273.

Mbodj-Pouye, Aïssatou and Cécile Van den Avenne. 2007. «C'est bambara et français mélangés». Analyser des écrits plurilingues à partir du cas de cahiers villageois recueillis au Mali. *Langage et société* 120 (juin 2007): 99-127.

Mbodj-Pouye, Aïssatou. 2008. Pages choisies. Ethnographie du cahier d'un agriculteur malien. *Sociologie et sociétés* Vol. 40 (n° 2, numéro thématique « L'archive personnelle des enquêtés, une source sociologique? »): 96-108.

Mbodj-Pouye, Aïssatou. 2009. Tenir un cahier dans la région cotonnière du Mali. Support d'écriture et rapport à soi. *Annales. Histoire, Sciences Sociales* 64ᵉ année (juillet-août, n° 4): 855-885.

Mbodj-Pouye, Aïssatou. Forthcoming. *Le fil de l'écrit. Anthropologie de l'alphabétisation dans la région cotonnière du Mali.* Lyon: ENS-Editions.

McNaughton, Patrick R. 1988. *The Mande Blacksmiths: Knowledge, Power and Art in West Africa.* Bloomington: Indiana University Press.

Schmitz, Jean and Marie-Eve Humery. 2008. La vallée du Sénégal entre (co)développement et transnationalisme. Irrigation, alphabétisation et migration ou les illusions perdues. *Politique africaine* 109: 56-72.

Schulz, Dorothea. 2000. Communities of Sentiment. Local Radio Stations and the Emergence of New Spheres of Public Communication in Mali. In *Neue Medien und Öffentlichkeiten. Politik und Tele-Kommunikation in Asien, Afrika, und Lateinamerika, (vol. 2)*, ed. Stefan Brüne, 36-62. Hamburg: Deutsches Übersee-Institut.

Schulz, Dorothea. 2002. The world is made by talk: Female youth culture, pop music consumption, and mass-mediated forms of sociality in urban Mali. *Cahiers d'études africaines* 168 (42): 797-829.

Scribner, Sylvia and Michael Cole. 1981. *The Psychology of Literacy.* Cambridge, Massachusetts: Harvard University Press.

Vigh, Henrik. 2009. Wayward migration: On imagined futures and technological voids, *Ethnos* 74: 91-109.

Notes

1　I wish to thank Thomas Fouquet for his careful reading of a previous version of this chapter.

2　Understandably, the fact that Mali organized the Africa Cup of Nations (Coupe d'Afrique des Nations) in 2002 was recorded more widely, even by senior writers, as a national event.

3　Names and private information (such as telephone numbers) have been blurred on the photographs, and pseudonyms are used throughout this chapter.

4　Local radios are at the centre of a wide array of practices, such as direct intervention through letter-writing or live phone-calls, song-requests, recording music or radio broadcasts. See

Schulz 2000 for an overview of local radios and their audiences, and on female youth culture Schulz 2002.

5 Of course, this knowledge is itself characterized by forms of mobility of great extension. Secrets are very often gained through migration or from foreigners (see the description by McNaughton of the way the magical and medicinal lore of blacksmiths is acquired, 1988). My use of the term 'local' refers here to the fact that this knowledge is given a local character by the writers, who refer to it is as 'Bamanan'.

6 I pursue this analysis of the transformation of Islamic knowledge in relation to print culture and writing practices in an on-going collaboration with Francesco Zappa.

7 The results of these classes are controversial: see Dombrowsky, Dumestre and Simonis 1993 for a critical evaluation around Koutiala, a Minyanka-speaking region where literacy in Bamanan poses specific linguistic difficulties. I conducted my research in the Northern part of the CMDT region in a Bamanan-speaking village.

8 Written culture in Africa is an emergent field of interest for historians and anthropologists. For a study of the imposition of writing under colonial rule in Ghana see Hawkins 2002. Writing, even imposed, has at once been subjected to cultural dynamics of appropriation (Barber 2006).

9 Though French remains the only official language of Mali, several 'national languages' (currently 13) have been acknowledged as useful for literacy classes, schooling and uses in the media. However the bilingual school, especially at its beginning, was strongly oriented towards the acquisition of French.

10 This broad panorama can be narrowed down with the use of statistical data collected through a survey that I conducted in every household of the village. The literacy rate obtained coincides with the national figure at the time: 19% of the adult residents can read and write a letter, in any language (9% of the women, and 30% of the men). The language distribution runs as follows: 18% of the adults state they can read and write a letter in Bamanan, 9% in French, and less than 1% (4 people) in Arabic.

11 I rely on interviews, notably with the former students of literacy classes in the village as well as with the first pupils to graduate from the bilingual school. For this last group, I conducted interviews in Fana and Bamako with those settled there. I rely also on observations and on a corpus of 301 photographs of pages of notebooks kept by 23 writers in the village. Though letter-writing is almost always the first use of literacy mentioned by villagers, I have been able to collect or observe very few letters, in comparison to other personal writings.

12 In the survey, I defined 'migration' quite loosely as having spent at least one month outside the village – *contra* for instance 'spending at least 3 months out of the village' in a much more detailed and large survey quoted above (Lesclingand 2004). The detailed answers regarding the length of stay show that, for all destinations, most of the stays are over one year.

13 Though I do not know the individual stories of these two men, it is tempting to see in this new development a consequence of the pauperization of the area, due to the crisis in the cotton market and the disorganization of the CMDT. It seems that the region will no longer be exempt from the phenomenon of international migration.

14 The high percentage of youths who have not moved is due to the fact that youths who have migrated are not covered by the sample; the population considered here is the resident population, and students or economic migrant are already out of the village but not yet back, and do not appear in these figures. In other words, these figures capture past migrations, so they make sense for those who have moved and returned to the village.

15 A full outline of the local history of migration is beyond the scope of this chapter. The elements provided here are drawn from interviews and informal discussions.

16 The first woman to have been in Bamako by herself as an unmarried woman was born in 1967, so feminine migration to Bamako can be dated back to the beginning of the 1980s. For an analysis of the negotiations around female migration and the way it becomes integral to local culture (in a context where it developed much earlier) see the contribution by Michael Lambert on the Jola (Lambert 2007).

17 Very few are already heads of households (*dutigiw*) themselves. One of them, who left his uncle's household, alternates periods of several years in the village and periods of the same length in neighbouring cities (Ségou, Koutiala). His case is quite exceptional though – he has withdrawn his farm from the village association of cotton-producers, and grows only food-producing crops. Migration, especially when it exceeds the dry-season, is incompatible with being the head of a farm.

18 I rely on the elaboration by Appadurai on the concept of locality as 'a complex phenomenological quality' which is 'primarily relational and contextual rather than ... scalar or spatial' (Appadurai 1996, 178). He contrasts it with the term 'neighborhood' which refers to 'the actually existing social forms in which locality, as a dimension or value, is variably realized' (Appadurai 1996, 179). I follow his line of argument here, as far as production of locality is defined as a historically-determined process that the nation-state attempted to shape to its advantage by developing its own disciplinary modes of localization (Appadurai 1996, 189-191).

19 A full-length transcription and a more detailed analysis of this notebook appear in (Mbodj-Pouye 2008).

20 A sociolinguistic analysis of the writings helps to unfold this apparent paradox: see (Mbodj-Pouye and Van den Avenne 2007).

21 During my fieldwork there were no phones in the village. When I returned in 2007 and 2009, mobile phone coverage had extended to the village, so the communication practices described here have changed drastically.

Engaging the world
on the Alexandria waterfront

Samuli Schielke

An intersection of possibilities

Mukhtar Shehata, a frustrated and underpaid teacher in an informal area in the east of Alexandria, lives just a block inland from the Abu Qir suburban train line which divides the up-market seaside from the 'popular' (*sha'bi*) inland of the city. Unlike in Cairo where upmarket districts are increasingly physically apart from the rest of the city, many of Alexandria's upmarket districts are in everybody's reach due to the double role of the seafront Corniche Road as a main area for middle class outings (the true elites are drawn to the more exclusive resorts east and west of the city) and as the city's main thoroughfare. Mukhtar and his family live just half a kilometre from the Corniche, and he often jokingly explains that he lives 'next to the Sheraton'. There are a few sites accessible to him and his family, such as the Fathallah super-market which offers a sense of global consumerism at very competitive prices. But in general, his very modest lower middle class standard of living is precarious at best, and the other side of the railway line is his for walking and window-shopping only (see Abaza 2006, 258). And like for so many other people in Alexandria, walking along the waterfront and dreaming is one of his favourite pastimes.

> When I sit on the seafront, it depends on my mood which way I look. When I'm in an optimistic mood I look away from the sea towards the high-rise buildings and think about the life of the people who live in them. When I'm depressed I look at the sea and think about the other side. And

> I imagine that on the other side there is someone who, miserable and depressed just like me, looks across the sea and dreams of the other side.

On the waterfront in Alexandria different promises of the good life come closer together than anywhere else in Egypt. One is the wealth and comfort of affluent Egyptians who spend weekends and vacations in holiday apartments overlooking the sea in Alexandria. Another is travel across the sea as a migrant worker, a prospect of which the Mediterranean Sea is a constant reminder. In January and February 2011, a third one quite suddenly entered the scene, as the Corniche Road became the site of huge demonstrations demanding the removal of president Hosni Mubarak and the system of corruption and oppression associated with him. During those short and intense days, Mukhtar, his wife, and their two children were among the hundreds of thousands of demonstrators who turned the waterfront of Alexandria into one of the key sites of Egypt's peaceful revolution, a political space of better future.

As an intersection of aspirations and possible paths of action, the Alexandrian waterfront offers a starting point for linking issues of movement and diaspora with the issue of aspiration for a good life at home, embedded in a vision of a wider world. In this chapter I look at the expectations, the constraints, and the possible dynamics involved in the state of 'dreaming of the other side', to borrow Mukhtar's words. My enquiry is devoted to an attempt to make sense of where and what that other side stands for, and what dreaming about it can do to one. But first, a few words about the notion of dreaming are necessary. If in this chapter I often use 'dreams' and 'aspirations' almost synonymously, it is because in doing so I am orienting on colloquial Egyptian usage of the word *hilm* 'dream'. To have a dream is to have guiding, driving ideas, something to pursue. Dreams in this sense of something to pursue raise the question of their realization. Unlike nighttime dreams, or even daydreaming, such aspirational dreams can be more or less realistic. However, there is a peculiar logic of imagination and action that greatly complicates the relationship between dreams and reality. Whether a dream can be acted out is one thing. What is actually accomplished through the act of pursuing a dream can be quite different (cf. Jackson 1996, 34).

The ideas I present in this chapter are strongly indebted to my shared work with Daniela Swarowsky on her documentary film project *Messages from Paradise*, the first part of which we shot in Egypt and with Egyptians in Austria (Swarowsky and Schielke 2009), and with Mukhtar Shehata who was my host in Alexandria and together with whom I have developed many ideas. Inspired to such a high degree by shared work and thinking, this chapter is to an important degree also theirs.

The people who appear in this chapter all hail from one village in the Nile Delta. Most of them live in Alexandria. Some of their paths are very conventional, while others, notably Mukhtar's and Tawfiq's literary engagements, are less so. While their particular trajectories may not be representative in quantitative terms, the conditions with which they struggle are shared by a very large proportion of men in Egypt. Furthermore, I argue that precisely this tension between conventional paths and unlikely detours is instrumental to teasing out the two powers of imagination involved in the gaze towards the other side.

Cosmopolitanism as a longing

The gaze towards the other side includes at once a vision of there being a world made up of different, interconnected parts, and the recognition that the relationship between these parts is marked by inequality and exclusion. Grounded as it is in an imagined world of possibilities and promises, the gaze towards the other side is a case in point of the social practice of imagination (Appadurai 1996) that shapes the scope of possible actions and trajectories. And in today's Egypt possible actions and trajectories are saturated by globally marketed and mediated commodities, promises of middle class prosperity and the good life, and various kinds of travelling theories. They are all over the place, in new houses built with migrant money, in furniture oriented at European models (even if they are impractical for Egyptian ways of living), in youth fashion oriented towards global tastes, in the spread of Salafi-inspired religiosity, in the fan culture around Lebanese singers, Egyptian and Hollywood movie stars and European football players, in the Turkish television series, Saudi Arabian sermons and Egyptian and American films through which people narrate their lives. And yet Egypt has not become like Italy, Saudi Arabia, the United States, or Turkey. Rather than a direct emulation of these goods and ideas, what appears to be going on is attempts by people to transform their own world to make it seem valuable in the face of these powers and promises (see Weiss 2009, 36).

There is a growing tendency in contemporary anthropology to study this condition as a cosmopolitan one in order to account for the fact that not only the wealthy and intellectual, but also people of very modest means, live lives that exceed the limits of what earlier generations of anthropologists called indigenous, traditional, or local. They aspire to make global modernity their own, without becoming homogenized or fully connected in the sense evoked by globalization (see Rouch 1958; Larkin 1997; Piot 1999; Behrend 2002; Weiss 2009; de Koning 2009; Elsayed 2010;

Gable 2010). Cosmopolitanism, in this sense, is about versatility in and belonging to 'the world', of 'ways of living at home abroad or abroad at home – ways of inhabiting multiple places at once, of being different beings simultaneously, of seeing the larger picture stereoscopically with the smaller' (Pollock et al. 2002, 11). As such, cosmopolitanism is a modality of both action and imagination. It is not only about life trajectories that exceed borders, but also expectations that exceed borders.

'Cosmopolitanism' has a flavour of being a privilege of the global elites. But when looked at from the point of view of the practice of 'open-ended subjectivities' (Marsden 2007; 2008, 215), cosmopolitanism is not the privilege of any particular class or place in the world, nor is it detached from particularistic local identities and hierarchies. The world evoked by cosmopolitanism in this sense is not a world without borders, but a world full of borders, inhabited by people who try to cross them.

There is good reason, then, to think of Mukhtar's stroll along the waterfront of Alexandria as a cosmopolitan one. With its intersection of different milieus of a stratified class society, and with the Mediterranean Sea reminding one of the presence of the overseas beyond the horizon, the Corniche is a cosmopolitan site par excellence. Crucially, Mukhtar also describes the experience of walking along the waterfront as one that often comes along with depression and frustration. The longing for a world of material comfort and money and a life of dignity and freedom (I come back to the details of this a little later) is an unfulfilled one in most cases, and even moments of modest material success are usually relativized by the undiminished sense of pressure that comes along with the race for material improvement. A world of fantastic promises is also a world of deep disappointments.

Sites of possibility

But what possibilities are we talking about? What kind of place is the world which the young men of provincial backgrounds and middle class aspirations aim for? And what are the promises they hope to fulfil by migration and its primary aim, social advancement? Like Mukhtar's different visions at the Corniche, the different moments and sites of aspiration together make up a bigger picture of the world of possibilities. To pursue these different moments, I move my focus for a while away from the Corniche, to Mukhtar's native village Nazlat al-Rayyis, some 80 kilometres from Alexandria, where since 2006 I have spent much time discussing the prospects of social advancement, political change, and labour migration with young men (and fewer women). In Nazlat al-Rayyis, as in much of Egypt, the years before 2011 were a time in which sustained economic growth made the cities' streets fill with private cars, and new red brick buildings of up to six floors transformed the appearance of villages. But it was also a time when almost everybody would bitterly complain about increasing economic pressure, corruption and nepotism, and deepening social divisions. During this time, three sites rose above others when people imagined and discussed the world and the possibilities it offered.

The first of these sites is the wealthy strata of class society in Egypt, the imagined and actual lifestyles of the Egyptian upper and upper-middle classes which are omnipresent in advertisement, cinema, television, popular culture, and the notions of wealth and happiness evoked in them. This is a fancy world, but the actual dreams of the good life it inspires are not extravagant. The stereotypical dream of a comfortable life that people I know express consists of marriage, children, a reasonably large and well-equipped house, and a private car – a decidedly middle-class fantasy. One of the particular features of contemporary consumer-oriented capitalism is that while it produces striking inequalities, the social utopia of the good life it offers is that of the middle class, 'middle' evoking a sense of being at the centre of society as one of the good, decent people Schielke (2012). What is important about this dream beyond its resonance with a worldwide capitalist sensibility is that, even in a time of an omnipresent pressure to migrate, it is primarily located in Egypt. The most important kind of social movement that people with such modest middle class aspirations expect is a movement upwards (or perhaps from the margins towards the middle), towards the lifestyle and standard of living of affluent Egyptians.

And yet precisely this movement appears also to be the most difficult of all. A major heritage of Arab socialism, the system of state education and public sector jobs continues to be the main hope for people of lower middle class background or aspiration. At the same time, however, all possible paths of advancement to the more privileged positions in the public sector have become regulated by *wasta*, networks of nepotist and clientelist dependency. Without *wasta*, one has no hope of entering anything except the lowest jobs in the public sector. In the private sector the situation is slightly less dominated by *wasta*, but more by the educational capital of having attended the right schools. People with government school degrees have little or no hope of entering good private sector careers. It was in this situation, where people's main aim was to build a comfortable middle class life in Egypt but where the means of reaching that aim were increasingly socially exclusive, that migration came to appear to be *the* solution over all others.

When people think about migration abroad, they think essentially about two sites: the West (that is, Europe and Northern America) and the Arab Gulf States.

Both sites are associated with complex expectations, promises, and perils. The Gulf is perhaps the most common site of migration for Egyptians. It has always been and continues to be more accessible for Egyptians to migrate to, although the highly exploitative contracts of labour agents also significantly diminish the profits of migrants. The Gulf is a site associated with highly contradictory sentiments. It is an Arab and Muslim place, and this gives it an aura of proximity and familiarity. Saudi Arabia in particular, with its privileged position as the country of the holy places of Islam and a globally successful centre of the Salafi current of Islam, enjoys a bright aura of Islam. This is clearly reflected in the way women's migration is primarily directed to the Gulf States, which are considered more appropriate for women than the culturally more different and morally more liberal, or decadent, western countries. But the positive aspects of the Gulf as a familiar Muslim Arab place are countered by a very negative image of the Gulf as an uncivilized place of arrogant, immoral hypocrites, ruthless exploitation of workers, and therefore also perilous to women. If most Egyptians see Europeans and Americans as irresponsibly materialistic and individualistic, their view of the Gulf Arabs is hardly better – rather worse. This negative stereotype is partly due to historical competition about who represents the cultural centre of modernity in the Arab world. More immediately, perhaps, it is due to the actual experiences of Egyptian migrant workers who often face extreme exploitation and humiliation, further aggravated because of the cultural familiarity and shared religion that would make one expect better treatment.

Europe and Northern America, in turn, stand for a different, equally complex and contradictory set of promises and concerns. While perhaps less accessible than those of the Gulf, the promises of America and Europe are in many ways even more attractive for and present in the lives of Egyptians. The increasing sense of nationalist and religious confrontation and paranoia that marked the first decade of the 21st century has not for a moment diminished the aura of a western (that is, mainly American) way of life. The same people who hold militantly nationalist, anti-American, anti-Jewish, and Islamist views of world politics are also enthusiastic consumers of Hollywood fiction, global brands of consumer goods, and European football. They identify with the global fan community of Real Madrid, refer to Hollywood plots to make sense of their own lives, argue that the world is driven to ruin by an American-Zionist conspiracy, express solidarity with the global community of Muslims, and look up to the Western industrial nations as examples of social and political progress.

It is in the nature of hegemony that certain powers and places cannot be ignored, whether one likes it or not. As an Egyptian from the provinces, it is very difficult to think about social mobility without reckoning with the wealth and possibilities of Cairo. And as an Egyptian from anywhere, it is very difficult to think about a better life without reckoning with the Gulf, Europe, and the United States. The very power of these sites to determine possible paths of progress makes the ways people engage them necessarily differentiated and complex. More fruitful than looking for moments of rejection or affirmation is therefore to look at some of the specific desires and concerns which people express when they think about their prospects in relation to places like 'Cairo', 'The West', and 'the Gulf'. In what follows I take up two issues which are closely related to the issue of migration, and which, simple as they seem, evoke quite complex frameworks of aspiration for good life: money and freedom.

Money and freedom

In December 2009, I showed the documentary film *Messages from Paradise #1* to a family I had befriended in Nazlat al-Rayyis. The family had just invested its modest but well-managed savings in building a house in an informal area on the outskirts of Alexandria. The widowed mother of the three sons hoped that her youngest son would be able to make a career as a doctor in Egypt, but the older two, Mustafa and Salah, she encouraged to think about migration. Both Salah and Mustafa were in fact seriously thinking about it at the time, albeit in somewhat different ways from their mother. Watching the film, which begins in Egypt and then moves to show the stories of Egyptian migrants in Vienna, one scene in particular caught their attention. In that scene Magdi, a former boxer and now civil servant in Vienna, declares that his entire life is now in Vienna and that he does not want to return to Egypt except on holiday. He even wants to be buried in Austria (most Egyptian migrants, even if they never return, hope to be buried at 'home'). Their mother expressed her discontent with the idea, and saw it as a kind of failure, even betrayal of the proper meaning of migration, which in her view would be to go abroad with a clear plan, achieve it, and return. Salah contradicted her: "No, he's right." His view of migration, too, was about making money to build a life, but he also looked forward to the idea of building a life in Europe.

After seeing the film, the three brothers, two other friends and I went to a café in the village, where we continued to discuss motivations and plans to migrate in more detail. In the course of the discussion, they developed money and freedom as the two essential motivations to migrate – not exclusive, but complementary. Those who just want money, they argued, are more likely to go to the Gulf States which are more accessible but also less attractive to live in. In any case, they said, the plan of the Gulf-bound is always clear and simple: go abroad and collect money to 'build a life' at home. Those, on the other hand, they argued, who also want freedom are more likely to want to go to Europe or, even better, America where they can live a life free of the constraints and oppression they experience in Egypt.

The way these young men, and like them many others, used 'money' and 'freedom' as evident shorthand terms for entire sets of aspirations and subjectivity makes it necessary to take a closer look at these two notions.

'Money', to start with, is not just about getting money. It is very strongly associated with quite specific things money is needed for, commonly expressed by the phrase 'building a life'. For a man, to build a life implies all the conventional responsibilities and assets that make a respectable man: marriage, an apartment or a house (a necessary precondition for marriage), and a comfortable standard of living (the most important marker of which at the moment is a private car). All this, in the imaginary evoked by 'money', is to take place in or near one's place of origin, be it in a new floor over one's parental house, a new house in the fields outside the village, or an apartment in a nearby city. 'Money' thus evokes a sense of establishing oneself as a respected and wealthy man in the already existing web of family relations, moving upwards while remaining connected, which significantly involves also being willing to provide financial assistance to less well-off relatives.

While there is some money to be earned even for the poor in Egypt, it is hardly ever enough to qualify as 'money' in this sense of sufficient resources for social advancement. Yet at the same time, money is absolutely indispensable in an informally privatized economy of a public sector where *wasta* and bribes are the only paths to good jobs. It is in this situation where, in order to move upwards, one *first* needs to have money that migration appears as *the* path over all others to a middle class existence.

'Freedom', in turn, is not quite what Europeans often assume it to imply for people from the Middle East. While the Western popular political imagination associates freedom with an individualistic sense of a freedom of choice – of lifestyle, of partner, of sexual orientation, etc., freedom is used by young Egyptians as a more complex notion and less exclusively centred on choice. Choice certainly is an issue, notably so in regard to sexual freedom, an issue that at once greatly animates the fantasy of young men but also appears as something dangerous, especially with regard to women (in the sense both that men's sexual freedom can endanger women, and that women's sexual freedom is seen as dangerous). But while freedom of choice is an ambiguous issue, another sense of freedom is almost unanimously phrased as positive: having rights.

Salah's brother Mustafa argued on another occasion that migration to Europe is, of course, about money, but also about enjoying a degree of freedom and rights. When I commented that it is no fun to be an Arab Muslim in Europe at the moment, he replied, "Even if the law discriminates against me as a Muslim and an Arab, I will know where the law stands and where I stand." A similar idea was put forward by Tawfiq, a young man who was pursuing several plans to migrate at the same time as we interviewed him for *Messages from Paradise #1* in the autumn of 2007:

> My uncle told me that once a friend of his sent him a letter from America. He wrote: I am in a country where five garbagemen can demonstrate in front of the White House and return to their homes safely. Here it could never happen. Here the judges get beaten up. Imagine what would happen if the garbagemen tried to demonstrate here.

This view of America may appear excessively optimistic in the light of the many civil rights violations that the past decade has witnessed. But in light of the routine and haphazard brutality of the Egyptian state, Tawfiq's appraisal of the garbagemen's demonstration and Mustafa's hyperbolic claim that it is better to be discriminated against by a rule of law than to be subject to a state of lawlessness are telling of a longing for freedom that is about predictable justice and, most fundamentally, human dignity in the face of a brutal and demoralizing social and political reality. And just as the idea of migration for the sake of money is really about living a better life at home, so also the idea of migration for the sake of freedom in the sense of rights is very much about the frustrating injustice, humiliation, and inequality at home.

Eventually, 'freedom' (*hurriya*) and 'dignity' (*karama*) were to become two of the key demands of the 25 January revolution, so evidently interconnected that one could not be thought of without the other. Also in the way developed here by Mustafa and Tawfiq, the demand for freedom is a demand for dignity, directed against one and the same sense of oppression and humiliation. Importantly, Tawfiq in fact came to be one of the revolutionaries of the first hour, joining the very first demonstration in Tahrir Square on 25 January 2011. That event puts the relationship of migration and freedom in a somewhat different light, and I will get back to his story towards the end of this chapter.

The two powers of imagination

So far I have spoken about the world, and being included in it by means of social advancement and migration, as an expectation, a potentiality. But how does this potentiality connect with action? Actually migrating is the most obvious kind of action involved. But there is more to it, and in a way actual migration may be less important and less insightful than other forms of action. Developing my enquiry to a conclusion with this question about dreams as a socially and existentially constructive activity, I want to highlight the question about how to find paths of action in a world of vast possibilities and limited means.

The tragic twist of migration as actual practice is that while it seems to be about widening one's scope of action and imagination, the actual experience of migration may rather narrow down one's horizon of expectation. When one really is there, working in a restaurant in Italy, selling newspapers in Vienna or guarding a bank in Doha, life is utterly monotonous and boring, completely ruled by very few questions: how much money can I save this month? Do I have enough to get engaged on my next holiday?

For Tawfiq, who dreamed of migration for both money and freedom, this was a very disheartening experience. In early 2008, he got a two-year contract as a guard for an international security company in Doha, Qatar. Although the Gulf was not where he really wanted to go, he was hopeful that going there would open up new possibilities for moving ahead. In October 2009 I went to Doha and met him there, living an utterly monotonous life between the bank where he worked and a workers' hostel in the outskirts of the city. He was very disillusioned about his situation which, he said, brought him some useful experience, but a lot less money than he had hoped, and a life under conditions of virtual slavery. Back in 2007 when I had asked him whether he would return if he could leave Egypt he had replied, "If you were released from prison, would you want to return?" In Doha, I asked him what he thought about it now.

> It turned out to be a bigger prison. The problem is how to know the borders of your prison. It's a prison of many walls. After crossing one wall you find another wall. It's like you're in the beginning in the innermost circle, and when you jump the wall you find yourself only in the next circle of the prison. You have to know where the borders of your prison are so that you know how to jump all the way over the outermost wall. But how to know which wall is the outermost? That's the problem.

Tawfiq's reply is a philosophical reflection about the condition of people who try to cross borders in a world full of borders (and there never may be that outermost wall). The problem he has with migration is that it has not offered him any practical means of pursuing different trajectories of life. On the contrary, the centrality of money – salary, cost of living, savings, remittances, presents – in the everyday life of migrant workers means that 'money', in the sense of the conventional things money must buy, simply becomes more powerful. And the biggest problem is that the little money which the migrant workers do earn is usually much less than they hoped for, and rather than return home with a fortune to 'build a life' they more often than not end up living in a more or less permanent state of migrancy to sustain that life.

The trouble with migration as actual practice, then, is even bigger than the lack of freedom outlined by Tawfiq. Even if one were only and exclusively after 'money', the problem is that migration troubles, even breaks, precisely that sense of connectedness so central to the social imaginary of the things money must buy. Migrants end up living far from their families, and instead of helping to live out a conservative social ideal, their economical profit often comes at the cost of personal tragedy.

This is the first of the two powers of imagination: the power of dreams that are so compelling that they become almost inescapable. In this regard, the expectation of migration is an imaginative, world-making practice of the tragic kind, because the imaginaries of the proper social roles of the migrant and the dynamics of migrant labour compel people to pursue dreams that greatly limit their capacity to dream. Because it can be acted out, and because there is some real money to be earned abroad, actual migration is a realistic dream. But what it accomplishes is often a troubling limbo; precisely those good things in life one really wanted to build with the money from abroad keep eluding one.

Tawfiq returned from Qatar exactly two years after his departure, without extending his contract. It was a difficult decision, because by staying he could have saved at least some money, while back at home his meagre civil servant's salary does not even cover running expenses. Back in Egypt, he told me that reading Paulo Coelho's novel *The Alchemist* in Arabic translation (Coelho 1996 [1988]) several times over during his time in Doha was what gave him the strength to return. *The Alchemist* is a parable of quite explicit symbolism, a story of winding paths to the fulfilment of a dream, and a plea for a life of individual self-realization guided by one's unique, true potential. If reading this novel could be powerful enough to help one to take a step against the compelling stream of migration, then this certainly raises a question about the power of imagination not only to create paths so compelling that other paths become almost impossible, but also to create alternative paths in spite of their apparent impossibility.

If the 'realistic' (in the sense of the socially accepted plan evoked by Salah's mother) dreams of migration often end up limiting one's horizon of fantasy, unrealistic dreams have the advantage that their practical relevance is not bound to their practicability. Mukhtar Shehata whose stroll at the waterfront in Alexandria opened this chapter is one of the most unrealistic dreamers I know in Egypt, and his own experiments in the relationship of dreams and practice offer some important insights into this second power of the imagination.

Now, you are the other side

Mukhtar has often considered migrating, and on two occasions he tried to get a visa to work in the Gulf States, but without success. But for him, migration for money was always secondary to travelling to widen one's horizon, as he explained in an interview for *Messages from Paradise #1* in 2007:

> It wasn't my dream to marry and have children, a house, a family. But it was my dream to go abroad. I didn't want to migrate to change my situation here. I wanted to migrate to find other dreams.

As Tawfiq's account reminds us, migration can be a disappointing way to search for other dreams. Yet Mukhtar, unable to migrate even to the Gulf, turned to fantasy as a means of imaginary travel. In 2007 he started to write a novel, the plot of which he explained to me on one of our strolls along the Corniche. After many difficulties (publishing a book costs money in Egypt), he finally managed to publish it in the spring of 2010. Entitled *No to Alexandria* (Mukhtar Shehata 2010), it is the puzzle-like story of Said (Arabic for 'happy'), a deeply unhappy man who reacts to a personal tragedy by emigrating, a journey that leads him from Egypt through Saudi Arabia and Afghanistan to Germany, with his only true friends being the spies set after him by Arab and Western intelligence agencies. A psychological novel in the guise of a spy story, *No to Alexandria* turns the themes of migration and global politics into a wider engagement with the Other, an issue that is central to Mukhtar's creative work.

Pursuing the theme of the Other, Mukhtar began to write a second novel which, located in Alexandria and the United States, tells the story of the fraught relationship between Christians and Muslims in the city. It is also a story of the city and the class boundaries that divide it, and the Abu Qir railway plays a major role in it. In Summer 2009, discussing my research about migration and his ideas about the railway and the Other, we decided to produce together an experimental short film about the topic(s).

The film, entitled *The Other Side* (Shehata and Schielke 2010), in nine minutes tells the absurd story of a man of extremist looks (played by Mukhtar himself) who at first seems to plan a suicide attack on the Abu Qir railway, but then turns out to pursue quite different objectives that appear to be related to an unhappy love story across class boundaries. Finally the hero finds himself on the waterfront, expressing the very thoughts about seafront that I cited at the beginning of this chapter. And in the film there *is* indeed another across the sea, longing for the other side just like the hero. The film ends with a leap by both the hero and his other towards the sea, leaving it open whether that boundary can be overcome or not.

Both the novel and the film develop the issue of migration through themes of unfulfilled search and the engagement with the Other. Both works look at situations in which migration appears as the only possible choice after other choices have become impossible in the eyes of the characters. These works leave their protagonists in a state of never arriving, always about to take yet another step forward. This makes hope and loss into an intimate pair, with the characters repeatedly finding themselves in situations where they desperately hold on to the dreams that once motivated them, but now those dreams are there to overcome their experience of exile. In this moment, the dream itself becomes the homeland they long for.[1]

Mukhtar's work, which also crosses over the boundaries that usually differentiate between the anthropologists and their interlocutors, is interesting in several respects. First, it is interesting because of what it has to say. At another level, it is interesting because of what the actual practice of writing and publishing a novel and producing a short film has accomplished. For one thing, it offered Mukhtar the chance to visit Germany and Mali as an author and filmmaker to present his vision. In this regard, his collaboration with me has been instrumental. But of course most people who enter the path of creative practice do not collaborate with anthropologists, and there is a reason why Mukhtar's literary and cinematic work is relevant beyond our encounter, and also beyond his arguably idiosyncratic personal trajectory.

Mukhtar's novel, as well as the colloquial poetry he is publishing on the Internet, is part of a new wave of writing that emerged in Egypt in the first decade of the 21st century. After a long period of stagnating readership of literature, the past decade has witnessed the rise of new, accessible styles of novels (see, e.g., al-Aswany 2002; al-Ayidi 2003) and colloquial poetry (Salama 2007; al-Jakh 2010; Sa'id Shehata

2010), and an entirely new genre of sarcastic observations about daily life (e.g. Fadl 2005; al-Khamisi 2006; Ez El-Din 2010.). These forms of writing, which are often published online before (if at all) they appear in print, share a stylistic proximity to colloquial Arabic, distribution beyond and past established literary circles, and a strong focus on critical social commentary. In the years before 2011 when politics was a dangerous, frustrating and unfruitful terrain, this social commentary developed into an important channel of critical political imagination.[2] And eventually writers and readers of this wave turned out to be among the most enthusiastic revolutionaries in the spring of 2011. In a way, engagement with literature did to a certain section of young Egyptians what reading Coelho did to Tawfiq: it opened up unlikely paths of action in spite of the odds.

Of course this is not to say that becoming writers would be the solution to the problems of frustrated young men and women in Egypt. Writing is a distinctive practice in its own way, requiring as it does education, support, and a degree of obsession. In any case it is almost never a way to make money. And the biggest problems in the lives of young Egyptians are economic in one way or another. And yet the rare occurrence of a revolution – even a politically unsuccessful one – makes visible in a dramatic way what the imaginative search for alternative paths usually accomplishes in undramatic, less visible ways. One's horizon of expectation and action is determined not only by the landscape of structures, powers, and promises one looks at, but also by one's way of looking at it. What the practice of imagination can accomplish under favourable conditions is a change in the way the world appears to one, and thus a change in one's possible paths of action. The power of flights of fantasy lies in their ability to give birth to new dreams (see Masquelier 2009).

It remains a difficult and uncertain path. Some new paths have opened up to the people this chapter tells about, but the problems of economy, inequality, borders, and the deep structures of securitarian state power remain unchanged. Tawfiq, back in Egypt from Qatar, turned into a very capable political activist in his village in the months after the revolution. But in May 2011, he nevertheless left for the Gulf again for a new two-year contract. Although this was a time when Egyptians were more hopeful than I had ever seen them before, the pressure to migrate had only grown due to the difficult economic situation after the revolution. But there is a different tone to migration now. Tawfiq's first migration to the Gulf in 2008 was undertaken by a bored young man so completely disillusioned about his society that he intended to leave forever. His second migration is that of a still young man, now extremely politicized and experienced in running a revolutionary movement in his village, but realistic enough to see the need to save some cash to overcome the difficult years and to get married.

Tawfiq's trajectory is telling of the dialectic relationship between the capacity to generate new dreams, on the one hand, and the recognition of the sturdy power of political economy. Just as it would be mistaken to assume that people are simply determined by the conditions to which they are subjected, it would also be illusory to assume that they could simply change those conditions by choosing to think and act otherwise. However, even this is only a partial picture. People do not face abstract conditions. They face other people, material objects and technologies, and these encounters – be they immediate, virtual, or imagined – are the conditions under which we all live. There is thus a third, relational aspect to this relationship of imagination and the material world that takes us back to the moment of gazing at the other side.

In 2011, the relationality of cosmopolitan imagination became very tangible around the Mediterranean. For a rare and exceptional moment, ordinary Egyptians were not compelled to compare themselves with Europe, America, or the Gulf, but occupied the centre stage of history when protest movements in Bahrain, the US, Spain, and France emulated the tactics of peaceful resistance developed in Tunisia and Egypt. Egypt itself became a site of possibility. In this spirit, I was inspired to comment to Mukhtar, "Now, you are the other side." And this is, of course, what the idea of gazing across the sea is all about. The idea that also on the opposite shore there is someone longing for the other side crystallizes the moral implicit in cosmopolitan longing. As Eric Gable (2010) pointed out, it is not only about wanting to be like (or equal to) the wider world, but also about expecting the wider world to be like oneself. This sense of 'moral mutuality' (Gable 2010, 89) is an important part of what a cosmopolitan horizon is about: being able to see one's predicament as one that is shared by others. In this sense, engaging the world on the Alexandria waterfront involves not only a demand for inclusion (Ferguson 2007), but also the more fundamental question about why the world is full of borders, and what could be done about it.

References

Abaza, Mona. 2006. *The Changing Consumer Cultures of Modern Egypt: Cairo's Urban Reshaping.* Cairo: The American University in Cairo Press.

Appadurai, Arjun. 1996. *Modernity at Large: Cultural Dimensions of Globalization.* Minneapolis: University of Minnesota Press.

al-Aswany, Alaa. 2002. *'Imarat Ya'qubiyan*. Cairo: Madbuli.

al-'Ayidi, Ahmad. 2003. *An takun 'Abbas al-'Abd*. Cairo: Merit.

Behrend, Heike. 2002. 'I am like a movie star in my street': Photographic self-creation in post-colonial Kenya. In *Postcolonial Subjectivities in Africa*, ed. Richard Werbner, 44-62. London and New York: Zed Books.

Coelho, Paolo. 1996 [1988]. *Al-Khimiya'i*. Transl. Bahaa Taher. Cairo: Dar al-Hilal.

Elsayed, Heba. 2010. The Unlikely Young Cosmopolitans of Cairo. *Arab Media & Society* 12: http://www.arabmediasociety.com/?article=760. Retrieved 6 June 2011.

Ez El-Din, Amr. 2010. *Khaltabita: Koktel misri sakhir*. Cairo: Dar Layla.

Fadl, Bilal. 2005. *Bani Bagam*. Cairo: Merit.

Ferguson, James. 2007. *Global Shadows. Africa in the Neoliberal World Order*. Durham and London: Duke University Press.

Gable, Eric. 2010. Worldliness in out of the way places. *Cadernos de Estudos Africanos* 18/19: 75-90.

Hirschkind, Charles. 2011. The Road to Tahrir. *The Immanent Frame* 9 February. Online Document: http://blogs.ssrc.org/tif/2011/02/09/the-road-to-tahrir/. Retrieved 27 June 2011.

Jackson, Michael, ed. 1996. *Things as They Are: New Directions in Phenomenological Anthropology*. Bloomington: Indiana University Press.

al-Jakh, Hisham. 2010. *Juha*. Online Video: http://www.youtube.com/watch?v=27jVymklmtU. Retrieved 27 June 2011.

Jurkiewicz, Sarah. 2011. Blogging as counterpublic? The Lebanese and the Egyptian blogosphere in comparison. In *Social Dynamics 2.0: Researching Change in Times of Media Convergence*, ed. Nadja-Christina Schneider and Bettina Gräf, 27-47. Berlin: Frank & Timme.

al-Khamisi, Khalid. 2006. *Taxi*. Cairo: Shorouk.

de Koning, Anouk. 2009. *Global Dreams: Class, Gender and Public Space in Cosmopolitan Cairo*. Cairo: American University in Cairo Press.

Larkin, Brian. 1997. Indian films and Nigerian lovers: Media and the creation of parallel modernities. *Africa* 67 (3): 406-440.

Marsden, Magnus. 2007. Cosmopolitanism on Pakistan's frontier. *ISIM Review* 19: 6-7.

Marsden, Magnus. 2008. Muslim cosmopolitans? Transnational life in northern Pakistan. *The Journal of Asian Studies* 67 (1): 213-247.

Masquelier, Adeline. 2009. Lessons from Rubí: Love, Poverty, and the Educational Value of Televised Dramas in Niger. In *Love in Africa*, ed. Jennifer Cole and Lynn M. Thomas, 204-228. Chicago: University of Chicago Press.

Onodera, Henri. 2009. The Kifaya Generation: Politics of change among youth in Egypt. *Suomen Antropologi: Journal of the Finnish Anthropological Society* 34 (4): 44-64.

Piot, Charles. 1999. *Remotely Global: Village Modernity in West Africa*. Chicago and London: University of Chicago Press.

Pollock, Sheldon. 2002. Cosmopolitan and vernacular in history. In *Cosmopolitanism*, ed. Sheldon Pollock, Homi K. Bhabha, Carol A. Breckenridge, Dipesh Chakrabarty, 15-53. Durham, NC.: Duke University Press.

Rouch, Jean. 1958. *Moi, un noir (Treichville)*. Documentary film. France.

Salama, Ali. 2007. *'Ala bab sifarit Canada*. Online Video: http://www.youtube.com/watch?v=vh8qFVFnfVw. Retrieved 27 June 2011.

Schielke, Samuli. 2012. Living in the Future Tense: Aspiring for World an Class in Provincial Egypt. In *The Global Middle Class: Theorizing through Ethnography*, ed. Carla Freeman, Rachel Heiman and Mark Liechty, 31-56. Santa Fe, NM: School for Advanced Research Press.

Shehata, Mukhtar Saad. 2010. *La li-l-Iskandariya*. Cairo: Arabesque.

Shehata, Mukhtar Saad and Samuli Schielke. 2010. *Al-Nahya al-Tanya* (The Other Side). Short film. Egypt and the Netherlands.

Shehata, Sa'id Sa'd. 2010. *Halimt bih.. wi-nsit: Ash'ar bi al-'ammiya al-misriya*. Cairo: Kitab al-Yawm/al-Qira'a li al-gami'.

Swarowsky, Daniela and Samuli Schielke. 2009. *Messages from Paradise #1: Egypt-Austria: About the permanent longing for elsewhere*. Documentary film. Austria, Egypt and the Netherlands.

Weiss, Brad. 2009. *Street Dreams & Hip Hop Barbershops: Global Fantasy in Urban Tanzania*. Bloomington: Indiana University Press.

Notes

1 This paragraph is a free translation of an Arabic abstract about the novel and the film by Mukhtar Shehata.

2 Blogs and bloggers are the internationally best-known and best studied part of this trend of writing, but the phenomenon is wider, blogs being only one aspect of it. See Onodera 2009; Jurkiewicz 2011; Hirschkind 2011.

Afterword

Michael Jackson

Throughout the 1990s, anthropological studies of migration were largely assimilated to the study of processes of globalization, emphasizing 'transnational social fields' and social networks based on new technologies of international communication, new forms of social mobility, economic opportunity, and fluid or hybrid identities. As Knut Graw and Samuli Schielke note, this perspective reflected the public preoccupations, governmental policies, and media-driven discourse of the receiving countries, and usually left the lived experiences of migrants unexplored. *The Global Horizon* marks the coming of age of a paradigm that Sarah Mahler calls 'transnationalism from below' (Mahler 1998), focused on the personal expectations, moral dilemmas, and changing worldviews of African migrants. The leitmotif is mobility – geographic, social, and existential – and the critical questions concern the forms of subjectivity and intersubjectivity, both fantasized and realized, among young Africans moving in the shadows of the global village, testing the limits of what is possible and endurable, trying out new tactics for crossing entrenched boundaries, and doing things their forefathers could only have dreamed of. To some extent Arjun Appadurai registers this shift from a Euro-American statist discourse to a phenomenology of African modes of being-in-the-world in *Fear of Small Numbers* (2006, ix) where he remarks that his earlier work, *Modernity at Large* (1996), had painted a somewhat too rosy picture of globalization and neglected to explore the violence, exclusion and inequality that characterized the poor and dispossessed who sought to improve their life chances by migrating to the global north. The shift is also noted by James Ferguson, who writes of the need to centre discussions of the global 'less on transnational flows and images of unfettered connection than on the social relations that *selectively* constitute global society' (Ferguson 2006, 23, emphasis added).

Though the present volume was anticipated by the publication of *Hard Work, Hard Times: Global Volatility and African Subjectivities* (Makhulu, Buggenhagen and Jackson, 2010), Knut Graw and Samuli Schielke provide a sophisticated theoretical prolegomenon to a more 'experience-near' anthropology of migration and mobility, together with a set of in-depth empirical explorations of migrant lives and imaginaries that afford new insights into the various motives, tactics, dilemmas, dreams, and disappointments that characterize migration within and out of Africa in the early 21st century. What I find singularly impressive in many of these essays is a sensitivity to the ways in which the quandaries of African migrants are not entirely unique to Africa or to people moving between 'traditional' and 'modern' lifeworlds. While more intensely felt by the young seeking to find a way out of a world of limited opportunity and circumscribed values, these aporias of transition are familiar to us all, whatever our age, gender, ethnicity or social status – namely, the impossibility of calculating what one may lose in leaving a settled life or homeplace and what one may gain by risking oneself in an alien environment, the difficulty of striking a balance between personal fulfillment and the moral claims of kinship, and the struggle to know the difference between what Ernst Bloch called 'concrete' and 'abstract' utopias (the first reasonable and worth pursuing; the second hopelessly unattainable). It interests me that the anthropologist's quest to do justice to these lives in limbo also entails a dilemma, for how can we judge when it is helpful to have recourse to abstract, experience-distant models of transnationality, global processes, collapsed capitalism, failed states, neoliberalism, and postcolonial or post-Cold War policies (to mention only a few of the terms currently deployed), and when it is more edifying to provide experience-near accounts of what Knut Graw calls 'the existential aspects of migration' and the widening, disorienting 'horizons' that take people to the very limit of what can be coped with or comprehended. Because many of the essays in this volume succeed in interweaving these discursive and descriptive modes of writing, and not allowing one to overwhelm the other, it is possible for the reader to decide for himself or herself which perspective gives the greater explanatory yield.

Some of the most compelling passages concern the kinds of strategies – behavioural as well as imaginative – that migrants invent or conjure in negotiating foreign terrains and adverse circumstances. To find oneself stuck, at an impasse, unable to make anything happen, waiting for one's luck to change or something to turn up, defines one of the most dispiriting situations in which a person can find himself or herself. To be immobilized is to be deprived agency, not to be able to make choices or exercise judgement, to be beholden to others or bound by circumstance. Mobility is crucial. To feel that one is on the move and getting somewhere is to possess, if only for a moment, what Bourdieu called illusio – a sense of forthcoming that bolsters one's conviction that one's hard work and suffering will secure a just reward, that one's investments of time and effort will pay off, that freedom is not a pipe dream, that hope is warranted (Bourdieu 2000, 208-213). But all too often one's minimal gains fail to compensate for what one wagered and lost. The life on which one staked everything sometimes turns out to be a life barely worth living (Lucht 2011). A mobile phone puts one instantly in touch with a scattered network of family and friends, but the love and solidarity of a face-to-face community no longer exists. One's small successes in a foreign country do not make up for one's estrangement from one's natal land. Instead of becoming somebody, a person of substance, one may experience oneself as a nobody, one's hands empty, one's morale exhausted. The migrant is often locked in an endless struggle, not only for an income, for food, for a safe haven; he is desperate to be seen as a success in the eyes of the folks back home as well as to gain a sense of legitimacy and normalcy in the face of everyday reminders that he is illegitimate, excluded, unwanted, and outside the law in the country to which he migrated (Agamben 1998, 21). The migrant's struggle for ontological security is a struggle against stigma, against being diminished, degraded or unfairly treated in his everyday dealings with locals, and of having to constantly justify to himself and others the sacrifice he has made in leaving kith and kin for an ostensibly better life abroad. And yet the migrant seldom doubts his *human* right to be given a chance, to vindicate his claim to a share of the bounty of the society he has entered. A logic of sacrifice informs the migrant imagination – the axiom that one must give up in order to gain, empty oneself in order to be filled, place one's hope in another, elsewhere, in order to achieve personal autonomy (Jackson 2011, 70-72). The assumption of common humanity, and an implicit ethic of generalized reciprocity, transcends the worldview that worth is relative to birth. It implies a cosmopolitan sense that one inhabits not so much a world without borders as a world in which one is entitled to cross those borders in quest of a better life (Schielke this volume, Chapter 9), to see it for oneself, whatever the risks and whatever the cost (Alpes this volume, Chapter 2). For many young people in Sierra Leone, their patience with the powers that be, whether traditional chiefs or contemporary politicians, has worn thin. For them, their due is merited by *need* not social status, by their *humanity* not their nationality. And because need is more of a subjective matter than a matter of what is decided for one by others, the question arises for anthropology as to whether we may now speak of a historically unprecedented and radical break from 'traditional' values, centred on the eternal recapitulation of time-honoured ancestral protocols, respect for elders, subsistence economies and stoic values (God's time') or whether what is ostensibly new is simply a variant of archetypal forms, either cultural or human. This argument for rupture finds expression in Charles Piot's recent observation that Africa is now characterized by 'a culture and imaginary of exile' in which everyone is searching for exit strategies that will carry them away to a utopian elsewhere either through geographical migration or occult forms of transport and affective transformation (Piot 2010, 3-4), and in Achille Mbembe's pronouncement that Africa 'is turning inwards on itself in a very serious way' (Mbembe 2001, 68). However, ethnographies of the longue durée and in-depth ethnographic biographies cast doubt on this model of radical discontinuity and call into question the analytical usefulness of antinomies like modernity/tradition, global/local, social/psychological. Classic African ethnographies have documented the tensions and antagonisms between the old and the young, between gerontocratic regimes and local cult associations, and between communal constraints and private yearnings. Migration has always been two-way (as locals depart, 'strangers' arrive), with migrants fantasizing return as well facing the ethical dilemma of how individual gains made in the wider world (the symbolic 'bush') may also serve the social weal. In her penetrating exploration of the trope of seeing among the Kasena of northern Ghana, Ann Cassiman (Chapter 7), shows how an imagery of enlightenment pervades both village rituals of transition, initiation and divination *and* the worldview of the migrant who seeks illumination and transfiguration abroad. The visual metaphor of understanding as seeing is reprised and applied as people explore new possibilities of making their way in the world. But there is continuity here, so that the ritual opening of the granary to a man's first-born son is like the opening of the world to the migrant, who hopes to sustain himself and his kin with the bounty potentially afforded by it. Filip De Boeck (Chapter 3) focuses on what is commonly called occult or libidonal economies to make a similar point. The proliferation of Pentecostal churches, informal economies, and NGOs in contemporary Kinshasa (and by extension, any contemporary African city) might appear to signal a dramatic shift toward new, future-oriented social imaginaries in which a person seeks fame and fortune either through divine intervention, successful migration, or ecstatic experience. But the utopian yearnings, mimetic desire, and magical thinking that find expression in a passion for lotteries, scams and pyramid schemes, fantasies of liaisons with foreigners, membership of churches that promise supernatural abundance, internet searches for exit strategies, and a turn to the intense if transient pleasures of sex, drugs and popular music have antecedents in alliances with djinn, blessings received from ancestors in return for sacrificial offerings and patience, not to mention dalliances, music-making, festivity and the fetishistic value placed on imported commodities and magical medicines (Jackson 2007, 130-131; 2011, 150-157). This is succinctly captured in Samuli Schielke's anecdote of a pecunious Alexandrian teacher who would walk along the waterfront, sometimes turning his eyes to the affluent high-rise buildings and sometimes to the sea, imagining 'that on the other side there is someone who, miserable and depressed just like me, looks across the sea and dreams of the other side.' In January and February 2011, a third dreaming site suddenly emerges, with demonstrations along the Corniche Road for the ouster of Hosni Mubarak and the end of the political corruption that had thwarted so many Egyptians in their search for a better life. Although De Boeck's essay on the social imaginaries of Kinshasa concludes that migration is not simply geographical but a form of 'mind travel, turning specific locales in both the North and South into virtual and imagined sites, or states of mind' he makes it clear that Congolese have always had recourse to such fantasized modes of mobility and techniques of the self, citing witchcraft and Lunda biographies to underline the fact that people have, under certain circumstances, always transgressed cultural, gender and status constraints in their opportunistic and inventive quests for greater agency and more viable lives. It may be generally true that an emphasis on inwardness, affect and self-realization stands in dramatic contrast to the prevailing ethos of a 'traditional' culture where duty, forbearance and respect for elders imply an acceptance of life as one finds it, and the suppression of thoughts and feelings that challenge the status quo. One might also say that, traditionally, lip service was paid to the idea that one must sacrifice personal gratification and spontaneous self-expression to attain adulthood *and* make sociality viable (the implication being that what is good for the many will prove good for the individual), and that collective rituals and everyday practices of commensality, neighbourliness and cooperation reinforced the common good. But one must be wary of seeing 'modernity' and 'tradition' as competing ontologies, or of supposing that one or the other of these theoretical extremes dominates every human consciousness simply because it dominates *public* discourse. Moreover, it must be pointed out that the appearance or disappearance of any episteme is never adventitious. The foregrounding or backgrounding of any language for describing human being-in-the-world usually follows radical disruptions to the social fabric – civil war, famine, epidemic illness, displacement and urbanization. The essays in this volume succeed in depicting these backgrounds of deprivation, crisis and scarcity without, however, seeing migration as an intrinsically new phenomenon that we can interpret as a sign of the times, a symptom of general anomie tied to failed states, global economic decline, media scenarios, or foreign ideologies. By describing actual lives and life experiences, the authors of these essays succeed in showing that statistical pictures, media images and migration patterns hide as much reality as they reveal, and that migration is

not an option for everyone. Africa has always been much more open to new possibilities, much more opportunistic in its attitude to outside religions, medicines,
strangers and commodities, than the Eurocentric cliché of closed societies and closed
minds has ever allowed. But, as in any human society, strategies for resolving a crisis
will be entertained and explored with caution and ambivalence. What is seen as a
source of hope today may plunge one into despair tomorrow. That which promises
new life for oneself may spell death for another. And so migration will be experienced
differently by men and women, mothers and sons, old and young, subsistence farmers and urban-dwellers, rich and poor. For some it is a real possibility; for others it
is the stuff of folktales. Only by complementing ethnography with biography may
we see how complex the phenomenon is, and how wary we must be in clustering
diverse experience under a seemingly unitary label. The cult of inwardness and the
cultivation of emotional and affective life that accompanied the rise of the urban
bourgeoisie in Europe did not preclude cultures of communitas and nostalgia for
the agrarian past, and it is perhaps this tension *between* traditional and modernity,
played out in the lived dilemmas of individuals, that we need to describe in more
detail in order to temper the search for explanatory generalizations with descriptions
of the inventiveness and resourcefulness of people, whatever category we assign
them to, so reminding us that human lives are as shaped by historical events as they
give shape to them. Filip De Boeck puts it very well.

> In order to capture and read into the realities of these different trajecto-
> ries, movements and migrations, I believe it is absolutely necessary to stay
> close to the actual lives of those who move through these various worlds,
> close to the specific lines these lives describe, the specific itineraries that
> unfold in the processes of living in contexts that are indeed often marked
> by a lack of opportunity, a lack that – paradoxically – often creates op-
> portunities on other levels. (De Boeck this volume, 82)

In as much as lives do not unfold in straight lines, our attempts to narrate and
explain these lives should avoid the same cause-effect models of linearity and history, for there are many temporalities within history, such as the subjective time
of reverie and dream, of memory, of crisis and impasse. Anthropology is only now
recovering a sense of these penumbral and irreducible worlds of limit experience
and quotidian struggle.

References

Agamben, Giorgio. 1998. *Homo Sacer: Sovereign Power and Bare Life*. Stanford: Stanford University Press.

Appadurai, Arjun. 1996. *Modernity at Large: Cultural Dimensions of Globalization*. Minneapolis: University of Minnesota Press.

Appadurai, Arjun. 2006. *Fear of Small Numbers: An Essay on the Geography of Anger*. Durham: Duke University Press.

Bourdieu, Pierre. 2000. *Pascalian Meditations*. Transl. Richard Nice. Cambridge: Polity.

Ferguson, James. 2006. *Global Shadows: Africa in the Neo-liberal World Order*. Durham: Duke University Press.

Jackson, Michael. 2007. *Excursions*. Durham: Duke University Press.

Jackson, Michael. 2011. *Life within Limits: Well-Being in a World of Want.* Durham: Duke University Press.

Lucht, Hans. 2011. *Darkness before Daybreak*: *African Migrants Living on the Margins in Southern Italy Today*. Berkeley: University of California Press.

Makhulu, Anne-Maria, Beth A. Buggenhagen and Stephen Jackson. 2010. *Hard Work, Hard Times: Global Volatility and African Subjectivities*. Berkeley: University of California Press.

Mahler, Sarah J. 1998. Theoretical and Empirical Contributions toward a Research Agenda for Transnationalism. In *Transnationalism from Below,* ed. Michael Peter Smith and Luis Eduardo Guarnizo, 64-100. New Brunswick, N.J.: Transaction Publishers.

Mbembe, Achille. 2001. *On the Postcolony*. Berkeley: University of California Press.

Piot, Charles. 2010. *Nostalgia for the Future: West Africa after the Cold War*. Chicago: University of Chicago Press.

Contributors

Maybritt Jill Alpes works as a post-doctoral researcher at the Faculty of Law at the VU University Amsterdam and teaches anthropology and migration as an external lecturer at Sciences Po Paris.

Filip De Boeck is professor at and coordinator of the Institute for Anthropological Research in Africa (IARA) at the Catholic University of Leuven, Belgium.

Ann Cassiman is associate professor at the Institute for Anthropological Research in Africa at the Catholic University of Leuven, Belgium.

Denise Dias Barros is a researcher and lecturer at the São Paulo University Faculty of Medicine and Interdisciplinary Centre for the Imaginary and Memory (NIME).

Paolo Gaibazzi is a post-doctoral researcher at Zentrum Moderner Orient in Berlin.

Knut Graw is a senior researcher at the Institute for Anthropological research in Africa (IARA) at the University of Leuven and associated researcher at Zentrum Moderner Orient (ZMO) in Berlin.

Michael Jackson has taught at the anthropology departments of Indiana University and the University of Copenhagen, and is currently a distinguished visiting professor of world religions at Harvard Divinity School.

Gunvor Jónsson is a PhD student at the School of Oriental and African Studies of the University of London.

Aïssatou Mbodj-Pouye is a researcher at the Centre national de la recherche scientifique (CNRS), affiliated to the Centre d'études des mondes africains in Paris.

Samuli Schielke is a research fellow at Zentrum Moderner Orient in Berlin and teaches visual anthropology as an external lecturer at the Free University of Berlin.